Dynamic Capacity Management for Healthcare

Advanced Methods and Tools for Optimization

Dynamic Capacity Management for Healthcare

Advanced Methods and Tools for Optimization

Pierce Story
MPHM, DSHS

CRC Press
Taylor & Francis Group
Boca Raton   London   New York

CRC Press is an imprint of the
Taylor & Francis Group, an **informa** business
A PRODUCTIVITY PRESS BOOK

CRC Press
Taylor & Francis Group
6000 Broken Sound Parkway NW, Suite 300
Boca Raton, FL 33487-2742

© 2011 by Pierce Story
CRC Press is an imprint of Taylor & Francis Group, an Informa business

No claim to original U.S. Government works

Printed in the United States of America on acid-free paper
Version Date: 20110609

International Standard Book Number: 978-1-4398-1975-3 (Hardback)

Library of Congress Cataloging-in-Publication Data

Story, Pierce.
    Dynamic capacity management for healthcare : advanced methods and tools for optimization / Pierce Story.
       p. ; cm.
    Includes bibliographical references and index.
    Summary: "Presenting new approaches, tools, and perspectives, this book facilitates the effective management of the complexities and "dynamism" unique to health care operations. It introduces healthcare managers and professionals to state-of-the-art concepts designed to improve both process- and dynamic systems-focused performance and develop appropriately dynamic process-level solutions to complex systems level issues. Employing common methodologies such as Lean, Sigma Six, and CQI, the "Dynamic Capacity Management" approach addresses the analysis and improvement of hospital- and department-wide capacity, patient flow, resource allocation, and performance optimization"--Provided by publisher.
    ISBN 978-1-4398-1975-3 (hardcover : alk. paper)
    1. Hospitals--Administration. I. Title.
    [DNLM: 1. Hospital Administration--methods--United States. 2. Efficiency, Organizational--United States. 3. Health Services Needs and Demand--organization & administration--United States. 4. Hospital Bed Capacity--United States. 5. Organizational Innovation--United States. 6. Quality of Health Care--organization & administration--United States. WX 150 AA1 S887d 2011]

RA971.D96 2011
362.11068--dc22
                           2010022596

Visit the Taylor & Francis Web site at
http://www.taylorandfrancis.com

and the CRC Press Web site at
http://www.crcpress.com

Contents

Acknowledgments

Naturally, I want to first thank almighty God for giving me a passion for healthcare, as well as the time and energy to write this text, at His perfect time. Regardless of how this is received by colleagues and the industry, I consider myself blessed to have done what I can for an industry I care deeply about.

Of course, I would be remiss to avoid crediting those whose thankless efforts resulted in the rearing of a son who had the wherewithal to do anything good in this world, my parents. Moms are always proud, but I'll bet her copy (free, of course) gets put on the mantel above the fireplace. (My beloved brother may have a PhD in chemical engineering and eight patents to his name, but he's only written articles. Haha! I win!)

I would also be remiss if I didn't mention Kristin Meader Story, who tolerated many lonely weekends of closed office doors, delayed house projects, a shabby lawn, and mildew-infested roses for the sake of this effort. Her undying support and insistence that my effort would someday be a *New York Times* best-seller gave me inspiration and drive. May she always be one of my biggest supporters.

I would also like to thank the many colleagues and friends who supported this effort, challenged my thinking, and assisted with the production. Special thanks go out to Dr. David Eitel, who assisted in the review and critique of these concepts and ideas. His feedback was and remains instrumental. Dr. Alexander Kolker of the University of Wisconsin Children's Hospital also reviewed parts of this text. Andy Day, the best boss I've ever had and one of the brightest people I've ever met.

Also, the Society for Health Systems (SHS), a division of the Institute for Industrial Engineers (IIE), has been instrumental in allowing me to be involved and engaged with the work about which this text is focused. Without SHS/IIE, this text would surely never have been written.

Furthermore, the staff at Productivity Press (a division of Taylor & Francis), and especially Kris Mednansky, have been very supportive and cooperative in this effort. If ever I take on another such project, I can only hope that I can work with them again. (I promise the next one will be on time.)

Finally, I must mention perhaps the biggest influence on my thinking and my work, Dr. Brian Scott, PhD, whose influence continues to be felt. Sadly, he passed away in the prime of his life and career as a brilliant simulationist and creative thinker. Even sadder, he left behind two beautiful children who will never know how much he really loved them. He was a wonderfully generous, patient, and kind man whom I often miss.

There are many others whose influence and direction no doubt influenced this text. I wish them all great and humble thanks.

Prologue: Kenji's Story

Kenji was on his way in for his 7 a.m. shift, expecting the typical, average day. His role at the big Toyota plant was to install dashboards in shiny new Corollas as they rolled down the long, steadily paced production conveyor. He was also regularly involved in the ongoing process of perfecting the operations of his workstation and the entire factory, so he was also planning a Kaizen event at the wheel alignment station. Kenji had become an expert in the art and science of the Lean philosophy, trained to instinctively look for waste everywhere. It often drove his wife crazy, since he took his Lean thinking home to the kitchen, bathroom, chores, yard work, and even trips to the grocery store. It was definitely a part of him now, one that he would never shake.

Kenji drove casually along Center Street, knowing he would be early to the plant. He had dropped his young son at school unusually early for a special band rehearsal. The sun was up though dim through the dreary, wet sky. As he merged onto the main plant road with a few equally early workers from other parts of his small Alabama town, he noticed a stream of large trucks going the other direction and away from the plant. Odd, he thought to himself. He'd never seen such a large number of supply trucks leaving at such an early hour.

He parked his car closer than his usual space, based on his arrival time at the plant. Maybe he would arrive earlier every day and save himself a few wasted steps, he thought! How much time would he save each year? How much time would he save if he did this every day? Quickly forgetting his self-imposed analysis, he gazed toward the plant as he slid out of his pickup with his lunchbox. From here, in the dim light of the morning, through the row of small pine trees lining the parking lot, he could see the loading dock of the huge, cavernous building where supplies and parts were brought each day. Though still a hundred yards or so away, he thought he could see something unusual: Trucks. Lots of trucks.

His curiosity piqued, he eyed the loading dock area as he walked through the side gate and showed his ID badge to a sleepy, inattentive guard. As he got closer, he could see large boxes, metal containers, and chassis being offloaded by workers from the evening shift. The area was congested and busy, with forklifts scurrying to move the goods off the incoming trucks, searching for space inside or outside the plant. A truck was backed up to each of the three dock bays, and four more waited just to the side, idling their engines while waiting their turn. Kenji got a sinking feeling of the unfamiliar in his stomach. His gut was telling him something bad was happening.

He stopped along the fence by the sidewalk leading to the south employee entrance and peered through. So much is wrong there, he thought, but he couldn't even begin to put his finger on where to start with any quick analysis. This level of activity was highly unusual. He'd never seen so much going on at once. Truck drivers were yelling at the forklift drivers, who were shouting to the workers on the ground. Workers ran in and out, splashing through puddles of rain, moving and rearranging anything they could touch. How would anyone stop that madness long enough to discern the problems? There was just too much going on, too much chaos.

Chaos? At this plant? Impossible! His plant ran like a huge machine, like some gigantic ticking clock. New Corollas roll off the assembling line with the precise timing of a Bolshoi ballet. Every source of waste or error or inefficiency had been identified and eliminated, with all the zest and vigor the many Kaizen teams could muster. Every section of the production line was synchronized perfectly with every other section so that each car could be assembled without stopping. Each subprocessing station was perfected in its own right, so that within each operation there was little, if any, waste. It was a world near perfection. But now this? This definitely wasn't the usual perfection. What was happening?

Kenji entered the plant to find what his gut had feared: breakdown. Total system breakdown. Nothing was moving. The production line had long ago stopped. He didn't even know where to start. The worker from the previous shift he would replace wasn't at the workstation. All available resources had been called to the front and back end of the assembly lines. Workers ran everywhere. Supervisors yelled out instructions as if a war had started and they had all become generals on the front lines.

Since Kenji was early to arrive that day, few of his fellow 7 a.m. workers were there. Kenji did what his instinct and loyalty to his company and job told him to do: find a way to help ... now! His first thought was to find a supervisor to find out what was going on. This wasn't hard, since he'd worked in the factory since it opened seven years ago, and he knew everyone by name. He spotted Allen Boatwright, supervisor of the chassis assembly station. Allen had an almost panicked look on his face, which was somewhat relieved upon seeing Kenji. He knew Kenji would help if anyone could. Kenji was a Sensei in training and would someday move up in Toyota to become a plant manager or master production specialist. Kenji was a rising star, and knew his stuff.

Allen quickly explained that a series of simultaneous events had caused the system to fall apart. Totally outside the norm, a seemingly random set of breakdowns throughout the plant had occurred over the course of the last twelve hours, throwing the entire plant into near meltdown. Some of the problems seemed to have started at the back end of the plant in paint finishing. Or maybe it was the storage area for new cars, where the vehicles await pickup and delivery to their new location. It didn't matter ... both were locked up like an engine without oil.

Allen and Kenji began walking, or rather speed walking, through the plant toward the loading area. Allen couldn't run and talk, so he walked as fast as he could while speaking. The new software just installed in the paint finishing area was full of bugs, and required workers to use a dual manual entry and to rework defective parts. This threw off the average processing time for each vehicle, which had literally slowed the entire plant down. Allen then explained that the software might not have mattered, since the new car storage area had become jammed with new cars. Winter storms as far south as Virginia, west to Dallas, and north to New Hampshire had shut down highway travel in the past week. Blizzard conditions had been widespread in the Midwest, and ice storms north of the plant had brought traffic to a standstill. Kenji heard about the storms, but all they had gotten locally was a lot of cold rain and a few icy spots on the bridges. They had been spared, at least from the weather. But because the car haulers from the north and west could not get to the plant, the new cars simply had nowhere to go. The back end of the plant was clogged.

But what about all the supply trucks? Kenji remembered the jammed loading area and asked about all the trucks. "Where did *they* all come from?" Kenji demanded. Allen scoffed as he breathed harder from his walking workout. "The supply trucks were coming from the south and Mexico, so they were able to get through. I almost wish they'd been stuck too!"

As they passed silent, motionless cars in decreasing states of completion, Allen continued. The recent economic turnaround, low inventories, and big new sales incentives had given a huge, unexpected boost to sales and expectations of sales. Demand had spiked in a way not seen before. The trucks at the loading dock were full of the parts needed to build the additional cars. The plant technically had additional capacity, but it was being demanded too quickly for the capacity to react. As if that were not enough, the bolus of parts orders had been exacerbated by customs issues at the border of Mexico, as new federal regulations on truck weight limits and drivers had taken effect. The supply trucks from Mexico had all showed up at once last night, just after Kenji's shift had ended and two days after they were all released from the border. Other trucks from Louisiana suppliers arrived in the pre-dawn hours, as usual. But since there were not enough workers to manage the late arrival of the first trucks, everything on the loading docks had been backed up. And since the cars in the new car storage area were not moving and paint finishing was bottlenecked, the entire plant quickly seized up like a hose with the end pinched shut. The collapse had come hard and fast.

"And don't even get me started on this damnable flu season, either! I am amazed to see anyone walk through the doors! I think we have about a 20-percent call-in rate right now. And with the damned unions trying to organize, we dare not call in temps, even for the day," Allen said.

The feeling in the pit of Kenji's stomach began to grow worse as they finally arrived at the loading area, or as close as they could get. Kenji's jaw dropped open at the mountains of metal containers stacked where there should have been small kanban bins. Workers from every part of the plant scurried to find room for the new goods and organize new storage areas to accommodate the boluses. The parts storage areas had been built to specifically house a certain amount of parts, just enough for a given, short period of time. The just-in-time inventory system served them well financially, putting the onus on the suppliers to have the right amounts available at the right time while avoiding large inventory waste and cost. Normally, this was relatively easy since production was scheduled weeks and sometimes months in advance. But someone, somewhere, probably in sales and marketing, had pushed a big red panic button, fearing Hyundai's ability to better service the quickly growing demand.

With more trucks waiting, Kenji could see why the containers were being stacked outside. They simply had nowhere else to go, since there was no room inside, there wasn't another plant in the state or a local warehouse to send them to. The parts would simply have to wait anywhere the workers could find space. But Kenji has lived in the area long enough to know that waiting outside in the traditional, seasonal rainy weather would cause wet containers, boxes, and wet parts. This would mean extra inspections and processing once they were inside and on the assembly lines. Documentation demands would go through the roof, as each part would have to be inspected more thoroughly to ensure against residual moisture. Despite this growing mess and wet parts, quality would not be allowed to slip, even if it meant extra processing and, yes, waste.

Only once had Kenji seen this kind of thing before. Years ago when he worked in the now-defunct air conditioner manufacturing plant, he saw this kind of chaos. It happened every summer, it seemed, when the demand for air conditioners jumped with the summer temperatures. He was always frustrated with the inability of the management team to predict the very predictable demand spikes. Every year, it happened. Maybe not the exact same number, but certainly the demand trend was there every year. So each spring and summer they turned steady work into chaos, overtime pay, and lots and lots of waste. That, at least, could have been predicted.

Kenji's flashbacks of his old job were jolted away by a huge explosion at the other end of the factory. He whirled to see the back of the factory collapse, its ceiling caving in. A cloud of white smoke and dust consumed the line of cars and perfected workstations as the walls of the plant fell like dominos toward him. He whirled toward the dock bay doors to escape, only to see them blocked by growing stacks of containers. More and more containers, stacking higher and higher. As he stared up in horror, the ceiling gave way to a dark, rainy sky as the containers piled up and the roof fell away above them. He turned to Allen, just as Allen's head began to swell like a balloon. His eyes bulged like a fish. The whiskers on his stubbly beard stood straight out and began to erupt from his swollen face. Allen's head grew then popped with a whoosh of air, his face falling in stiff, painted pieces to the floor, shattered like an old vase.

Kenji gasped and turned to run away, but his feet couldn't get traction. He looked down to see the polished concrete floors melting into a gray mud. His feet became covered in the sticky ooze. He was immediately frozen in place, unable to move. He and everything around him began to sink. His body, the machines, the cars all began to shrink away as the floor turned to mush. He realized he was drowning. His legs were quickly being covered. He groped for something, anything, to grab onto. But everything was being sucked in. His perfectly Lean factory was being swallowed whole before his eyes. The enormous conveyor creaked loudly as it sank, as if screaming in horror, warping and twisting as it slid in deeper. White clouds of ceiling dust swirled innocently above as the walls and ceiling behind him continued to cave in toward him, splatting hard into the thick ooze as they fell. He pawed at the thick, gray mud trying to swim. His legs and arms became frozen, trapped against the weight of the thick, wet goo as it lapped against his neck. He tried to scream. Only a soft, low groan came from his gaping mouth as the walls of his perfect factory fell in around him. His head fell back, he gasped upward for the last bit of air. As his eyes gaped open toward the fading light, his head slid softly under the surface.

Suddenly, Kenji felt a strong hand on his arm, grabbing him tightly, pulling him from the sinking ooze. "Sir." A deep, strong voice spoke softly, "Sir!" Kenji jolted to awareness. He looked around, dazed at first. An elderly man in a white T-shirt repeated, "Sir, you were making noises and groaning. Maybe you were having a terrible dream, I think. I didn't want you to die right here in the emergency department or wake the boy." Kenji put his hands over his eyes and rubbed hard, shook away the horrible images and looked down at his son who was sleeping peacefully in a chair next to him. Thank goodness, at least he was resting.

He looked blankly at the old man. "Thanks. Thank you. Oh … sorry. I hope I didn't disturb anyone." Kenji grunted as reality settled in and the horror of the production meltdown and the gray ooze and Allen's huge head slipped from his mind. "Looks like we got in before the rush. This place is packed!" he said as he looked around the crowded emergency department. Standing-room only for sure, he thought. "What time is it, anyway?" Kenji asked. "Twelve-thirty a.m. Too damned late to be here, that's for sure," said the old man.

Seven hours and twenty minutes since he and his son had arrived. Kenji stood to stretch. His butt and back hurt from sleeping in a stiff plastic chair. He looked down at his son again, then over to the reception area where a crowd of people stood and waited to be registered. His son really needed to be seen. But there was nowhere else to go.

What the heck was taking so long?

Preface: Blasphemy!

> Hospitals are more like busy airports or battlefields than Toyota production lines. So why do we rely on manufacturing-based methodologies to solve all of our hospitals' problems?

OK, Stephen King, I'm not! But to further the analogy of that statement and Kenji's nightmare, a Toyota plant worker doesn't show up for his 7 a.m. shift to find forty chasses unexpectedly stacked up on the loading dock awaiting processing. But an emergency department (ED) physician might show up with an unexpectedly overloaded ED and a waiting room full of sick patients. Hence, it might make sense to see if the differences in the two types of systems (manufacturing and hospitals) might warrant different analytical tools and performance improvement methodologies. Yet that is blasphemy to many Lean and Six Sigma proponents and consultants.

Existing performance and process improvement (PPI) methodologies (such as Lean, Continuous Quality Improvement [CQI], etc.) use a variety of tools and concepts to achieve their success. Working at the process level and improving individual departments and subdepartment processes, 5S, "go to Gemba," value stream mapping, DMAIC (define, measure, analyze, improve, control), control charts, and so forth are all useful in their own ways. If incorporated effectively into an overall performance and process improvement strategy, these tools can be useful in achieving at least some degree of impact.

Furthermore, Lean, as a management philosophy focused on seeing waste wherever it may lie, is highly valuable in a host of environments, especially healthcare. Waste is literally everywhere in the typical hospital. Likewise, Six Sigma's "philosophical" attention to variability and data analysis is quite valuable to healthcare. Indeed, you'll see all these concepts purported in this text!

Yet, what I have generally seen over the years is the ineffectiveness of many of these methodologies to get past the process level and truly improve our healthcare systems writ large. Our PPI efforts have been traditionally focused on specific departments, such as the ED or the OR (operating room), or specific processes such as registration or discharge. Meanwhile, at the hospital-wide, or system level, we often play Whack-A-Mole™ with our problems, chasing bottlenecks around our hospitals from situation to situation and department to department, while failing to move the needle of the entire system's performance. Or, we find solutions that work during some circumstances or seasons of year, and not so well in others. Developed solutions that work on Tuesdays fall apart on the weekends when the variables of the system dramatically change. Or, we improve individual processes, sometimes for the sake of only that process, without considering the potential up- and downstream results. The adopted manufacturing methodologies simply are not getting the job done.

All this seems to be due to a fundamental inability to account for and analytically incorporate some key differences between healthcare environments and those of other industries such as manufacturing. There are many attributes that make healthcare altogether unique and much more difficult to improve. For the purpose of this text, we will hone in on a few of these, including: variability, complex interdependencies, the dynamism of our systems, and the evolution of our systems over time. This text will describe these and other concepts, what they mean for analysis and solution development, and how they might be brought into a more holistic and effective approach to improving our unique operational environs.

Let me be clear that these new methodologies, tools, and concepts purported herein are in no way meant to replace or even supersede existing PPI methodologies, including Lean, LSS, and Six Sigma. Rather, they are meant to be adjunctive, complimenting the existing work and allowing healthcare providers to become more effective in their efforts to achieve optimal performance within the context of their very dynamic worlds.

Many of the "old-timers" of industrial engineering scoff at the newest buzzwords and the latest craze in process improvement, thinking that much of it is little more than good, ol' fashioned industrial engineering with a new name. Managers, they'll say, flock to whatever acronyms seem to be in vogue, driven by the often unique but well-publicized successes of a few select companies. I assume that those same experts will find some very familiar thinking in these pages, and say it's nothing more than systems thinking in a new box.[1] Nonetheless, I hope to add a small piece to the bigger picture of healthcare performance and process improvement so as to help us achieve greater results in the years ahead.

Note

1. Systems thinking is largely attributed to the work of Peter Senge, whose *The Fifth Discipline: The Art and Practice of the Learning Organization* was a huge hit when it was published in 1990 (Doubleday/Currency Press). Systems thinking is an analytical framework based on the concept that the component parts of a system can best be understood within the context of interrelationships and interdependencies between each other and the larger system(s), rather than in isolation. The only way to fully understand why a problem occurs and persists is to understand it in relation to the system in which it exists. Thus, the problems of healthcare should be analyzed within the contexts of the larger care provision systems in which the problems exist.

Chapter 1

Introduction

> Hospitals are dynamic systems and must be analyzed and managed as such. We need dynamic tools and thinking to fix healthcare's dynamic systems.

The healthcare world is dynamic, changing every hour of every day in a seemingly constant state of flux. Although other work environments also change, few are as dynamic and complex as healthcare. Care provision is specialized down to the patient, who is treated with the individuality of a snowflake. The processes required to take thousands of these unique patients from sick and diseased to cured or improved are perhaps as complex as any. Thus, healthcare systems are known more for their complexity and chaos than their standardization and regimen. Nurses, doctors, and administrators are therefore correct to claim that healthcare is indeed different from other industries.

But because we are caring for fellow human beings, with lives and loves and livelihoods at stake, healthcare systems are expected to yield nothing short of perfection, yet do so efficiently. Though they may not be designed to achieve the desired results, patients, insurers, and regulators expect healthcare systems to function flawlessly. Cost controls, therefore, cannot dictate lowered quality standards or excuses for errors. Product recalls don't apply here, and well-heeled, greed-inspired lawyers await every mistake.

Furthermore, in the future, healthcare providers will be expected to achieve even better results with reduced compensation, fewer resources, lower capital expenditures, even stricter regulations and restrictions, and more litigation. As "health reform" oozes from Washington's political powerbrokers into the real world of patients and providers, the financial future of healthcare provision has never looked scarier. This means that efficiency and performance optimization will be of even greater importance as we try to perfect the processes of the care provided within the constraints of reduced or existing capacity, higher per-patient costs, and reduced compensation. The provision of services must yield high quality and optimal clinical outcomes yet be provided at the lowest possible cost. Therefore, improving the efficiency of the complex and dynamic operations of care delivery may be one of the best ways to ensure the survival of health facilities.

A Child of Our Own

Given the dynamic world of the provision of healthcare and the inherent unique-ness of its operations and processes, it is ironic that healthcare hasn't developed its own performance and process improvement (PPI) methodologies. We tend to try to improve healthcare systems with tools and methodologies adopted from other, very different and less dynamic industries. Throughout the last twenty years, we have seen various and sundry manufacturing performance and process improvement methodologies become the "play of the day" or the "flavor of the month." These methodologies can and have worked well, bringing with them new thinking and perspectives which have allowed healthcare systems to see dramatic improvements. Oftentimes, however, they fail in the face of the ever-changing complexities.

We commonly adopt the latest improvement concepts without enough custom-ization to the unique environs of care delivery, resulting in frustration and reduced impact. We might tweak them, or blend several concepts together, so as to force relatively static methodologies to fit into our dynamic systems. Yet even this has failed to move the needle enough.

Too much simply doesn't apply well to healthcare to allow for the achievement of the desired, dramatic, and long-lasting results. As when learning to speak an alien language, much can be lost in the translation between one environment and another, leaving us constantly groping for the next big thing. Indeed, many hospi-tals that have seen dramatic improvements using Lean or Six Sigma concepts over the years have, in practice, gone well past the basic tenets of these philosophies, incorporating tools and improvement ideas of their own making to achieve greater results. This is a testament to the need for more specificity.

The history of healthcare PPI is thus replete with great leaps forward, frus-trating setbacks and wasted effort, and far too much stasis. Although we can and should learn from the improvement efforts, tools, and methodologies of other, less dynamic industries, we should expect that healthcare's unique environment requires us to create a custom PPI system. In fact, since healthcare is so much different *we need tools and methodologies that won't apply at all to the world of manufacturing.*

That, essentially, is the premise and the reason behind this text. Herein, I would like to shed some light on the nuances and uniqueness of healthcare operations, challenge the current thinking about healthcare performance improvement, and offer some new ways to think about the management of hospitals and healthcare systems. With these new concepts added to other methodologies, philosophies, and tools, I hope we can profoundly change the way hospitals are managed.

Dynamic Capacity Analysis, Matching, and Management (DCAMM): Concept Overview

The purpose of this text is to bring forward some new thinking and analysis to persistent and consistent issues in healthcare PPI.[1] The essentials are summed up in the following paragraphs. If you don't understand the concepts and terminology, fear not—you aren't supposed to just yet. By the end of the book, I hope that you will. The concepts go something like this: Healthcare systems are dynamic. Variable demand comes to us from the community through various entry points, changing constantly throughout each day, week, and season. This demand is met with variable service capacity, which also changes over time. Because these elements are ever-changing, healthcare environments are inherently difficult to manage, since "dynamically matching dynamic demand with dynamic capacity" can be problematic, at best.

The most common analytical tools, such as spreadsheets and flowcharts, fail us, often terribly. The use of averages to represent system performance deceives, since averages fail to capture the real variability and dynamics of our complex systems. Instead, averages can yield incorrect conclusions and create misguided solutions. The *dynamism* (defined herein as the combination of the inherent variability and interdependencies in complex systems) in the demand–capacity continuum is simply too complicated to be effectively represented by a simple average. Thus, the complexity begs for better analytics by which we can better understand our dynamic systems, proactively manage them, and better care for patients.

Fortunately, at least some of the system's dynamism has patterns by which we can discern current and future behavior. Indeed, in many instances, some 80 percent to 90 percent of the variance occurs within relatively tight ranges around the commonly used yet misleading averages, creating discernable patterns. These patterns offer the realization that our systems are not as random and chaotic as we might think. Based on the patterns of historical behavior, we can often say that 80 percent to 90 percent of the dynamism can and should be dealt with as commonplace, standard, and "in-range." This helps us develop solutions to manage limited variance without requiring that we manage chaos. Furthermore, these patterns, when and where they exist, offer the means by which to study system behavior within the context of the dynamism of the system. More important, the patterns are the key to *predictive analytics* by which we can predict system behavior by hour of day, day of week, week of month, and season of year.

At certain points, the system may tip into an *outlier status*—circumstances and conditions that are among the more rare and unusual, but are relatively unpredictable. This relatively small percentage of the dynamism, which falls outside the 80- to 90-percent range of occurrences, are the truly random and unpredictable events that drive the systems over the edge and cause breakdowns. And cause great impacts on the system's overall performance. *Outliers* as thus become recognized for what they are.

The points at which the system leaves its standard range and moves into outlier status are the system's *break points*. Break points must therefore be recognized and their causality predicted, so as to help us discern and predict when the in-range performance can no longer be expected, and when perhaps some change to the standardized processes needs to occur. This helps us create unique solutions for these particular scenarios, which may differ from the in-range solutions. *Dynamic Standardization* then allows us to flex to the inevitable whims and outliers of variable demand, while maintaining quality and optimizing capacity and flow. Using our predictive analytics and tools, we can do this well in advance of occurrence. Our thinking therefore shifts from managing every day as if it's an outlier to managing outliers as outliers. Since it is the outliers that cause the most pain and suffering, and since the in-range metrics can be predicted relatively well, we should focus on the former and not the latter. This becomes a new way of thinking about the management of dynamic systems, known as *outlier management*, which should be the locus of our tactical and strategic analytical and managerial efforts. This in turn, gives us the confidence to *manage to* the ever-changing environment, rather than reacting to it and being managed by it.

As we see and predict the demand–capacity continuum and its impact on performance, we begin to see how we can influence the up- and downstream demand patterns in the system so as to have a truly systemic impact. Thus we move from reacting to static averages toward dynamically and proactively managing the dynamic demand–capacity continuum based on a better and more realistic understanding of the system's actual dynamic performance. We now have new ways to understand and better manage the capacity we make available for our communities, herein known as *dynamic capacity management*. This is the heart of DCAMM—dynamic capacity analysis, matching, and management.

As I stated earlier, don't be concerned if that makes little or even no sense to you at this point. If it still makes no sense after reading this text, then *I* have the problem!

In order to proceed through this text, we will need to define some specific terms (many of these will be repeated and elaborated later).

Dynamic capacity analysis, matching, and management (DCAMM)—The proactive, predictive management of dynamic capacity to meet, with the precision possible, the dynamic demand of the communities we serve.

Service capacity—The sum of the ability to meet some level of demand for a given service. In this text, *capacity* will be synonymous with service capacity.

Variability—The range of performance measurements, values, or outcomes around the average which represents all the possible results of a given process, function, or operation.

Interdependencies—The causal impact of one process or operation on another within a given process flow or system. Also, those links between one system component and another which result in some sort of impact(s) on either, both, or other components of the system.

Dynamism—The product and state of a system's performance capabilities resulting from the combination of process variability and system interdependencies.

In-range—A range of performance measurements, values, or outcomes of a given process, function, or operation which falls within a specified degree of commonality or rate of occurrence. The range may vary, depending on the degree of variability of the system in question. Commonly, it is the 80 percent to 90 percent of all occurrences.

Outlier—A performance measurement, value, or outcome of a given process, function, or operation that falls outside a specified degree of commonality or rate of occurrence.

Break point—A condition or set of conditions that result in the performance measurements, values, or outcomes varying outside a given range of expectations (aka, in-range performance). Break points occur as performance gives way to outlier status. The consistent presence of a break point and an outlier can indicate the evolution of the system.

Evolution—In this text, evolution will refer to the changes within or to the system that take a performance measurement, value, or outcome of a given process, function, or operation from an outlier to some new standard and expected level of occurrence, or vice versa. Systems evolve as the outliers become in-range metrics, or in-range metrics become outliers.

Dynamic standardization—The use of a variety of standardized processes or operations for the same given function to achieve a specific performance standard for that function.

Predictive analytics—The use of data, modeling, and an understanding of a system's dynamic behavior to predict future performance based on current performance or a hypothetical combination of input variables.

What-if scenario—The construction of a hypothetical situation created from the combination of system input variables so as to generate an understanding of the expected performance measurements, values, or outcomes of a given process, function, or operation in that situation. Used with a variety of simulation and other analytical tools.

The concepts will be expounded in the coming text. With these concepts in hand, I hope to be able to shed light on a new way to approach our most persistent and troubling PI issues, including throughput, patient flow, staffing, and perhaps even supply chain management.

A Caveat to the Text

I would like to be able to say that DCAMM is the end-all-be-all solution to all of hospital flow and capacity issues. Sadly, it is not. Yes, it's a critical part of the solution, and huge leap over where we are and have been heading. But it still requires more than it alone can offer. Having worked in DCAMM projects over the past several years, I can personally attest to the need for a truly holistic approach to the issue, which includes clinical consulting (to perfect the new clinical workflows required), Lean to remove the waste, Six Sigma to squeeze the variability, and management/industrial engineers to work with it all. Furthermore, there are all the financial metrics and quality considerations involved in profoundly changing the way hospitals are managed and reducing the cost of the provision of care, while maintaining high standards of excellence. Successful implementation also requires senior management skill and vision (sorely lacking in today's executive suites), and an admission that one methodology, toolset, philosophy, or concept is not enough to solve the problem. I freely admit that here, but there are many "Leaners" (dogmatic adherents to Lean) who have tried to say that these tools and concepts are not at all necessary. This attitude is almost as dangerous to progress as doing nothing at all.

I hope you will find these concepts and tools useful in your quest to optimize the performance of your facilities and your systems.

Note

1. Though these concepts could apply to physician offices, clinics, nursing homes, and other care areas, the foci of these tools will be the hospital and its many departments.

Chapter 2

Variability: Killer of Capacity

Before we can discuss some of the heavier topics of the book, we must first (re-) establish a knowledge of the core principles, building blocks, and essential elements of the dynamic capacity management concepts. One of the essential elements to an understanding of dynamic systems is variability. This chapter is devoted to an overview of the concepts, analysis, and impacts of variability within the complex systems in which we work.

Variability is such an important factor because it can have a tremendous impact (usually negative) on our operations and our efforts to improve. Thus an understanding of, and appreciation for, variability is critical to any performance improvement effort, whether at the process level or the systems level. For the purpose of this chapter and subject, we will stay away from heavy statistics and instead will reference important concepts that are commonly supported with statistical analysis. For example, standard deviations and other statistical tools are commonly used to assess the degree and impact of variability. In this chapter and book, however, we will only discuss the practical applications of these tools as they apply to change management. So rather than explaining how you would calculate the standard deviation of a given data set, we will discuss how the range of data points within the data allows you to determine the impact on process and change.

The degree of the impact of variability is driven, of course, by the extent of the variability and the number of variables and variable steps in a process or system. Since it can have such a significant impact, variability is known and studied throughout the process improvement literature and methodologies, particularly Six Sigma. Indeed, a core principle of the Six Sigma methodology is the identification, classification, and elimination of (unwanted) variability. Thus, the literature on Six Sigma is replete with information on the use of statistical analytics to study (and hopefully eliminate) variability in everything from process to parts specifications to time. According to Michael George, "The source of defects is almost always linked to variation in some form," to which he adds time. "That's why the fundamental thesis of Six Sigma is that *variation is evil* [author's emphasis] because a high level of variation means customers will not get what they want."[1]

The Lean or TPM (total productive maintenance) methodologies utilize a different, sometimes indirect approach to the elimination of variability through focus on concepts such as work standardization and takt time analysis. Some have even suggested that certain kinds of controllable and unwanted variability is another (eighth) form of waste for the Lean methodology.[2] Unfortunately, many Lean authors and consultants fail to even mention variability in their methodologies. The word *variability* isn't even listed in the index of Womack's infamous and world-renowned book, *Lean Thinking*,[3] Martin's best-seller *Kaizen Event Planner*,[4] or most of the other Lean texts.

In the book *Making Hospitals Work*,[5] a Lean story of hospital improvement based on a UK experience, the authors conveniently dance around the issue of variability and safely assume that all variability ultimately becomes the average over time. Meaning they assume perfect bell curves for all variation.

With due and great respect to these and other authors and consultants, theirs may be a different level of focus and analysis that might not constitute the analysis of variability. Nonetheless, variability and its impact do not seem to be quite as commonly addressed as it is in Six Sigma, despite its importance in healthcare process analysis. This, in my opinion, leaves a gaping hole through which project failure can often creep. Though most if not all will agree to its existence, many are not familiar with its impact or the need for its analysis.

There is a host of reasons for the neglect of this important factor. In part, variability is difficult to easily represent, either graphically or statistically, without significant training. Representing variability to a nonstatistician, who doesn't quickly grasp the significance of a standard deviation formula, is difficult without graphs, charts, and lots of data points and explanations. Furthermore, our data systems typically kick out single numbers for analysis, rather than extensive histograms, candlestick charts, control charts, or other graphical representations of variability. Thus, the "average," as a simple and only somewhat telling statistic, is a standard metric. Just think of all the averages used in healthcare, such as average …

- Length of stay
- Waiting time
- Operating room (OR) time
- Turnaround time
- Labs per day
- Procedures per hour

Table 2.1   The Limitations of Relying on Averages for Analytical Metrics

Set #	Sample Data									AVG
Set 1	5	6	7	7	5	6	5	6	7	6
Set 2	6	3	9	3	6	9	6	3	9	6
Set 3	1	6	11	6	1	11	11	1	6	6

The list goes on.

Yet ask yourself a very important question: Do I understand the variability around the average that I am using as my key metric? If you don't understand the variability of your processes and outcomes, you may not understand your process well enough to effectively analyze and improve it. If you don't know whether your process has only a little variability or a great deal of variability around its average, you won't know the range and spread of possible outcomes that lead to the average you are using. You might also lose sight of the possible solution, the extent of possible improvement, and perhaps even the need for any improvement effort. Furthermore, the range of the variability around the average has a tremendous impact on how chaotic a system might feel, and how much cushion is needed in resources and supply allocation. Lastly, the variability in your process may have significant impacts on other processes in the system, which can cause both you and others significant issues. This can be shown using a simple spreadsheet and a calculation of averages (see Table 2.1).

In Table 2.1 the sets of numbers all have the same average, but have vastly different highs and lows. This is a simplistic yet revealing example of the impact of variability on the decisions made with averages. If this were numbers of patients admitted to a unit on Tuesday afternoons, nurses would find the situation created by Set 1 much less chaotic than that of Set 3. Since the range of Set 1 is very tight, between five and seven admissions, it will feel less chaotic that the range of Set 3, which goes anywhere from one admission to eleven. Think about trying to staff for the Set 3 situation versus the others.

The Look and Feel of Variance

Variability can appear in several forms, including the time it takes to complete a process, or the actual process by which a task is completed, or the number of arrivals per hour. The former, process time variability, can result from different operators performing a task, experience and training with the task, and external variables such as weather conditions. Variability of a process task, or the way in which a process is completed, can be the result of training differences, process workarounds that vary among staff members, external factors such as physician preferences, and so forth. Since one often leads to the other, we commonly deal with the time it takes to complete a process. This is sometimes called tact time, processing time, turnaround time, or throughput time. The variability of arrivals, demand, and processing can also have a significant impact on our systems, as this variability throws off our resource availability and the consistency of our flows. Keep these various types of variability in mind as we move forward, especially later as we discuss root causes, contributing factors, evolution, and other concepts.

What does variability look like in a process? Think of the graph in Figure 2.1 depicting emergency department (ED) length of stay. The histogram depicts a sample distribution of variability in length of stay (LOS) across all patient types in a given ED. This histogram represented the number of times that a given LOS shows up in the data set (grouped, for simplicity's sake, into hour buckets). So, for instance, 122 patients have LOS in the four- to five-hour range. A histogram is a good visual representation of the distribution of data points for a given process. The line sticking up between four and five hours showing the average length of stay, based on all the data points in the sample data set, which in this example occurs roughly at 4.88 hours. This single number is what most ED managers study and report. Yet, charts like the one shown can be developed from historical data. Using a month's or year's data, one can take all the LOSs and plot them on a histogram like the one in Figure 2.1. Graphically and visually, it quickly demonstrates the variability in LOS of patients in this ED during the period in question.

An alternative to charting the number of patients is to use percentages and probabilities of LOS. This convenient and informative histogram will help you to readily grasp the probability and impact of a given LOS within the spectrum of occurrences. (You can look ahead to Figure 2.8 to see an example of the use of percentages.)

Furthermore, the average may not be as indicative as the most common LOS (known as the *mode*) or the exact middle number of the range (aka the *median*). The mode or the median might be a more telling number about an ED's LOS, depending on the distribution/variability of the data and how the data is distributed within the range. Depending on the spread of data to the left or right of the average, other metrics can become important and informative, since skewing of the average can be visually and statistically deceiving. This is why it is always best to report at least a few numbers when referring to system or process performance, since a single number can be quite misleading.

Visually, we readily see in Figure 2.1 that most of our patients are getting in and out of the ED in less than six hours. However, we also see that, based on the distribution of the number of times a given LOS occurs, the exact average number rarely occurs. If our data were more precise, using many decimal points (such as 4.887562 hours), the actual average would occur even less frequently.

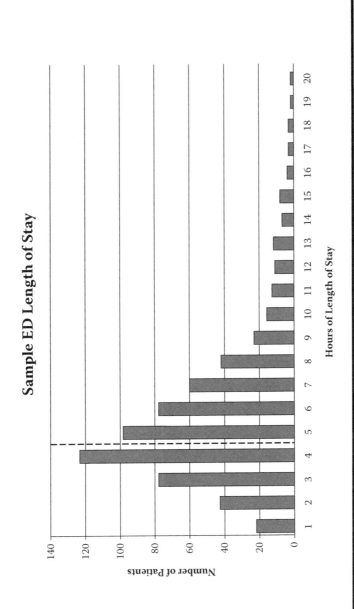

Figure 2.1   Sample ED length of stay for all patients.

We also see a long tail on our distribution, or the area that spreads out to the right side of the chart. The number of patients with very long LOSs gets much smaller as the LOS goes up, as is expected. In our ED, these might be mental health and intoxicated patients, abdominal pain patients, patients awaiting an inpatient bed, or other patients with long workups. If there were more patients in this tail of the curve (more patients with higher LOSs on the right side of the chart), the average LOS would be pulled to the right and would go up. With fewer patients in the tail, average LOS shifts leftward and goes down. Logical enough, right? Therefore, we want our curves to be "high, tight, and left." Meaning, no right-side tails on our distributions. If our processes ran like production line machines, there might be no variability at all. Then (and only then) would we use the average without concern.

The patients at the far ends of a distribution of data (whether on the short end or the long end, but most commonly on the long end) are known as *outliers*. Outliers are those data points that lie on the outer fringes of our operational outcomes. (Of course, outliers can occur on the short end, wherein this case LOS is lower than the average. But we are typically trying to create more of these, thus we don't refer to them as outliers (a negative connotation) even though they technically fall into the category. Again, these patients might be awaiting inpatient beds, might be intoxicated and require time to sober up, or require longer work-ups. Importantly, they may indicate a potential systemic problem (e.g., patient throughput or inpatient capacity constraints) and can have a huge impact on the system's overall performance. Think of Pareto's principle (the 80–20 rule), which would tell us to focus on the 20 percent outliers who make up the 80 percent of our issues and problems.

But because of the inherent difficulty in easily conveying variability to the layman we will commonly quote one number: the average. However, just using the average doesn't tell much about the potential improvement possible in the process, or about the important variability in the process, or even about what we should do to improve the process. Just look at Figure 2.1 and see all the information that would be missing by simply reporting the average. The average doesn't tell us anything about how long the tail is, how many patients are in the tail, by how much the tail can be reduced, nor the impact of the elimination of the tail. Thus, again, the average is a very poor indicator of both performance and potential. Therefore, averages can be quite deceiving if used in isolation.

The Deception of the Average

The use of averages becomes even less informative when we look at a series of processes, whether within a given department or throughout a facility. A series of processes, each with its own variability, results in a total process time that can be very different from the sum of the averages. If we were only analyzing a single process, there would be no upstream or downstream consequences of the variability, so there would be no need to concern ourselves with the process variability other than that which impacts the single process. Likewise, if there were no variability in the process, or if the variance was tightly distributed around the average (as shown in Figure 2.2) then there would be less need to use something other than the average. (Even Figure 2.2 shows enough variability to be of concern.)

If, however, there are multiple processes to be analyzed and if each process has some significant degree of variability, then the issue of variability becomes even more important to the study of the system, its outcomes, and its potential for improvement. To demonstrate this, let's look at the impact of variability in a four-step process using a simple analytical simulation model depicting a simple ED flow.

A discrete event simulation model (hereinafter simply *simulation*) will be used here to demonstrate the impact of variability and assumptions about a system's performance. As we will see in later chapters, they will also be used to analyze interdependencies, outliers, and predict the outcomes of changes to system components and demand patterns. Discrete event simulation is quite good at capturing the impact of variability on key metrics, like throughput. In fact, that's one of the primary reasons they were developed back in the 1970s. Using simulation, an entire system can be replicated, or modeled, complete with its dynamism and other important attributes such that the process itself can be more effectively and accurately analyzed. Furthermore, accurate replication of a given process gives us the power to see what might happen in real life if a part of the process were changed.

For this example, let's use historical data to create a data distribution representing the first step in our four-step process: triage processing time in an ED. The histogram looks like the one shown in Figure 2.3, with the average being around 7 minutes, as shown by the vertical dotted line. Typically, if we were trying to analyze the triage process, we would just use the average as being indicative of the effectiveness and efficiency of triage. However, we can see the same issues in doing so as before, based on the spread of the range of actual data points. We "feel" this variability in the flow, perhaps as an elderly woman takes much more time to properly triage. We all know how that can back up the process for future patients.

If you look at all the numbers in the distribution, representing all the process times that took place throughout the period, we see that the average process time of 7 minutes rarely happens in real life. It is not even the most common data point, as is often the case with widely distributed data sets. So how do we replicate the variability for our analysis. To truly and accurately represent the process, rather than using just the average to represent a process, one would need to account for all the possible data points in the distribution. This is so that the process is accurately represented when it generates outliers as well as when it generates something

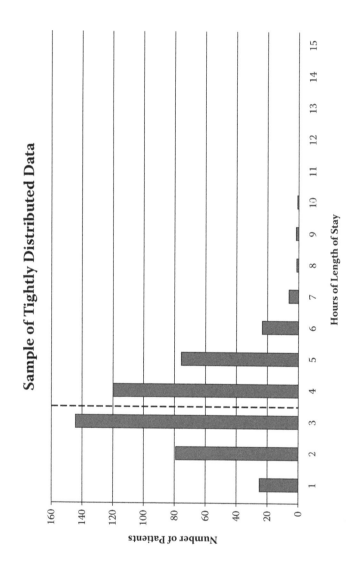

Figure 2.2   Tight distribution of data around an average.

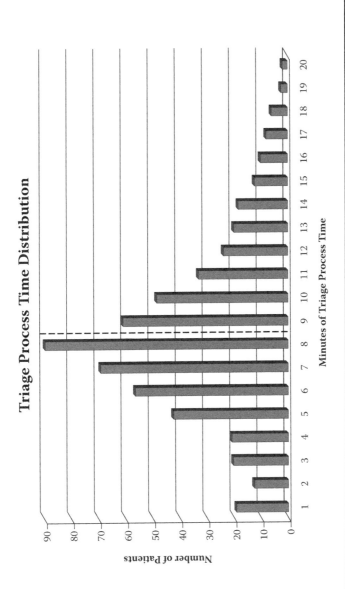

Figure 2.3   Triage process time.

closer to the average. You would no more want to represent your process with an outlier than you would with an average—we need them all. To do that, two things must happen.

First, the model needs to run (or replicate) the process over and over and over in order to give the process a chance to run enough iterations, with enough variable process times, such that all the process variability can be replicated. And, second, the simulation needs to select data points from the distribution representing various process times that might occur. For this, a random number generator is used. The *random number generator* uses a mathematical formula representing the data distribution we created, and randomly selects a process time for each occurrence of the process. Thus, for one occurrence of our triage process, the randomly selected process time might be 5.9 minutes. The next occurrence of the process might take a randomly selected 11.5 minutes. The next 13.2, and the next 8.9. As the model repeatedly and randomly selects data from the distribution for each time the process occurs, it more accurately mimics what might actually happen if the process were taking place over time before our eyes. Thus, the variablility of process times is represented accurately as it occurs in real life, and the process is thereby replicated accurately. Using a model, we might run a process hundreds or thousands of times in order to gauge the impacts of the variability and other attributes of a complex system. With modern computers, we can analyze in minutes a system that might normally take weeks or even years to observe in real time.

The triage process alone, in isolation, would not necessarily require the study of variability. Indeed, the ultimate result of statistical analysis on a single process would be the same average number we had when we started. The only practical lesson we might learn is the range of the variability around the average, which might help us to understand just how chaotic ("out of control" in Six Sigma-ese) our triage process might be.

However, let's assume that we want to study something more complex. For instance, let's model a system consisting of four individual, exclusive ED processes: triage, registration, disposition, and discharge. Each has its own process time, variability, and process time distribution (typically pulled from historical data or developed for future state analysis based on assumptions about the future system's performance).

The simulation in Figure 2.4 depicts the same four processes twice to help us differentiate the impacts of variability. In the top process, each process step is represented by an average number. That is, each time a process happens, it takes the same average process time, each time. So, let's say that triage takes an average of seven minutes and disposition takes ten minutes. In the top model, each time that triage takes place, it will take exactly seven minutes. No more and no less. Similarly, each time the disposition process takes place, it will take the same average ten minutes every time. The model will not need its random number generator to develop a distribution—the distribution consists of a single number, the average.

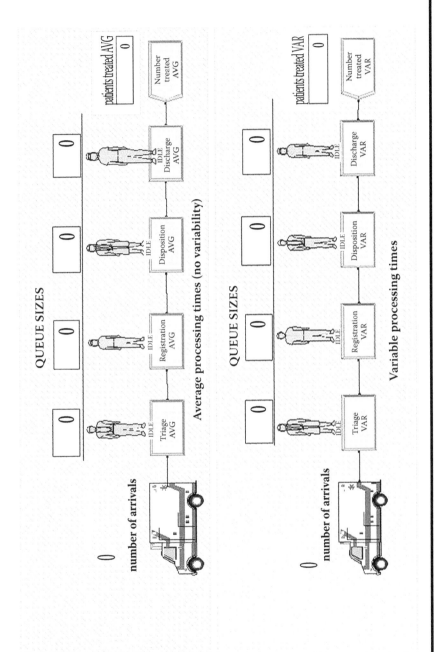

Figure 2.4   Simulation model interface of a simple, four-step process.

Table 2.2 Average Process Times for the Four-Step Process

Process	Triage	Registration	Disposition	Discharge
Average process time	7 min	8 min	10 min	10 min

This is essentially what happens when we use *static* analysis, such as spreadsheets and value stream maps to analyze our processes—we use a single number to represent each process in the system. The process times of each process step are shown in Table 2.2.

In contrast, the lower process in Figure 2.4 will include variability in each step like the one we used in Figure 2.3. So, each time the triage process takes place, the model will draw from the triage distribution as described earlier. The process times for each of the other three processes will be represented by distributions representing the variability in their process times. For example, the disposition process will still have its average of ten minutes, but the random number generator will allow for variability in each individual occurrence of the disposition process, just as in real life. All four process steps will therefore vary, such that the registration, disposition, and discharge process will all have their individual variability represented. Furthermore, and most important, the entire process will have its variability more accurately represented.

Before we start our analysis, there is one more bit of variance we'd like to represent: the arrival patterns of patients. Patients do not arrive as we would like them to, spaced out evenly and predictably, with the same number arriving each hour of each day. In reality, there is variation in the arrival pattern that will need to be replicated to accurately assess our little system. Fortunately, simulation models can also vary the arrival patterns of patients, just as happens in real life.

Each half of the model will use its respective arrival patterns. The upper model, which is using average process times, will use the same average number of arrivals per hour, consistent across hours and days (which is what one does when using an average daily or annual volume to represent a system). The lower model's arrivals will vary in number throughout each hour and day, so as to effectively replicate the variability in the number of arrivals per hour. This, too, is represented mathematically via formulas such that variability is accurately replicated. (If necessary, simulations can easily replicate different arrivals patterns for different days of the week, seasons of the year, or patient types, though we won't go to that extreme here. This feature is nonetheless very handy for the analysis of complex systems like hospitals.)

What we have hereby created is two very different worlds. One, the upper model, uses average numbers to represent a simple ED throughput system. The lower model accounts for variability to represent the system. It is important to remember that the *average process times for each respective process step in the two systems is roughly the same.* Here is the key issue to consider: If the use of averages accurately represents the performance of a system, then the throughput, LOS, and other key metrics of the two models should be the same. This seems, in a deceptively logical way, to be correct. After all, the variability in the four process steps in the lower model will ultimately result in four average numbers, right? If those four average numbers were added together, we should logically get the same total average obtained from the upper model. The averages should, in essence, average out. However, this is the deception of averages. Look at the results, shown in the screenshots from a simulation model and its outputs in Figure 2.5a.

Patients enter on the left, and a total of roughly 265 have arrived into both systems. Look at the last little boxes on the far right-hand side of each flow—the total throughput, or the number of patients making it all the way through the system in the given amount of time. What you see right away is that the throughput of the two systems is different. Depending on when the model is stopped, that difference can range from 10 percent to 20 percent. The bottom (variable) model is always and inevitably the poorer performer, especially as the model runs longer (assuming endless arrivals).

Furthermore, we see the bottlenecks throughout the system. We see that disposition time is highly variable, and isn't balanced with the rest of the system, and thus causes the greatest number of patients waiting. Interestingly, if we repeatedly stopped the model throughout its run, we would get bottlenecks opening and closing, getting worse or better, as the variability plays itself out throughout the four steps. So, for a period, there might be a large queue in triage. Fifty patients later, there might be a large delay in registration and small delay in discharge. As we see in Figure 2.5b, the physicians become bottlenecked in disposition, with over thirty patients queued at once. This is, in part, why static methodologies make it so difficult to create true system balance within a set of variable processes.

Why doesn't the average average out? Think of it this way. If the first process at some point takes longer than its average (as it inevitably will), it forces the next process to wait to begin. This backs up the second process and then possibly the third and fourth. The entire system is thus slowed. In order for the system to remain at its average performance, one or all of processes two through four would have to instantly speed up to accommodate the slowed first process and catch the entire system back up. Furthermore, even if the second process is quicker than its average, it might not be quick enough to catch up from the initial delay. The system is then bottlenecked, at least temporarily, and steps three and four might also need to speed up. Furthermore, since all the processes in the lower model system (Figures 2.4, 2.5a, and 2.5b) have variability, any of the process steps could slow the system, causing upstream and downstream waits and delays.

So, let's assume that our first process is slower than its average, for whatever reason (e.g., our patient takes a long time to explain his chief complaint and medical history). The second process, which might be finished with the previous patient, is

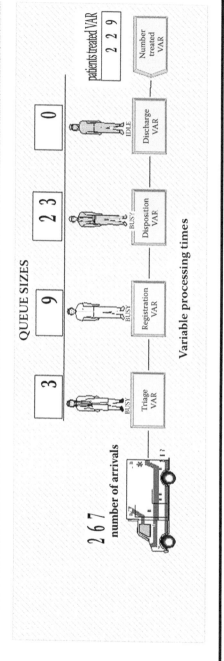

Figure 2.5a   Simple simulation model output comparison.

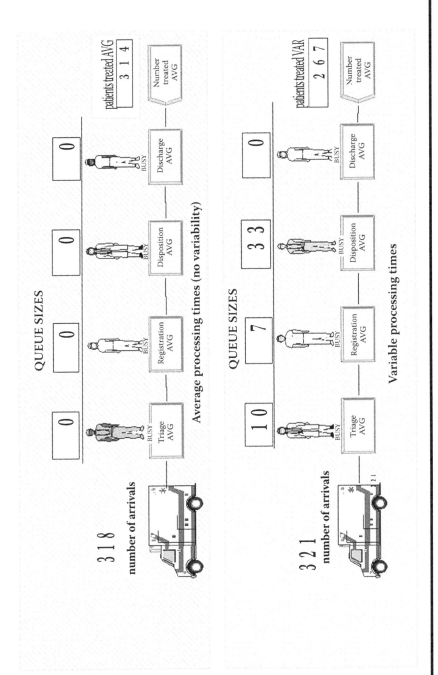

QUEUE SIZES

3 1 8

number of arrivals

0 | 0 | 0 | 0

Triage AVG — Registration AVG — Disposition AVG — Discharge AVG

BUSY | BUSY | BUSY | BUSY

patients treated AVG 3 1 4

Number treated AVG

Average processing times (no variability)

QUEUE SIZES

3 2 1

number of arrivals

1 0 | 7 | 3 3 | 0

Triage AVG — Registration AVG — Disposition AVG — Discharge AVG

BUSY | BUSY | BUSY | BUSY

patients treated VAR 2 6 7

Number treated AVG

Variable processing times

Figure 2.5b   Simple simulation model, physician bottlenecked.

now idle and waiting for triage to complete. Meanwhile, more patients arrive but have to wait just a bit until the slower patient leaves triage. The LOS is now being altered from the average, as wait times creep in. Several slow patients in a row can thus significantly slow the entire system. So, a slowdown at discharge might impact the process all the way back to triage. A slowdown in triage might cause wait times downstream as the flow becomes inconsistent. Sound familiar?

If there is great variability in a process step (i.e., a wide range around the average) the impact will be greater. Recall from Table 2.1, the three data sets representing ranges around the average of six minutes. If one or more of our four processes is represented by the more variable Set 3, the range of variance would cause a greater impact on the process and thus the system's performance. If all our processes had a large range in performance, our system might seem very chaotic.

What about our average process? It hums along with each process step taking the same predicted, average process time. The total process time is little more than the sum of the averages of the four processes. Bottlenecks occur here only to the extent that one process step's average process time is longer than the previous process average, or the arrival pattern is quicker than the initial process allows. Then, there might be a backup while the upstream process waits on the downstream process (as can happen in the variable process). But because there is no variation, we can easily and accurately predict exactly how long a wait will be generated from each such occurrence, and even accurately predict the total wait time through simple addition and subtraction. Furthermore, to make our average system improve, all we'd have to do is figure out which of the four process steps is the longest, then simply bring its process time down to the same average as the others, thus optimizing the entire system's performance. If only it were that easy, right?

So, from this little four-step model we see that variation has a significant impact. Food for thought as you consider variability in your own systems:

- Even when using identical process averages for the respective processes in the two systems, the results of the entire processes are not the same.
- A process flow with variability inherently has reduced throughput and a longer total cycle time than a process based strictly on average numbers.
- We see that variability can randomly impact our system, with little predictability in the timing of the impacts. The degree of impact on the system depends on the degree of variability of the process step(s) in the system, and their respective impacts on upstream and downstream processes.

"But," you insist, "I know my historical system average." All this said, why bother with it if you already know the average of the system performance (for example, our ED's average length of stay)? Why understand how we came to get to that average, or what component variability led to it?

It really only matters if you are studying and somehow want to improve the performance of your system. If all you want to do is know and report the average LOS for your ED, you might not care about the variability around that average. However, if you are trying to improve the performance of the system, it is imperative that you account for the variability of the system and in all the relevant component parts. This is because improving one part of the system may or may not yield a desired outcome on the system due to the other variables within the system. In other words, variability has a great deal to do with whether we are successful in improving our entire systems as we improve component parts. (Interdependencies play a huge role here as well, and we'll discuss that in the next chapter.)

System Demand, Patterns, and Variability

To recap, variability can impact individual process performance as well as system performance, causing degradation from the average over time. We have also established that the average is a risky number, if taken as the sole or primary indicator of process and system performance. This is particularly true when looking at multi-process systems, like the complex, interdependent systems of healthcare.

Now that we have established that variability has a tremendous impact on the performance of our systems and processes, we need to re-examine one important element of the upstream—the arrival patterns. These arrival patterns in our small, four-step model formed the demand patterns for all downstream processes. When a patient arrives, processes begin to occur throughout the downstream system. These processes can occur over several days or weeks for admitted patients, since an arrival triggers all subsequent demand in the system for a given patient, much like a turn of an ignition key starts other engine parts in motion. Thus the arrival patterns are the starting points for all subsequent demand.

Downstream demand is generated based on a realization of a specific need for services, actions, products, and so forth. We will refer to demand as the need/desire itself as well as the time at which that need/desire is generated. For example, demand is generated when …

- A patient arrives in the ED
- A patient calls for 911 service
- A patient needs a medication
- A physician places an order
- A nurse sees the need for a dressing change
- An ED physician realizes the need for an admission

Some of these are upstream demands, which initiate other, interdependent downstream demands. Without an understanding of the initial arrival/demand patterns, fixing downstream processes may be much more difficult, perhaps causing us to merely shift flow constraints from one process to the next. This is because the demand patterns on the front end of the process impact the other (variable) processes in the system, particularly if those arrival patterns are highly variable rather than steady and static. For instance, imagine trying to fix the ED triage process without first understanding when and how many patients show up, when they arrive, and how acute they are (believe it or not, many have tried).

Furthermore, the variability in the arrival/demand is exacerbated by any variability in downstream processes, as we saw in our small model. (Recall the variable triage process in the model was consistently bottlenecked because the process time for triage could not accommodate the arrival pattern of patients. The variable arrival patterns complicated this situation, creating a larger bottleneck. Demand variability analysis will impact the changes and degree of improvement necessary throughout the system.

Analyzing this demand variability is slightly different than process variability. In healthcare systems, demand should also be sliced to reflect differences within a given larger set of data. For instance, knowing the total average daily volume of ED patients isn't as helpful as knowing the number and patient types by hour on Mondays, or any physician-specific testing variances, and types of procedures performed. Data parsing should also reflect the source of the demand and an appropriate timestamp. In the OR, the initial demand is the patient arrival. For the downstream processes, the demand initiation might be case start time, or perhaps the time into PACU for patients being admitted. For direct admits, it is the time at which the physician's office calls for the admission and the bed is reserved. All these demand points and patterns, and most important their variability, must be thoroughly understood if we are to address demand and capacity, and even come close to dynamic capacity management.

Patterns in Demand Variability

In healthcare, we intuitively know that certain arrival and demand patterns are not typically produced in a steady stream. Even scheduled surgery cases which start on time at 7:30 a.m. do not necessarily end at a specific, predetermined time. Nor are patients always on time for their surgeries. In fact, we often consider our systems to be chaotic, ruled by completely random events. This is particularly true of ED and direct admit arrivals, admissions, and patient flow. Yet hospital systems are not as chaotic as some might believe. Variable, yes, but not completely random. More often than not, patterns exist, even where there appear to be none. Understanding the patterns in demand variability begins with probabilities in the data. For instance, the bars of the histogram in Figure 2.6 show the percentage of the total patient population that arrives during a given hour. Statistically, with

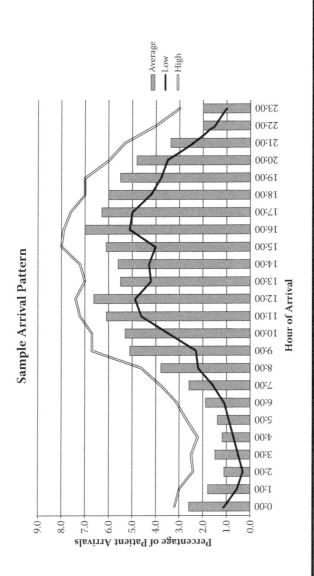

Figure 2.6 Sample arrival pattern.

enough data, we can also measure the probability that a given data point will occur. From this we can determine that, say, 80 percent of the occurrence of demand volume is less than X and more than Y patients. This is shown via the lines above and below the average. Combining the demand variation for specific time slots into larger time slots, such as entire days or weeks, allows us to visualize the variation across an entire period. So, we can see that 80 percent of the time demand occurs within a given range of variance from the average over time. Importantly, without an understanding of these patterns, proactively matching capacity with demand will be much more difficult.

As we have seen, it is critical for process analysis to know that registration takes between eight and fourteen minutes. Yet it is equally critical for demand–capacity analysis to understand the variability in the number of patients that arrive on each day of week during a given interval. Without knowing the demand variance, we will never be able to allocate resources efficiently and manage the flow of patients into and out of the registration process, making the former issue worse. We might only "staff to the average," which may not yield optimal results, especially if there are wide swings in patient volumes. What we therefore need to understand is *the range of demand* in a given time period and the *probability* that a specific amount of demand (i.e., number of demand units) will be generated. Fortunately again, definitive ranges in the variability exist, such that patterns can be ascertained.

The ranges in variability essentially represent the distribution of data and offer us insights into the relative degree of variability in our demand. Refer again to Figure 2.6. We can see not only the average but the most common highs and lows and the relative occurrence of each. This is far more informative than a simple average or other single reading. Thus, just as with the variability in process time, the variability in demand can and should be understood and taken into account to effectively analyze our system. Using either percentiles (e.g., 20th percentile), the entire range of the data set (e.g., the true high and low), or by kicking out the worst outliers (e.g., Pareto analysis, using 80 percent to represent the bulk of the occurrences/arrivals) we can see the ranges in the data that will tell us what we need to know about the demand variance. As we begin to study the common ranges in demand patterns, we can begin to better understand the performance of our systems in relationship to the commonly used averages and the inevitable outliers.

These patterns can be surprisingly consistent, and can therefore reveal a great deal about our systems, as we will see later. By using patterns and ranges, rather than trying to select a specific number like the average, we actually get a better understanding of the system's performance and the parameters that impact us over time. We will use patterns and ranges throughout this text, as they are invaluable indicators of performance in many, many respects.

Review Figure 2.7.

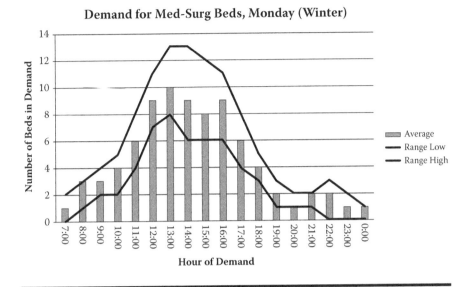

Figure 2.7   Demand pattern for med-surg beds, Monday during winter season.

The Importance of Ranges

The range is particularly crucial as we study our demand patterns, which is at the heart of any systems analysis. For example, let's look at the histogram of the demand for a medical-surgical (med-surg) bed on Mondays (Figure 2.7). Similar to the previous variability analysis, the bars represent the average demand for a med-surg bed during each given hour of the day, based on historical data. The lines on the graph represent the variability of the demand for each given hour. Important here is not the average (we typically already know that) but the range around the average by hour of day, since this tells us much more about the relative challenges of our system. If the range around the average is tight, meaning there is little variability, our demand for med-surg is relatively stable over the period in question. If the range is wide, meaning there is a great deal of variance, then we may have a system that requires upstream process improvement and change. Obviously, then, the range in the variability has a great deal to with the feel of a system or process, and the steps taken to manage it. In this case, the requirements for bed turnover, staffing, supplies, and coordination of care would change if the variability were wider. We might have to staff and stock supplies with a greater cushion, and be prepared with proper processes should the variance cause a dramatic upward shift in demand. On the other hand, if there were limited variability, we would be able to staff more tightly, reduce overhead and call-ins, reduce inventory levels, and generally run a tighter ship.

Ranges around the average tell us:

- The relative variability of the process, demand, and so forth
- The consistency of the variability over time
- The workload that we might commonly expect to see
- The degree to which we can allocate resources, alter processes, or flex to accommodate the variation
- The degree to which patterns of behavior might be seen and predicted (more on this later)

The range around the average is the critical factor in understanding how to manage the capacity of our systems and best match it to demand. Ranges simply give us a much better understanding of the actual reality in which we work. We cannot only better appreciate our system but also and more accurately understand it. With this comes additional benefits unattainable with the use of averages.

Probability of Outcomes

One critical element worth repeating is the analysis of the probability of a given outcome. Think of ED arrivals. Yes, once every fifteen years a major bus wreck causes the immediate influx of dozens of patients within minutes of one another. This is quite atypical and an extreme outlier, so we certainly would not include it in anything other than disaster planning scenarios. Since the probability of this happening is very low, it will show up on the very far end of a statistical distribution, and will not be seen in our range of common (80 percent-plus) demand. However, a more common data point might be within the typical range but still occurs less frequently than the most common number. Thus, we need to ensure that we account for the various probabilities of occurrence through proper statistical analysis, such that we can achieve more effective predictive analytics, resource and facilities planning, and so forth. Fortunately, this is already done through our histograms and distributions. The proper use of these tools in analytics helps to ensure that any replication of the data in a simulation model will be accurate and statistically valid. Simulation models are quite good at handling these issues and statistical analyses, which of course helps them to replicate variable systems.

Variability, Ranges and Patterns, and Predictive Analytics

If patterns exist, they should beget predictability. After all, that's what a pattern offers us—the ability to create quantifiable similarities between different periods of time. If there are patterns, then those patterns should offer us some degree of ability to predict the probability of the range within which the next event will occur (e.g., the next LOS range in the ED). Notice we did not say the probability of an exact occurrence of a specific number, as this would not likely be very accurate in our dynamic systems. A range is used since it will give a higher probability of being correct and more accurately reflect the variance in the actual occurrence. Therefore, our predictions can be far more accurate and more informative since we are now dealing with the predictability of ranges and not specific, single, average numbers.

For instance, take an ED LOS. Although I cannot say with any great certainty precisely what the next ED LOS for a specific patient type on a specific day will be, I can predict with great certainty that the next LOS will fall within a given range. Likewise, I cannot predict the exact number of admissions to the med-surg unit next Tuesday afternoon. Yet I can predict that the number of admits will fall within a certain range, 80 percent to 90 percent of the time. Based on our previous learning, that range will typically be relatively tight and more predictable than we might expect.

In point of fact, we do not need to be able to predict specific numbers of admissions to med-surg to more effectively manage our system. In fact, knowing the range of variance is actually more informative, since the range can help us understand the relative capacity requirements of the demand patterns we encounter. If our variance is small, great. We can plan on minimal variability in the demand for resources, for example, and thus can plan more easily. If our range is predictably wider, the range still gives us the percent probability that a given demand will occur. This information helps us determine how effectively our capacity matches our demand within the inevitable variation of the demand patterns. Knowing the demand patterns helps us do everything from predict resource requirements to plan for future space and physical plant. Furthermore, the ranges will help us understand any evolution that might be going on, as our ranges are consistently broken and change becomes evolution in our system. And this is extremely helpful as we get into outlier management later. We will discuss how predictability, variability, evolution, and outlier management all come together in the coming chapters.

Outliers and Break Points

As a refresher from the previous chapter, if the ranges would always hold, and the variability were always limited to the boundaries of expected, historical performance, we could more easily manage our systems. Alas, the 80 to 90 percent of variation that falls within our historical standard ranges still leaves an additional 10 to 20 percent that don't. These are the outliers of the system. As we'll see in the coming chapters, it is the outliers that cause us the most pain and suffering. You probably already know this from personal experience if you've worked more than a few days in a busy care environment. Outliers are manifested as "bus crash day" in the ED. We remember these outliers days most, and not the "typical" day when things run closer to averages for which we have planned. Outliers, by their very nature, are those occurrences which are neither fully predictable nor readily managed. As mentioned before, outliers are normally thought of in a negative sense, and as causing "bad" things to happen. In truth, outliers can happen on the "good" side too, but we typically don't deal with eliminating those, since we are usually wish we had more of them. And while our simulation can help us to understand what to do when the patterns fail, it cannot necessarily predict exactly when those patterns will fail to hold (else, these instances would be part of some predictable behavioral pattern). Fortunately, at least our models will help us to learn how to manage them as they occur.

Outliers come into play beyond some "break point." A break point is a set(s) of circumstances which cause the system to begin to lose significant performance integrity. As we'll see later, break points can occur in varying places to varying degrees, with varying impacts. For now, it is important to understand that a break point typically occurs with the presence of an outlier. However, this is not always the case, since a break point can occur within our typical (80 to 90 percent) range if our systems are not robust enough to handle the inherent variability in system demand and performance. In other words, if our systems are not set up to handle variability, and if our understanding of the variability and ranges is limited, our systems are susceptible to breaking down at many levels of variation. These are yet more reasons to study variability and develop robust approaches to help manage our dynamic worlds.

Patterns, Demand, and HODDOW WOMSOY

You knew before you picked up this text that there was variability in your processes and systems. We now know that there are commonly patterns to this variability, represented by the ranges around the average, and that our systems are not dominated by totally random events.

As we saw in the previous section, there are ways to show variability in system performance, arrival patterns, and so forth. Take the arrival pattern shown in Figure 2.8 for example. Does this ED arrival pattern seem familiar? Likely so, since many EDs exhibit similar arrival patterns. Similarly, there are patterns to the variability of these arrival patterns, as can be shown in candlestick charts or histograms with ranges. These can be derived from data over distinct periods of time, such as days of week and seasons, or for particular patient types. Indeed, to properly analyze the demand patterns as we do, one must necessarily differentiate between the various patterns and subpatterns of demand, such that patterns can be effectively ascertained, when possible, and capacity can be effectively matched.

For example, disaggregating the arrival patterns of mental health patients into a community clinic may show a different pattern than if we simply look at all arrivals. If we analyze the patterns of intraday arrivals, we might find particular

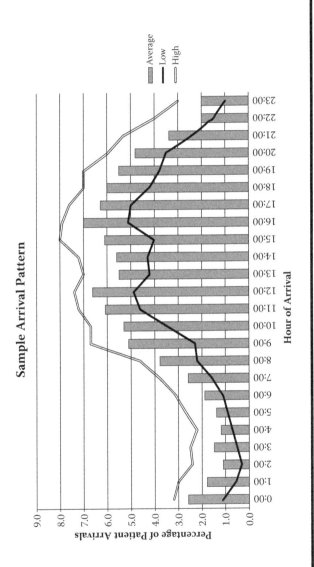

Figure 2.8   Sample arrival pattern.

hours are more prevalent or that there are patterns from week to week. Similarly, if we simply look at the total arrival volume of all patients into a Florida ED, by day of week, in winter, it might belie an unusual increase in chest pain patients on Monday mornings.

Thus, our variable patterns should be analyzed for what they can tell us about critical system components/departments during different time periods. What we need, then, is a better breakdown of the analysis of upstream demand patterns, which will tell us the initial demand for subsequent downstream processes. For this, think HODDOW WOMSOY. No, it's not a Native American translation of "demand pattern." It stands for:

Hour of day (HOD)
Day of week (DOW)
Week of month (WOM)
Season of year (SOY)

Breaking down your analysis of demand patterns, and even other variables in the system using these time groupings can assist you in effectively analyzing the variability throughout your systems, not just in demand.

Hour of day (HOD)—This should be obvious by now. Your demand patterns for both upstream and downstream processes vary throughout the day. Mornings are different than afternoons, which are different than nights. Without understanding the demand variability throughout the day, it will be much more difficult to later effectively allocate capacity.

Day of week (DOW)—This, too, should be obvious, yet we often fail to take advantage of this simple piece of information. Think of the demand for inpatient beds from the OR. Is it the same on Mondays as it is on Wednesdays? Specifically, is it the same for *each specific bed type* on each day of the week? Perhaps not. There is variance depending on the OR schedule and the types of cases seen. Furthermore, are admissions from the ED on Thursday mornings the same as Monday's? Unlikely. So, why do we fail to account for the differences between days (not to mention the variances within days)?

Week of month (WOM)—As it relates to inpatient bed demand from the OR or demand coming from other specific areas where events tend to be scheduled, is the demand consistent throughout the month? Probably not, since some physicians work every other week or shift cases around within their own schedules in patterns. Thus, week 1 of a month may be different from week 4.

Season of year (SOY)—Nothing is more befuddling to me than an ED that proclaims a specific ALOS as a standard, fixed metric, yet is taken aback when that LOS changes during flu season. SOY can mean tremendous changes in upstream and downstream demand patterns and thus must be accounted for in our analysis of our dynamic systems. Variability can change, as can volumes and patient/case types, so taking seasonality into account is critical.

Therefore, you should have as many single-digit metrics as are reflected by your systems' variability over the course of time. For an ED this might be, at a minimum, four for hours of day (at least morning, afternoon, evening, and night), seven days of week, plus four for seasonality. You should therefore not be at all surprised as your systems change over time due to the variances within and external to them.

Attribute Variation

Of course, the number of arrivals is certainly not the only attribute of a healthcare system which varies. Other demand attributes include acuity and patient types. These can be critical, particularly as they relate to seasonal variability. Flu season or even pregnancies are variances that can sometimes be patterned over time. Do not hesitate to examine the subpatterns within your patterns, as it may lead you to a better understanding of your systems. Some of the subpatterns you might study, as they relate to key metrics or outcomes, include

- Patient and/or acuity type
- Surgery type
- Physician specific (such as total LOS, number of tests, or disposition time)
- Unit or floor
- Admission source
- Shift or care team

Variability and Evolution

Variability happens over time. As that variability occurs in dynamic patterns, systemic changes can be detected. We call it *evolution*, as it reflects a permanent alteration in some aspect of a system's performance, variance, or pattern, which is more indicative of the future than the past. While evolution is difficult to detect while it is happening (since it often happens ever so slowly), it can indicate slow changes in critical variables such as demographics, economic conditions, insurance coverage, and health trends.

Furthermore, our systems change over time by our own hands. Improvements to processes are made, infrastructure and technology advance and decline with age, and external variables such as demand and acuity patterns change as services are added and expanded. All these are evolutionary in nature, and indicate the need for ongoing analysis of the system's variability and its respective impact on system performance, capacity requirements, and so forth.

First, evolution can take place in several ways. The outliers of a process can become more frequent and prevalent (on either end of the scale), causing them to become normalized within the performance patterns. Meaning, a previous outlier becomes part of the 80 percent-plus of our common occurrences. As the process evolves within the context of the larger system, the system itself might permanently evolve. Second, variability can be reduced or eliminated such that the process/system is in some way permanently altered. This happens as process improvement efforts squeeze the variability from a process/system such that it becomes more stable and even more predictable. This widens the 80 percent-plus range as more outliers fall into the more common range of occurrences. Third, some external variable is altered, such as growth in community demand based on a newly expanded ED capacity. This may make current outlier volumes the norm for the future. As one component of the system evolves (e.g., the ED expands its capacity), we must consider the other components to see how they too might evolve or need to be altered. Without doing so, we stand to lose whatever optimization we might have gained through the analysis of the variable system, since we mistakenly study the system's variability in a static way, as if it will never change or as if only part will change.

Therefore, it is critical to study both the variability of the entire system and its components as well as the "variability of the variability" to look for evolutionary patterns from which might come additional change requirements. Ongoing analysis of the system, its component variability, demand patterns and variability, and changes made to our systems are all critical to the ongoing understanding and optimization of system performance. Small changes to specific components can have large impacts on the rest of the system, as we will see in the next chapter.

Summary: Variability and Demand

Variability shows up throughout our hospital operations. Because humans are not robots with precise movements, identical capabilities, and regimented actions, there is inherent variability in the way we perform tasks. Even the simplest of tasks can have variability. The outcomes of this variability will depend on a number of factors, such as the degree of the variability and the number of times the process is performed.

We focus on demand in this text, as described in Chapter 1, because the demand drives everything else in the system, throughout the system. A patient's arrival in the ED triggers an entire chain of subsequent demand events, particularly if that patient is admitted to an inpatient unit. Thus, in order to analyze and improve our systems, we must have a very firm handle on the demand in the system. Without a deep and complete understanding of demand, we will continue to tweak the supply (e.g., the services demand is requesting) via reactive management and yet may fail to optimize the system because we are not actually matching demand with available capacity. Our goal here is to change the way hospitals think about their demand, its variability and predictability, and the opportunities for better service capacity through predictive analytics and outlier management.

Notes

1. Michael George, *Lean Six Sigma: Combining Six Sigma Quality with Lean Speed*, McGraw-Hill, New York, 2002, p. 17.
2. There are commonly seven wastes in the lean methodology. I use the acronym "Tim Wood" to remember them. They are, in order of the letters of the acronym, transport, inventory, movement (unnecessary), waiting, overproduction, overprocessing, and defects. These wastes form the basis of the concepts for the lean methodology and its assorted solutions and toolsets.
3. James P. Womack and Daniel T. Jones, *Lean Thinking*, Simon and Schuster, New York, 1996; index pages 335–350.
4. Karen Martin and Mike Osterling, *Kaizen Event Planner*, Productivity Press, New York, 2008.
5. Marc Baker and Ian Taylor, *Making Hospitals Work*, Lean Enterprise Academy, Boston, MA, 2009.
6. There are a number of simulation software packages available on the market. This particular software is called Arena™, from Rockwell Automation. There are also large and highly robust models that have been customized to replicate and analyze entire hospital-wide flow, such as that built by GE Healthcare.

Chapter 3

Interdependencies

In 1978, historian James Burke developed and aired the first in a brilliant BBC (British Broadcast Corporation) television series called *Connections*. Professor Burke had an interesting take on the "evolution" and developments that led to the modern-day era and current circumstances and technologies. In the initial series, he traced the development of thoughts, inventions, ideas, and concepts back through the ages to their origins, connecting the sometimes tiny and indiscernible dots within complex developmental interactions. Across continents, events, and huge spans of time, he found seemingly inconsequential incidents and causalities and wove them into contiguous streams of historical evolutionary flow to their illogical but nonetheless inevitable conclusion. His knack for finding the subtle relationships between seemingly disparate occurrences made for a fascinating trip through the course of human events and history. A Baltimore man invents the bottle, which lead to razors and clock springs, and eventually the Hubble telescope (episode 14). Or, in episode 16, a sick lawyer in eighteenth-century France forever changes farming and triggers the French Revolution and new concepts in medical research.

I believe it was the watching of this show that initially led me to become hooked on the complexities of large system interactions. It wasn't until many years later, when I was introduced to Venn diagrams, Peter Senge, spaghetti charts, and other such concepts and tools, that I became enamored of and fascinated with systems and interdependencies.

Interdependencies

What Burke called connections I will call interdependencies. His were global and historical in nature, whereas those we'll deal with here are much more finite though nonetheless complex. Regardless of scale, the concepts are similar.

Interdependencies in a given system are those links between one system component and another, which result in some sort of impact(s) on either, both, or other components of the system. Or, stated another way, the causal impact of one process or operation on another within a given process flow or system. While one component may not be absolutely dependent on another (meaning that its function cannot occur without the function of the other), the former can nonetheless be influenced by the other's outputs, actions, variability, and so forth. Thus interdependencies are causal in some way, in one or multiple directions. Interdependencies are part of every complex working system, from the human body to a hospital, and appear in myriad ways throughout a system's functionality.

Think of the little model we built in the previous chapter (Figure 3.1). The interdependencies of this simple system ([ED] triage, registration, disposition, and discharge) are easily seen. As we saw in the previous chapter, if triage takes more or less time than anticipated, it can have a significant impact on downstream processes and operations. Both the variability and the interdependency between system components can flow upstream as well as downstream, and can have more or less influence depending on the magnitude of the variables that influence the causality. Variance in arrival and demand patterns, process errors, misinformation, unexpected events, new variables, external input changes, and other factors can also influence the upstream or downstream of a given system, causing the impacts of interdependencies and the degree of their influence to expand, decrease, or change in some way.

In healthcare, as in our little variability model, interdependencies are everywhere. Think of the many years we grappled with improving an individual department's flow and function, such as the ED. Most often, we tried to "fix" the ED in isolation. That is, we tried to improve it within its own four walls, without accounting for and dealing with the external interdependencies of radiology, lab, admissions, inpatient resource availability, and other external (interrelated) variables. Furthermore, we often tried to fix it through static analytical tools and methodologies, ignoring or failing to see the variability inherent within and external to the department. While some of the internal ED issues could be dramatically improved (e.g., the flow from triage to physician), external factors can constrain or negate those improvements and prevent systemic impacts. For example, ED physician throughput might be constrained due to an admission flow constraint, thus negating the impact of an effort to improve triage throughput time and reduce overall ED LOS. The degree to which the various internal and external constraints impact various changes and improvements can be a mystery unless we have the right analytical tools to diagnose and predict the interdependencies. Furthermore, the degree to which improvements we might make will impact the system writ large can also be a mystery, since we cannot foresee the impacts of the system's upstream and downstream variability and interdependencies without the proper toolsets.

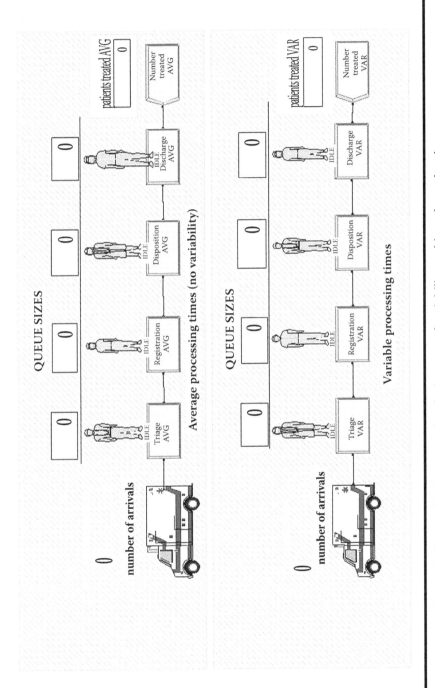

Figure 3.1 Sample simulation model demonstrating the impacts of variability and interdependencies.

Interdependencies in the Current PI Methodologies

In many process improvement (PI) methodologies, interdependencies are mentioned and even studied. For instance, any flowchart can be as detailed or as "systemic" as need be. A good, high-level flowchart can depict an entire system in a single diagram, complete with interdependencies. It is not uncommon to see the words *upstream* and *downstream* mentioned in Lean texts. Systemwide views are sometimes achieved through Lean's value stream maps (VSMs), which can show, for instance, entire supply chains (at a high level). Flowcharts, by whatever name, can and do depict nearly any level of system flow and thus are great starting points for analysis, if nothing else.

Six Sigma's failure mode and effects analysis (FMEA) is used to identify various and specific ways in which a given process, product, or service fails or becomes defective. FMEA is then used to develop ways to address identified issues.[1] Other tools such as fishbone diagrams (also used by Lean proponents, which they call Ishikawa diagrams) capture the impact a given set of inputs have on a given process output. Inputs are typically lumped into categories such as resources and equipment, for further detail, and definition.

Six Sigma and Lean Six Sigma (LSS) advocates often employ SIPOC analysis to study the upstream and downstream of a given system. SIPOC analyzes suppliers, inputs, process(s), outputs, and the customer in the relationships and flows of activities so as to draw attention to the various subcomponents and potential issues within the flow.

As another example, the theory of constraints (TOC), popularized by Goldratt in his educational novel, *The Goal*,[2] is all about the analysis of interdependent constraints and solving for key bottlenecks in factory flow (this notion was applied to the UK healthcare system, albeit rather poorly, in a book titled *We All Fall Down*[3]). Other related materials (all must-reads, if you ask me) include Senge's *Fifth Discipline*, which speaks of organizational dynamics and learning organizations on a systems level; Schrage's *Serious Play*[4] speaks on the complexities of design and new ways of thinking about creativity; and books from Gladwell (e.g., *The Tipping Point*[5]) speak of the relationships in human interactions and the impact on business growth, marketing, and product awareness.

The Missing Elements

Yet despite the availability of these tools and concepts, the analysis of complex interdependencies in healthcare, specifically hospital-wide patient flow and capacity, is only at a nascent and rudimentary stage. There are a number of reasons for this.

1. The human brain is simply not wired to think in these complexities. We lose our understanding of the system as it grows larger, more variable, and more complex. If understanding complex systems were so readily achieved, complex and variable

hospital-wide flow would not be so difficult to solve. Recall the statement from the beginning of this text, "Hospitals are more like busy airports or even battle-fields than Toyota production lines." Yet, assessing the interdependencies of such systems can often be a difficult exercise, at best. Interdependencies do not react the same way all the time, and these differences make the system more difficult to improve. The tendency is to be process focused rather than systems focused, since here we can sometimes have an impact.

2. In the early stages of improvement efforts, a narrowed process focus may be related to the degree of change necessary and the daunting scale of the tasks ahead. There may well be so much to fix that *any* change will be seen as productive and advantageous. Therefore, our process focus is seen as a start-ing point toward a larger end goal. Additionally, a process focus may keep us quite busy for a long time, as there may be many process issues to solve before delving into the more "advanced" analytics and solutions. However, this limited focus may, in the long run, inhibit optimization due to unfore-seen impacts on interdependent components.

3. In part, it is also due to the aforementioned tendency to solve problems in silos. We traditionally solve for one department or function, leaving the opti-mization of other departments and functions, and indeed the entire system, to other disconnected projects. (This allows for better finger pointing.) Even within more structured methodologies such as Lean, the tendency is to be process focused, leaving out the systemic impacts that might occur as a result of specific departmental or operational changes. Although Lean and other methodologies speak to the interdependencies of systems, only a few method-ologies specifically and directly attack this issue. And those, such as TOC, are not commonly used in healthcare. And even when these potentially valuable methodologies are used, they fail to account for the variability within the interdependencies since they do not utilize the correct analytical tools, as we will see in a moment. Thus, even these can fail.

4. It is often assumed that the "sum of the parts is greater than the whole," in the sense that improving critical individual components, such as the OR (operating room) and ED, inevitably yields a more optimal total sys-tem. Although the improvement of individual components is obviously required to yield an improved system, we most often fail to understand how improving or changing one component will impact others in the system. Upstream and downstream constraints can actually be *created* by the improvement we make at a given process level. Thus in fact, *it is the interrelationships between the various components that often dictate whether a given process change will yield its desired and expected outcomes.* For instance, even if the ED can improve its internal flow, external constraints such as transportation availability can reduce or mitigate improvements. So even though we might improve processes individually, the greater system may not benefit.

We thereby create an "optimized box of gears" rather than a functioning Swiss watch. The gears, though individually functional and optimized in their own right, do not mesh together dynamically to allow for a functional system.

5. There is also a tendency to discount the need for complex analytics. Lean users, in particular, often gloss over the need for detailed data analytics. I have often heard Leaners say that hospitals do not have good data anyway. (I know some Lean healthcare users who are actually frustrated Six Sigma converts, who grew weary of data requirements and detailed statistical analytics.) This narrowed process focus yields a "simpler" view of the issue, which in turn can yield a disregard of the true complexities and up- and downstream interdependencies that may exist. And while Lean is certainly fast and efficient, and the need for speed understandable, the lack of systemic analytics can lead to future impediments to achievement. So despite what might be the lack of data for the kind of analytics required, those analytics are still necessary.

Think of the last Kaizen or plan–do–check–act (PDCA) event you worked in or heard about. Did the actual improvement effort cross over departmental boundaries? Did it do so on a variety of days of the week or shifts of the day? Were all the upstream and downstream components included in the analysis? If so, you are far more advanced than most, and were probably well beyond the scope of traditional methodologies, using advanced tools and applications (and, by the way, hats off to you).

Six Sigma advocates are much more data driven and tend to focus on larger, more complex projects. Six Sigma's focus on data analytics is one of its better attributes. Yet, they still often fail to effectively predict the system's interdependencies and its influence of performance. Furthermore, projects do not necessarily reflect the right breadth and scope. Thus despite its data focus, Six Sigma can miss the mark without the additional tools and interdependency analytics of dynamic capacity analysis, matching, and management (DCAMM).

6. More importantly, healthcare analytics tend to be static in nature, failing to account for the very elements that make them inherently difficult to analyze and improve. It is not so much the methodologies themselves that prevent systems and interdependency analysis (though they can be a barrier). It is our focus, vision, mental capacity, and choice of analytical tools that ultimately inhibit our efforts. Thus even if the various methodologies were combined or used more heavily in the analysis of the systems' interrelationships, the tools and thinking necessary to effectively analyze these interdependent systems would still be desperately lacking. This is due in part to the particular nature of healthcare's complex interdependencies, the lack of familiarity with available tools, and the combination of interdependencies with the last chapter's villain, variability.

The Biggest Missing Element: Variability

In case you skipped Chapter 2 on "Variability," by far the biggest inhibitor to the proper analysis of healthcare's complex interdependencies is the lack of tools to account for and analyze variability. Variability, when it is combined with complex interdependencies, can make common analytical tools and methodologies less effective, if not useless, for systemic or complex process improvement. Were it not for variability and its inherent significant impact on process performance, the current and common methodologies could easily adapt and account for the interdependencies in our systems. A flowchart or value stream map would easily suffice to analyze and manage our systems. However, these can only show the flow of the system and not the impact of the variation within the flow. It is the additional complexity of variability that makes it the most important constraint to the effectiveness of existing methodologies.

(Please note: Do not misunderstand these considerations to be refutations of the value of these popular methodologies. To the contrary, I remain a strong supporter of just about any methodology that can improve processes. However, it is clear that there is a definitive need to expand the analytical capabilities and add a "tool to the tool box" in the form of DCAMM, such that individual process changes can yield their optimal value to the system.)

Interdependencies and Variability: The Origins of Dynamism

The combination of variability in and between processes and the interdependencies of those processes creates what we will call *dynamism*, or the dynamic component of this dynamic capacity management concept. Formally defined, dynamism is the causal and variable impact of one process or operation on another within a given process flow or system.

Dynamism is derived from the melding of variability and interdependent processes. A process that is variable will have variable outcomes. Variable processes that are causally knitted together make for a dynamic system. The relationship between one process and a downstream or upstream process creates crosscurrents of impact that can go in either or both directions. Dynamism is created and exacerbated as multiple, variable processes intersect, and the resulting variability begins to broadcast in multiple directions simultaneously. As we have seen, this variability has direct impacts on the other components of the system. For instance, the time at which a downstream process is able to begin (assuming no parallel processing) is impacted by delays in upstream flow. That impact is, in and of itself, variable, based on the degree of variability in the upstream process. Thus a variance in the registration process might yield a patient who is early, slightly delayed, or significantly delayed in seeing her physician by the appointed time. Furthermore, the degree of impact on the downstream process can vary, depending on the variance of the upstream process. For instance, a patient who is five minutes late to a scheduled appointment can still be seen without delaying others. However, a patient who is ten or more minutes late might be turned away or, if seen, delay later patients.

Furthermore, variability combines with interdependencies to create systems that change over time and may not react the same way under different or even very similar circumstances. The probability of various results becomes more important, creating a need to understand how multiple potential process outcomes impact the system's interdependencies. This dynamism makes the analysis of highly complex and variable systems all the more difficult.

Think, for instance, of an outpatient surgery center's upstream registration process and a downstream initial patient intake process. Such a simple system could be readily depicted in a value stream map or flowchart. However, lost is the capacity, processing capability, and actual throughput of even this simple flow.

The variability in the registration process has its own impacts on patient intake, since the upstream can delay the downstream processes, depending on the upstream variability. The downstream process can cause additional constraints insofar as it cannot handle the flow from the upstream process—for instance, if registration is particularly quick yet the patients are made to wait due to the rate of the intake process. The interrelationship between registration and a variable intake process creates a whole new set of issues if both are variable. Thus, one can further constrain the other, depending on the variability in and between the process times of the two components. This can mean that an otherwise simple process might see a reduction in its throughput and capacity, or at least total processing time.

To delve further into this example, let's assume intake cannot start before registration is complete (i.e., no parallel processing). Let's also assume that there is limited capacity in both, and that there is limited space for waiting patients. We'll say the typical range of processing time for registration is between nine and fifteen minutes. Patient intake requires between eleven and eighteen minutes. Now, let's assume that we have an outlier patient in both processes at roughly the same time. The registration process, due to a lack of proper insurance information, requires nineteen minutes, and the intake process for an elderly, obese patient requires twenty-three minutes. Both processes are now outliers and are constrained, and both impact each other as well as other processes in the system. From a flow perspective, the following questions arise:

- What sort of an upstream constraint has just been created for the next new patient arriving to be registered (perhaps in the form of wait time)?
- Will the waiting area be overfilled?
- What delay has been created for these and the next several patients, as well as the nurses and physicians, as the patients move through the care process?
- What impact has this delay created for the productivity of the staff?
- Is the system now in an outlier status, and how long will it be before it returns to its normal pattern?

To make the example more complex, let's say that Tuesdays are the busy clinic days, and Tuesday morning (rather than afternoon) is when the physicians prefer to see their patients. Furthermore, let's assume that Friday's schedule is left intentionally open to manage patients who need to be quickly scheduled. How does our flowchart work now? It might still show the flow of patients, but the details of that flow are now too complex for such an analytical tool. Given this new complexity, additional questions might include:

- What, then, are the throughput capabilities of the system on various days of the week?
- How will altering the schedule impact the wait time on Thursdays if Tuesday's patient schedule is realigned?
- If the above scenario occurred on a busy Thursday, would the impact(s) on the physicians' productivity be greater? If so, by how much?

Questions for the process analyst arise if the existing variability cannot be immediately reduced or managed, such as:

- What is the actual capability and capacity of the system within a given time frame? Is it the same each day?
- Will overtime be required, and if so, how much?
- How does one increase capacity given the variability within the system and limited resources?
- Does the variability in arrival patterns and processing times require different processes and operational models on different days?
- Does the variability in arrival patterns, processes, and process times create the need for different value stream maps? If so, what day of week or hour of day do you put into your additional value stream maps?
- Which day's scenario would go into your fishbone diagram when searching for root causes?
- If the variation is significant enough, how many value stream maps and diagrams are necessary to effectively capture all the possible scenarios, as the combination of the circumstances combine to create a variety of outcomes?

The issue of improving flow thus becomes more complicated. Which process should we try to impact and by how much? How much variability should be squeezed from the various processes to improve flow and capacity? Will anything we do in either process actually improve the throughput through the system on specific days of the week? While we might see an obvious bottleneck in registration, worse bottlenecks might be generated with specific patient types in patient intake. Thus it is important to remember: *It is the outliers, not the average, that break the system.* If there are outliers, driven by the dynamism of the system, average responses will fail to be effective.

This means that the analysis of the system's metrics will be inherently limited if not incorrect if we only use averages and fail to account for dynamism. This could lead us to false assumptions about both the performance of our systems and the solutions that might drive real and effective change.

The point here is that even the simplest of systems can be confounded by a little dynamism. Dynamism requires the addition of some analytical capabilities not common to healthcare.

Dynamism and Systems Analysis

The process analysis issue therefore evolves into: How do you effectively analyze and improve a dynamic system with a static tool like a process map or a static methodology such as LSS?. The short answer is: you can't. If there is enough dynamism, the complexity of the system is increased to the point that static analytical tools no longer effectively capture, and offer solutions for, system-level issues. Healthcare systems cannot be analyzed well using traditional static methodologies and tools, since these invariably rely on averages as analytical benchmarks of system performance (and we saw what averages mean for analysis in Chapter 2). Dr. Jeffrey Liker, Lean advocate, author, and guru, admits that "many manufacturers lose their … gains after a few years because managers fail to monitor their viability as sales volumes or other conditions change."[6] In other words, gains are lost because systems vary and evolve. Furthermore, much evidence shows that many, if not most, Lean healthcare projects fail[7]. To this, I say, "Well, duh!" This is exactly why DCAMM is necessary and why static methodologies inevitably falter.

As we now know, our patterns [in demand and capacity] yield a certain degree of predictability that similar results will occur if the conditions are replicated. Taking this one step further, if we assume that component-level dynamism can be patterned, then we can also assume that the system's dynamism can be patterned since it is directly linked to the components. That is, the components' patterns (and variations therein) ultimately add up to the system's patterns (and variations therein) even as the inherent interdependencies impact system performance (e.g., throughout HODDOW WOMSOY). Thus not only processes and components but entire systems can take on patterns, inclusive of the dynamism of the individual system components. System operations, initiated by upstream demand patterns and linked to capacity requirements and the component dynamism, can therefore be studied to the extent that demand and component patterns exist and can be detected. This in turn means that the performance of entire systems can be more effectively predicted, under a variety of circumstances, by accounting for the variability and interdependencies within and between operations and recognizing the patterns therein, within the context of the known historical patterns. This understanding is the beginning of true system-level predictive analytics and an entirely new world of management opportunities.

As we analyze the patterns that create the system's dynamism, we can also begin to ascertain what causes the system to begin to break down and under what circumstances outliers emerge within the patterns. As long as we are able to effectively capture the variability of the demand, and the dynamism of and between the system's components, we can predict the dynamism and HODDOW WOMSOY patterns of the entire system.

Unless our typical demand and component performance patterns cause us to routinely cross a "break point," either up- or downstream, we should expect and plan for this predetermined variability in the day-to-day management of the system. It should not be surprising, then, to see the in-range variation in demand, such as ED arrivals or number of cath lab cases. Only when our system flips over to outlier status and moves to the "wrong side" of a break point might our reaction be different. And even then, a deepened understanding of the system should lead to predetermined and effective solutions. This is especially true if the break points occur within the normal range of variation. Therefore we can study the entire system within its typical range, its reaction as it flips over to outlier status, and the root circumstances of both situations. Through the deep, strategic DCAMM analysis of the system, we can essentially create an ongoing, working knowledge of the causalities in the system that lead to the issues we face. And if this is possible, we can thereby proactively see the multiple triggers that yield the beginnings of operational breakdowns and aggressively manage these scenarios before they begin to have their full effect. As we will see later in Chapter 5, this sort of analysis is made infinitely easier with our simulation models, since they offer the capability to run scenarios before or after situations occur, so as to learn how, when, and where to react. In fact, this analysis would be impossible *without* our models.

This points us to the next level of management and a very necessary capability for our future interactions with our complex, variable systems: predictive analytics at a systems level. And of course, all this requires a change in the way we think about both the tools we use and the way we use them. We will cover this is greater detail in Chapters 5, 8, and 12.

Dynamism and Evolution

Recall that the evolution of performance takes place either as outliers fall into more predictable patterns that are then deemed normal or variability is reduced or eliminated, thus changing performance. In other words, a process that is changed due to efforts to alter it or changes in external factors that influence it may eventually evolve to a new state of performance or both. Thus processes evolve for a variety of reasons and under a variety of circumstances.

Changes in process that have downstream impacts may alter the system of which they are part. If evolution occurs within variability, and if variability and interdependencies combine to yield dynamism, it stands to reason that evolution occurs within the dynamism of the system as well. If, in other words, variability evolves, so does the impact variability has on the system to which it is related. And if the variability impacts the interdependencies and created dynamism, then that dynamism will reflect similar evolutionary changes.

Consider the multiple changes that might have gone on within your current facility over the years. These might include new technologies, process improvements, changes in demographics and acuity patterns, and the competitive landscape. Changes that impact only specific components of your system, such as acuity patterns, may have resulted in upstream and downstream systemic responses, whether good or bad, intentional or merely reactive. Additionally, changes in demand patterns to system components (such as the ED) likely yielded some downstream impacts that might have, or perhaps should have, been addressed through some form of change to the impacted components (such as radiology). Component evolution thus yields system evolution as the interdependencies are impacted by the changes at the component level. As the components change, so too can the impact on the system writ large. And if the components are altered to a significant enough degree, the entire system can be altered significantly and thus require larger, systemic adjustments.

Detecting the need for evolutionary adjustments requires understanding the drivers of component variation, the impact of changes on the components, interdependencies within the system, and the upstream and downstream impacts on the system itself. Most importantly, it requires an understanding of what constitutes outlier status and how new conditions might reflect a new normal. As the system components evolve, and the system reacts and evolves, predictive analytics and proactive management can foresee the new normal and proactively alter any necessary components to rebalance the system. In other words, once the system is better understood and key parameters are known, the system can be regularly analyzed for the need for rebalancing such that optimal overall system performance is attained/maintained.

Why Not a "Live" Test, PDCA, or Kaizen Event?

PDCA and other "live" tests such as Kaizen events are, in a way, inevitable in process improvement. At some point, regardless of whether you have modeled your systems, and regardless of whether you have effectively planned for change implementation, you must put process changes into action. By using the Kaizen events and PDCA, we analyze the systems as they will actually perform for a given period. However, these events are often done without deep consideration of the dynamism of system performance. A PDCA event conducted in May might result in significant improvements. However, the winter might bring new challenges, such as changes in demand patterns or other variables, which will alter one or more of the components and cause May's improvements to break down. It is thus not uncommon for even standard variation to require multiple solutions, or as we call it, *dynamic standardization*, rather than a single solution for a single set of circumstances.

And while Lean, PDCA, and other methodologies are responsible for tremendous change and improvements across multiple industries, including healthcare, improvements become harder and harder to come by as our efforts continue. As the low hanging fruit is picked, future advances toward optimization will inevitably require more effective solutions, typically because they involve cross-functional process change and systemic alterations of performance. And this is where the more static methodologies begin to lose their incredible power.

Last, recall that evolution and dynamism require that static methodologies constantly and repeatedly analyze complex systems. (By most definitions, isn't that rework?) As Liker so eloquently stated, Lean improvement can be lost as internal and external variables change. Thus while the various static methodologies might aid in short-term, process-level solutions, DCAMM is required to truly take management to the next level.

Therefore, additional analytical methodologies and tools, such as those described herein, are necessary to obtain more dynamic and optimized performance throughout the organization. As we will see, the results will be a more robust and effective analytical methodology: the dynamic analysis of system capacity.

Dynamism in Systems Thinking: An IOM/NAE Perspective

If you yet don't believe that dynamism impacts healthcare, take a look at some of the statements from the 2005 report titled *Building a Better Delivery System: A New Engineering/Health Care Partnership*. A joint effort from the Institute of Medicine (IOM) and National Academy of Engineering (NAE), the report should have been a groundbreaking, market-moving document. Covering the breadth of gaps in delivery, safety, efficiency, and thinking within care delivery, it presents both a call and a challenge to leaders, providers, and payers alike. Complete with recommendations for action, it serves, for some, as the foundation for advancements in the efficacy of the provision of healthcare.

Indeed, some progress has been made since the 2005 publication of the report, particularly in increasing the focus on quality operations and in improvements in information technology (IT). The concepts of a systems approach to the delivery of care and the need for systems engineering tools, however, seem relatively stillborn when compared to the work and advancements in quality and IT. Without a solid systems approach to the issues we face in healthcare, all other solutions and technologies risk ineffective design, erratic implementation, and inefficient utilization.

The authors of *Building a Better Delivery System* wisely anticipated the challenges facing healthcare and did not shy away from calling out gaps in expertise and the clear lack of vision. To quote from the influential first pages of the report:

> The health care sector as a whole has been slow to embrace [system engineering tools] however, even though they have been shown to yield valuable returns to the small but growing number of health care organizations

and clinicians that have applied them. ... Relatively few health care professionals or administrators are equipped to think analytically about health care delivery as a system or to appreciate the relevance of systems-engineering tools. Even fewer are equipped to work to apply these tools.[8]

Most profoundly, the report condemns when it states, "It is astounding that health-care has not made better use of the design, analysis, and control tools of systems engineering."[9] Sadly, this is almost as true today as in 2005.

Yet, change is beginning to take shape, and the healthcare market is beginning to see a shift towards the IOM and NAE's recommendations and goals. Herein is an outline of how changes are developing, where they are (it is hoped) leading, where gaps remain, and what can be done to advance these efforts.

The IOM and NAE specify a clear role for systems thinking, pointing out "a desperate need for systems engineering tools" like statistical process control, systems dynamic models, and complex neural networks.[10] The report also emphasizes the difference between improving the performance of all individual hospital units and optimizing the system as a whole, stating, "Optimization of the whole requires a clear understanding of the goal of the overall system, as well of interactions among the subsystems. The whole must be recognized as being greater than the sum of its parts."[11] Adopting and acting on a systems view require a change in not only thinking, but also staffing, investment, and training.

Perhaps the largest gap in implementing the recommendations of *Building a Better Delivery System* is training and leadership. In a conversation with a senior executive from one of the largest healthcare systems in the world, I asked about the difference between hospitals that succeed and those that struggle. Without needing even to ponder the question, her simple and obvious answer was firm and short: leadership.

The IOM and NAE are specific and blunt in recommending a call to "accelerate change."[12] For example, the report appeals to a plethora of resources—from the federal government to universities to the private sector—to establish learning centers for teaching and enhancing systems engineering. It calls for changes in education systems to allow for the teaching of systems thinking to all healthcare professionals, and it calls on Business Schools and Operations Research departments to add healthcare materials and case studies to their curriculum topics. At a higher level, it establishes the need for culture, habits, and systems to accommodate the new learning required to implement these changes.

Although we still have much work to do, especially at the local hospital level, some change is already under way to address the recommendations for the dissemination of systems engineering and systems thinking. In universities, industrial engineering departments have formed or are forming health systems engineering programs and tracks for graduate and undergraduate degrees. MBA programs are allowing the inclusion of public policy and healthcare-related studies, and MHA (Masters of Health Administration) programs are beginning to include greater emphasis on engineering topics. These programs will continue to train the leaders of tomorrow with a broadening focus and a more diverse skill set.

However, on-the-job training remains in short supply. Nursing and medical school programs must incorporate systems and process thinking into curricula to help graduates understand the complexities of the worlds in which they will work. Locally, staff nurses, physicians, technicians, and literally every employee at every level need to understand basic systems engineering concepts such as variability, queuing theory, and process control. Current staff must become not only familiar with but passionate about such concepts as a part of daily work to attain the con-current goals of efficiency and quality simultaneously.

Local hospital leadership must play a role, either becoming educated and passionate about systems engineering or stepping aside to allow forward progress. Government, payers, and patients can demand change, but leaders who remain unfamiliar with the concepts of systems engineering often slow or even prevent that change through a lack of passion, education, and vision. Without consistent education throughout hospitals, from the executive suite to staff, change will be difficult and slow. A meaningful transformation will not happen without the necessary passion and vision of local hospital leadership.

Fortunately, many organizations around the country actively work to advance systems engineering, not the least of which is the Society for Health Systems (SHS), (a division of the Institute of Industrial Engineers). But these are not the organizations of hospital leadership, who are often represented through the American College of Healthcare Executives (ACHE), the American Organization of Nurse Executives[4] (AONE), the American College of Physician Executives, and others. Though not a specific demand of the IOM/NAE report, these organizations must become conduits of communication, collaborative creativity, and shared solutions rather than serve their respective constituencies as siloed entities. Alignment and cross-pollination for these groups will serve their memberships through the exposure and advancement of systems engineering in hospitals' organizational and departmental structures, ultimately serving the true customer of the healthcare system, the patients. Starting within the communities of healthcare professionals will create the momentum and positive change the IOM/NAE report envisioned.

Tools for Interdependency Analysis

Obviously, the *A* (analysis) in DCAMM requires special tools. Spreadsheets, flowcharts, value stream maps, and other typical tools are too static to capture dynamic systems. We have already discussed several of the more important tools of the analysis of variability, specifically simulation tools and their random number generators. Fortunately, these same tools are handy for analyzing complex system interdependencies. As we will see in Chapter 5, there are several simulation tools that are quite handy for studying interdependencies, namely, discrete event, Monte

Carlo, and a few others. I prefer discrete event (aka process simulation) as it allows for the development of a more realistic flow within a complex system. Whatever tool you choose to use, the key is *how* you use it. Discrete-event simulation is my tool of choice for the study of complex interdependencies. Simulation works by accounting for each individual process as a discrete event. Meaning, each process occurs within the context of its own parameters, and is only influenced by other processes in the system insofar as the start time of each iteration, and any delay post-processing. So, let's take an ED process, physician evaluation. Each physician evaluation process takes a given amount of time to perform, represented by a distribution of process times since each iteration takes more or less time than the last one. The time of the actual process in not influenced by the time it takes to complete triage, registration, or discharge. The time still takes some amount of time represented within the distribution. This is what makes the "discrete" in "discrete event." The time at which the process can start is obviously influenced by the preceding processes. Similarly, the next process in the flow might not be able to start until the physician evaluation process is complete. Thus, flows and wait-times are generated. Yet, each discrete event is performed under its own parameters.

Therefore, we can study the interdependencies of a system. If we add capacity to the physician evaluation process by adding staff, we do not change the time it takes to perform that process, but can still double the throughput. Similarly, we can alter the process itself by adding technologies, such as portable iPads to speed order entry. Both will have up- and downstream impacts, as more resources and faster processes will allow for greater throughput through this individual process step. As each process is analyzed within the entire stream, we can see where, when, and to what degree bottlenecks occur, and how they might be managed within the context of the entire system. With the inclusion of process variability, we can begin to ascertain the complexities of, and assess solutions for, dynamic system interdependencies.

We start to detect the relative importance of some interdependencies on performance, such as pre-op testing in the OR, and radiology throughput times in the ED. We can discern which processes have the most impact on others, and to what degree and under what conditions those processes create bottlenecks. The important thing to remember is that you are seeking to predict *patterns* of system performance, based on dynamism in the system from its HODDOW WOMSOY, demand patterns, and available capacity variations. Of course, there are many internal and external variables that can influence the inputs and system performance, from staffing patterns to flu season. That is why an understanding of the system's interdependencies and outliers is so critical and why static methodologies fail to give us adequate analytics.

For the purpose of this discussion, it is critical to be able to glean the structure of the interdependencies and how those interdependencies react to a variety of circumstances. For instance, look again to our small ED model (see Figure 3.1 and Figure 3.2) to see how up- and downstream constraints impact other components of system

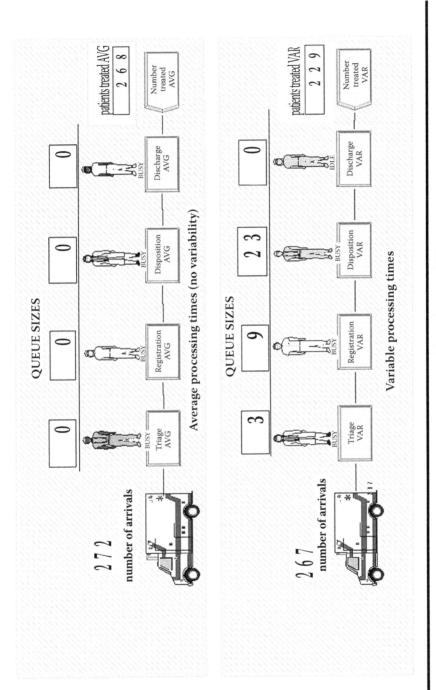

Figure 3.2 Sample simulation model outcomes for simple variable and nonvariable systems.

flow. Anyone who's worked in healthcare for more than a week fully understands this concept. Now, we can actually analyze it, dynamically, and proactively manage it.

Summary

Dynamic systems require dynamic analysis and unique improvement methodologies. The analytical tools common to manufacturing environments are not as effective when transposed into the dynamic systems of healthcare. Thus the use of static methodologies to try to improve healthcare can be frustrating and unproductive.

Variability, interdependencies, evolution, and the resulting dynamism make healthcare systems more complex and difficult to analyze with traditional methodologies. Lean, Six Sigma, and others fail to offer the dynamic analytics required to improve these systems. DCAMM is a new way to think, analyze, and improve. The methodology builds on the successes of Lean, Six Sigma, and others, adding the critically important concepts of dynamism, interdependencies, and variability. With this, we can begin to use predictive analytics to achieve new management success in the most complex of operational environments.

In the coming chapters, we will delve more deeply into predictive analytics and the resulting management tools that can come from its effective use.

Notes

1. For a great list of Six Sigma tools, see Michael Brassard, Lynda Finn, Dana Ginn, and Diane Ritter, *The Six Sigma Memory Jogger II*, GOAL/QPC, Salem, NH, 1994.
2. Eliyahu Goldratt, *The Goal*, North River Press, Croton-on-Hudson, NY, 1984.
3. Julie Wright and Russ King, *We All Fall Down: Goldratt's Theory of Constraints for Healthcare Systems*, North River Press, Great Barrington, MA, 2006.
4. Michael Schrage, *Serious Play*, Harvard University Press, Boston, 2000.
5. Malcolm Gladwell, *The Tipping Point*, Little, Brown, and Co., 2002.
6. Paul Davidson, Lean Manufacturing helps companies survive recession, *USA Today*, November 3, 2009, http://www.usatoday.com/money/industries/manufacturing/2009-11-01-lean-manufacturing-recession_N.htm
7. This percentage comes from various presentations and articles, and particularly from Virginia Mason Medical Center of Seattle.
8. P. Reid Proctor, W. Dale Compton, Jerome H. Grossman, and Gary Fanjiang, eds., Institute of Medicine and National Academy of Engineering, *Building a Better Delivery System: A New Engineering/Health Care Partnership*, National Academies Press, Washington, DC, 2005, 2–3.
9. Ibid, p. 14.
10. Ibid. Also see Table ES-1, p. 3.
11. Ibid, p. 23.
12. Ibid, p. 6.

Chapter 4

DCAMM Introduction

Capellini: The Better Spaghetti

Every process improvement tool seems to have a name, from fishbones to affinity diagrams to DMAIC (define, measure, analyze, improve, control) to Kano models. Many Lean tools and methods have really cool Japanese names, like Ishikawa, Gemba, Toppa, and Kaizen. So, I think our new concepts should have cool names, too. We've already started with a nice acronym, DCAMM (dynamic capacity analysis, matching, and management), but we have other tools in need of monikers.

The study of interdependencies isn't new, however, so it is hardly a patentable idea. Still, the visuals representing the concepts presented here seem to be unique enough to warrant a name, if for nothing else but this text. The moniker "spaghetti diagram" adequate fits the description of the diagram shown in Figure 4.1. The twisting and turning lines of interdependencies of a complex system could easily resemble a plate of spaghetti and meatballs. However, the name "spaghetti diagram" has already been taken in process improvement (PI) methodologies and refers to a number of types of flow and layout diagrams. For instance, in the Lean world, spaghetti diagrams represents the movement of workers within a given space as they perform their jobs, so as to seek out travel waste and other forms of waste. Spaghetti diagram also refers to a method of examining a systems dynamics model and high-level flow diagramming. So though it's a great descriptor, it already has several connotations.

I therefore settled on two potential naming conventions, one Japanese, one not: Shirataki and capellini. The former (Shirataki) is a thin, nearly translucent low-carb, high-fiber Japanese noodle made from the root of a konjac plant. If you're a Lean advocate who accepts the principles put forth in this text and prefers Japanese

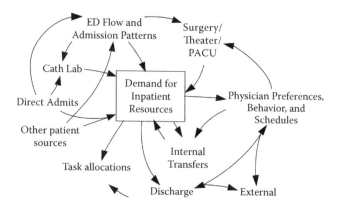

Figure 4.1   Hospital-wide demand–capacity capellini diagram.

nomenclature, you can call them Shirataki diagrams. The latter, capellini, is obvious to any pasta lover and is my favorite form of Italian pasta (it's the "skinny spaghetti," commonly known as angel hair). Capellini looks a lot like spaghetti so it fits with the existing spaghetti diagram concepts created in systems dynamics modeling. Systems dynamics diagrams show interdependencies and, using Monte Carlo and other similar tools, can depict limited variability. However, the reason these new DCAMM tools need their own unique name is their unique applications, and if for no other reason than as a differentiator in this text.

The capellini diagrams you'll see in this text are quite easy to create using VenSim™ and similar simulation tools. VenSim (from Ventana Systems, Inc.) is used with sensitivity analysis and parameter optimization, and can be a handy tool for many applications. Of course, you can draw them on a white board or a dinner napkin, whatever meets your analytical needs.

Capellinis display process interdependencies quite well. Based on the example shown in this chapter, it is clear which process is related to the other, and in which direction that relationship flows. The interdependent relationships can be shown with one or two arrows, or a double-ended arrow to show the flow to and from each component in the diagram. Additionally, the width of the arrow can represent the intensity of the relationship, the critical path of flow, or otherwise signify relative importance of the flow or relationship. The line width might also signify the degree of the process variability, the degree of wait time between the two components, the rate of flow, and so forth. The lines can be colored to reflect certain characteristics of the flow. Regardless of how the capellini is set up, you can see at a glance how complex the system is, where the interdependencies lie, and even where the bottlenecks might likely exist or potentially crop up.

Of course, capellini, like any visual representation, can become difficult to comprehend if taken to the extreme. Just as with a large and complex value stream or process map, the representation can lose its intended impact and become visually overwhelming if there are too many lines and icons. Thus, for some complex operations, multiple, interconnected capellinis will be necessary. Some will be high level, as our hospital-wide flow model seen herein. Others, as drill downs, will be more process- or department-specific representations. This allows for necessary detail while allowing for the interdependencies of the systems' operations to be effectively represented. Otherwise, diagrams can come to look like an actual bowl of capellini and meatballs, with too many crisscrossing lines going in too many directions.

Last, adding in the use of simulation tools into capellini aids in the inclusion of dynamism in the system. Through simulation, we can eliminate dependencies on averages, and develop a more robust and realistic analysis. Then, we can then achieve more realistic and dynamic what-if scenarios to aid with the analysis of possible solutions, future changes, and their impacts on system performance.

Capellini and Hospital-Wide Flow

If for no other reason, capellinis are good for visual display of complex interdependencies. Unlike value stream maps (VSMs) and flowcharts, capellini are better at showing the dynamism of a complex system than the more linear tools like Visio. Using the simple capellini diagram in Figure 4.1, we can see how and where the components and subsystems of hospital-wide flow intersect. With this simple visual, we can start to understand how, where, and why the systems begin to back up using dynamic analytics as described in this text. We can analyze how these interdependencies and the dynamism of the system changes from hour to hour, day to day, and season to season. We can then study the impact of that dynamism (remember, defined as "variability meeting interdependencies") and how dynamic our responses must be to impact the system itself and improve performance.

If we were to drill down into each of the these specific areas (e.g., the emergency department [ED], operating room [OR], or hospital discharge), we could dive into another capellini, or perhaps a VSM, swimlane diagram, or flowchart of a more detailed process flow. A capellini of the cath lab might look as illustrated in Figure 4.2. This shows the interdependencies of cath lab patient flow (at a high level) and where flow might break down, causing patients to wait. There are further drilldowns available herein, including radiology and inpatient admissions. The further we dive, the less appropriate this particular tool might be, and the more appropriate a tool such as a swimlane diagram, VSM, or root-cause analysis might become, with or without simulation. Remember, the appropriate use of simulation and its depicting of dynamism depends on the complexity of the process to be analyzed and the degree of dynamism therein. Capellinis are commonly used at a higher level, where there are systems issues to be analyzed. This is also where simulation can shine, since it effectively captures the dynamism of the system and its complexities.

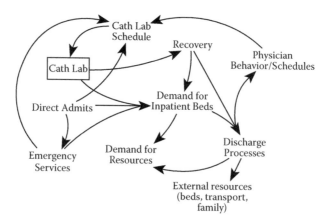

Figure 4.2 Cath lab capellini diagram.

The hospital-wide capellini shown in Figure 4.2 will be used throughout the remainder of this text as a visual reference for the concepts and tools purported.

Dynamic Capacity Analysis, Matching, and Management (DCAMM): Introduction and Refresher

DCAMM is the proactive, predictive, and effective management of complex, highly variable, interdependent systems. More specifically in this case, it is the dynamic management of hospital-wide patient flow operations to efficiently and proactively match capacity to the community's dynamic demand for healthcare services. Through the use of the DCAMM concepts, tools, and thinking, we can move away from reactive, high-cost "firefighter" management to a more cost-effective and efficient management methodology.

DCAMM starts with the analysis of initial demand patterns, which drive the need for downstream capacity, including resources, space, and time in a series of interrelated events and downstream patterns within the system. As the initial demand (e.g., arrivals to the ED) flows downstream, we can follow it throughout the system as additional demand is generated within system components (e.g., radiology or inpatient beds). We can thereby study the system interdependencies as they relate to resource requirements, space, and time. By studying the variability within the initial demand and downstream components, we can better analyze the upstream and downstream constraints generated by various system interactions and circumstances. This offers a deeper and more telling look at how the system actually reacts and performs over time. Mapping the system interdependencies, as well as the component variability, is therefore critical to understanding, managing, and predicting these dynamic systems.

To do this, we can most likely look within historical and proximal initial demand data for patterns in the demand as they change through the day, week, month, and season, aka HODDOW WOMSOY. With the right amount of data, we can also begin to assess the pattern variability (or, ranges around the averages) and the probability of event occurrence such that we can grasp the impact of the ranges on system performance. With this we can then study the impact on the upstream and downstream components. As we do so, the concept of outliers throughout the system begins to emerge as we detect data points that are atypical (occurring less than 5 percent to 20 percent of the time). Ranges can be thus used to point us to outlier versus in-range demand, in both the upstream and downstream components. Finally, we can begin to study the evolution of the system as internal and external influences play their roles in changing system performance.

When we analyze the variability in both the source and downstream demand, we can see whether and how that variability might be more effectively managed. Much like locks in a canal, system dynamism needs to be effectively managed such that negative influences are mitigated in upstream and downstream components. More dramatically, by understanding the HODDOW WOMSOY of system dynamism, we can further and more specifically ascertain how, when, and where dynamism impacts the system. Thus we can begin to study our system as it performs dynamically.

Importantly, this analysis will allow us to do some advanced predictive analytics. We have seen how to detect the patterns of demand, understand the variability in and between processes, and study the interdependencies of system operations. We can also analyze the critical ranges around the averages, and determine where, when, and by how much the system is out of range.[1] Combined, we can replicate the system using simple simulation models (Monte Carlo, etc.) to study the probabilities of certain outcomes and the impacts of various upstream and downstream events and circumstances, based on changes to system components and demand. *Knowing the range of system dynamism, we can thereby predict, to a great extent, how the downstream system will react to upstream change, and vice versa.*

Even where we cannot predict performance via solid patterns of behavior, we can use these same tools to aid us in predicting the outcomes of outlier circumstances on the system and its components. This is particularly important as we try to make changes to our system, whether through capacity enhancements, resource allocations, demand management, or some other forms of process improvement. If we fail to study the components and the dynamism that exists with them, we might find (for instance) our bigger, fancier, and new ED bottlenecked by a lack of inpatient resources and beds. Thus predictive analytics aids us in managing not only current operations but effectively planning for the future of the care system.

This will also help lead us to better and truer root-cause analysis. Often root causes change throughout the HODDOW WOMSOY. Yet, we tend to try to isolate one root cause during all circumstances. Without an understanding of the dynamism of the system, we can miss changes in upstream and downstream variables and parameters that cause the system to degrade. Missing this might lead us to look to the wrong problem and therefore the wrong solution. Even a concept as simple as starting with community demand patterns is often lost on the best consultants, who choose to look at one component process for solutions to system problems.

DCAMM involves all the elements we have studied thus far, plus a few more we will add. Variability, interdependencies, evolution, and dynamism are all part of the DCAMM world. In this and the coming chapters, we will add break-point analysis, dynamic resource allocation, dynamic standardization, workload analytics, and outlier management to the mix.

Capacity Entitlements and Acceptance Patterns

Two concepts are worth mentioning here.

Some of us work in highly constrained environments, in which demand simply exceeds even dynamically optimized capacity. As we'll see in later chapters, the concepts of Capacity Entitlement and Acceptance Patterns should then arise.

Capacity Entitlement is simply that amount of capacity that should be expected to be made available, based on the historical patterns of demand, regardless of the current demand. Simply put, if the optimized, dynamic capacity patterns show available capacity of, say, between 4 and 6 beds on Unit 4-West on Tuesdays between 2 p.m. and 5 p.m., we should expect that this can and will be made available each week. The Entitlement for capacity then becomes at least 4 beds. The onus is then on Unit 4-West to make the Entitlement available, such that the upstream components can anticipate available capacity.

Similarly, patterns of capacity can also be anticipated, even in the most over-crowded facilities. Even if, again, the demand far exceeds capacity, there is *some degree* of capacity made available though it may not fully satisfy the demand. The patterns by which this capacity is made available should be as consistent as possible, so as to allow for smooth and predictable flow within the system. Acceptance Patterns are simply the patterns by which downstream components accept the demand from upstream components, based on a well-matched DCAMM system. As the components are dynamically meshed together, the dynamically optimized capacity matches as much dynamic demand as possible, thus eliminating the typical scrambling we are used to in crowded hospitals.

We'll see these concepts applied later in the text.

Optimized versus Excess Capacity

Many hospitals, especially in the Midwestern US, are seeing the opposite of capacity constraints…they have excess capacity. Due to the changes in demographics, local employment and insurance coverage, and excessive building in recent decades, some hospitals are operating at less than 60 percent utilization. One would not naturally assume that these facilities need to be worrying about dynamically matching capacity with a lesser demand.

However, these hospitals may need DCAMM more than you'd think. Optimizing capacity to meet demand will still lead to a more efficient and cost-effective delivery of care, regardless of which direction your capacity needs to go. If your capacity needs to shrink, you still need to understand the patterns of demand, variation in upstream patterns, and the capacity you can and/or should make available. Otherwise, you risk having excess capacity available for a shrinking demand.

Again, our models will help here, as we test a variety of reduced demand and capacity scenarios to see how, when, and where to change capacity and better manage demand so as to reduce overall cost and increase efficiency of care delivery. As we do so, we can ensure that our reductions in capacity do not harm patient care, satisfaction, or staff satisfaction. We can also ensure that any capacity reductions we might make will result in the greatest reductions in variable and/or fixed cost.

These concepts will be shown in much greater detail in the coming chapters.

Summary: Why DCAMM Is Necessary

DCAMM is a methodology that allows for on-the-fly analysis in a dynamic world. DCAMM is necessary because of the highly variable environment of healthcare and the inherent need for quick reaction. The better our reactions to external and internal circumstances can be predicted, the more effectively we will manage our dynamic systems.

DCAMM is meant to be used with other, more process-focused methodologies such as Lean. DCAMM offers a more strategic, robust, and dynamic view of the system's performance, whereas Lean, the Toyota Production System (TPS), and others tend to look to individual, snapshot process improvements. These can be successful insofar as the processes they influence are static enough such that variability and complex interdependencies are not an issue (more commonly the case in manufacturing). Or the processes might be continually analyzed, such that the dynamism of the system is accounted for and managed through an ongoing effort. However, if the latter is the case, it seems natural that an easier way might exist through using DCAMM and the analysis of the dynamism. If, for example, there is a need for continuous analysis of the same process or department, it might be due to the inherent process/system dynamism, which would require continually updated snapshots of process performance. This, again, is part of the issue with Lean and other methodologies, which are static and only analyze snapshots of reality. (And isn't all that rework anyway?)

Using DCAMM analytics, however, we can now effectively predict and more precisely manage the system dynamism such that better and more robust analysis can be achieved initially, giving us the ability to anticipate the results of the ongoing change rather than reacting to it with a new project. DCAMM might eliminate some of the process analysis rework through the effective study of the system interdependencies and changes over time and a strategic understanding of the system's dynamism.

Lean and the others, alone, cannot solve healthcare's most pressing issue. DCAMM is brought forth as an additional tool in the belt of PI professionals and administrators to allow them to do more to optimize system flow. In the coming chapters, we will delve deeply into the application of the DCAMM methodology, picking up with up–down–up as well as outlier management and the other important concepts of DCAMM.

Note

1. In Six Sigma, this would be a control chart on an individual process that would show a process out of control or in control as it performs outside and within a given statistical range of precise variability. Thus, the concepts of ranges and control charts between the two methodologies are largely the same.

Chapter 5

Predictive Analytics

In this chapter we will take a deep dive into tools that analyze dynamism, how those tools work, and how they generate confidence in their predictive capabilities. This, for those who know simulation, will likely be repetitive. For those new to the tools, I will provide examples of dynamic capacity analysis, matching, and management (DCAMM) use and how it can be incorporated into current Process and Performance Improvement (PPI) methodologies to produce more accurate and useful analysis.

We can accurately predict trends and future behavior based on known history. Therefore, we can use the analysis of dynamism to proactively manage the typical variations in system and component performance, as well as define and better understand the less predictable outlier scenarios. And to the extent that we can determine seasonal variability, evolutionary patterns, and other changes to the systems' external and internal inputs, we can also predict the trends and behaviors associated with these changes, based on historical data. *Ideally we would take this to the next level and predict system performance based on anticipated or hypothetical changes in future external and internal variables.*

This would allow us to better understand how the vagaries of change will impact us, such that we can more effectively react if and when hypotheticals become reality.

Considerations of future change might include changes to demand patterns, component functionality and variability, long-term demographic and economic trends, differences between summer and winter volumes and acuity patterns, and even large-scale emergencies and disease outbreaks.

At the process level, we might want to study the impact of staffing changes or new government regulations. We may want to analyze the impact of changes to PACU admission process flow on PACU wait times. Or we might want to study the impact of the variability in arrival patterns on registration bottlenecks on certain days of the week. These questions, and their answers, might logically roll up into a larger, DCAMM analysis through which we would look at the relevant impacts of these process-level changes on system-wide capacity, flow, length of stay (LOS), and so forth (see Chapter 8 on up–down–up methodology).

Furthermore, we may want to understand where, when, and to what extent the system or its components begin to break down, so as to understand at what point(s) a solution(s) will be required, and which solution might be more effective. We might also want to stress test the system and its components to determine its robustness under a variety of circumstances, or determine which proposed changes will offer the biggest bang for our improvement effort(s).

In doing so, we might analyze the system in the face of its own dynamism, or map out potential short- and long-term interdependency issues between the various components. Additionally, we might want to study the impacts of future evolution, disaster scenarios, staffing changes, new government regulations, and so forth on key performance metrics. Also important, we many want to analyze *the impact of multiple parameter changes, since change rarely occurs singularly or in isolation.*

Rather than static analytics, or even dynamic analysis based on history, what we need is *dynamic predictive analytics* (DPA). DPA is an essential component of the DCAMM methodology, since the ability to accurately represent future scenarios is a key element of the proactive management of dynamic systems and their outliers. DPA can help in a number of ways.

First, it can offer a means by which to study the parameters of the current system as they relate to potential future system performance. This is quite handy as we run up against the questions about the impacts of potential process improvements on individual components as well as overall system performance. Or, it can aid in studying the current system parameters and their impacts on the robustness of the system and its various components. In fact, this capability is one of DCAMM's greatest attributes.

Second, it will allow for better analysis of the expected future performance of the system as changes are made, as it evolves over time, and as external variables change outside our immediate control. This helps in ascertaining the short- and long-term impacts of changes throughout the system. Third, it allows for developing new ideas and solutions, based on the results now more accurately foreseen. This important capability helps to develop new ideas faster while offering an environment for robust testing and vetting. Without a realistic, dynamic view into the future world of our dynamic performance, we rapidly lose confidence in the outcomes of the changes we wish to make.

Fourth, as DPA allows us to predict how to best proactively manage a variety of future scenarios, it helps us learn our systems more thoroughly. Using DPA, current and potential performance of systems, its component behavior, and the dynamism that drives its complexity can be more "scientifically" explored and understood. In doing so, we better understand the system itself, how its components fit together to make up the whole, and how it dynamically functions, changes, and evolves over time. And as we better know the system, we can begin to instinctively manage to the dynamism within the system, proactively asserting control over the issues that currently plague us rather than merely reacting to what seem to be random circumstances. Without this capability, the management of the system's dynamism and outliers would still be difficult.

"Managing To"

As a clarification, *managing to* is different than *management of.* Managing to is a more proactive mindset, as it involves aggressively predicting and managing the dynamism in component and system parameters before and as it occurs. Managing to means (1) we acknowledge that at least some of the parameters in our systems change outside our direct control, (2) we can nonetheless understand, predict, and proactively manage many of those changes, and (3) we should constantly and proactively pursue dynamism rather than waiting for it to happen. Managing to is thus different from management of based on the significance of the ability to predict the dynamism in systems and proactively move toward it. It is essentially the difference between playing offense and defense.

Simulation Models: The Tools of DCAMM and DPA

Fortunately, tools exist for DPA. We have already discussed the analytical power of discrete event simulation and other simulation tools. These tools can effectively replicate the variability and interdependencies of complex systems, such that they can be better evaluated. But because they can accurately replicate the complex systems, complete with each component's variability and all the system interdependencies, they can also accurately replicate, and thereby accurately predict, future performance based on changes to the modeled parameters. However, to trust the predicted outcomes of a model, and thus feel confident in taking action, one must first understand a few important points.

Discrete event models work in a way that allows them to replicate current process and operational realities. We have already discussed how they use distributions and random number generators to mimic process variability, and how interdependencies are modeled. However, the replication of interdependencies now requires some further explanation as we get into predictive analytics. Discrete-event models work by replicating each individual process occurrence as an individual event, with its own variability. For instance, using our four-step model from Chapter 2, the triage process time for the first patient that arrives into the model is randomly generated. After the allotted time, the patient then moves on to the next step of the process. Without getting into the gory details of model programming, the model can be made to send the patient to the next process step or a multitude of possible next steps, based on some criteria, such as a percentage, a prioritization, and so forth. So, for instance, 70 percent of the time a patient might go to registration, and 30 percent of the time a patient might go directly to an ED bed. Or, patients with a higher priority might be seen first or move to the front of a queue. Those with a lower priority might wait until all higher priority patients are treated (as in real life). This will aid us later in testing the impacts of possible flow or resource allocation changes. However, in the case of our sample model, we use a very simple flow in which the next step after triage is always registration. So 100 percent of the patients will move to registration after completing triage, with no accounting for prioritization. As triage finishes, patients are then ready to move on, and the model looks for the next step in the patient sequence.

If for some reason the next step in the patient process cannot accommodate that patient, the patient begins to wait until the downstream process can accommodate. (Typically, this wait time is recorded somewhere for later calculations and analysis). This delay is commonly due to some capacity constraint, such as a patient currently being processed, not enough resources or space, or simply too many higher-priority patients requesting the downstream process at once.

If there is available capacity downstream, the patient moves on. At registration, another random number is generated to represent the amount of time the registration process will take for that particular patient. However, this process time has nothing to do with where the patient came from, how long the previous process took, or how long the patient waited to be seen. Unless the model is programmed otherwise, the random number generator will generate a random process time for this patient in the same manner it would for any other patient. Thus, registration and triage are independent of each other in terms of their respective process times. In this simple model, the upstream influences the downstream only as it relates to when the downstream process can begin, which is of course driven by the upstream process step's process time.[1] Thus each occurrence of each process step throughout the modeled system is a discrete event, hence the name.

This means that interdependencies between process steps can thereby be accurately replicated since one process step can be made to be independent of the other. This is quite an important distinction from other modeling systems. For instance, the time it takes for the disposition of a given patient typically has little or nothing to do with the time it took to register that patient. However, the two processes can be quite interrelated, since backups and long wait times at either registration or disposition can influence the flow to or from the other. If the actual disposition process time were influenced by how long it took to get through registration, it would be difficult to isolate and analyze disposition as an individual process, particularly if a number of upstream processes fed into disposition. The two must necessarily be independent in order for distinct process analysis to occur. Disposition will, of course, be influenced by registration to the extent that flow interruptions occur.

But the processes themselves, including process times, resources, and so forth, are and must be discrete. Because each event in the flow is independent of the previous or next event's treatment of the patient, we can therefore replicate each process step's unique characteristics, and therefore how each process step impacts, and is impacted by, the others in the system.

Taken to a much larger scale, we can begin to see how a model might replicate a highly complex system. As each process step in completed, patients are routed to the next process step. In larger models and systems, this next step can be based on complex *attribution*, or the characteristics of the particular patient, such as acuity or patient type. So, for instance, we can program our little ED model to generate a certain percentage of patients in each Emergency Severity Index (ESI) level. Patients are then randomly attributed as having a given ESI level as they arrive, based on some total percentage of each acuity level in the total patient population. This is much like an ID tag that a patient might wear to identify them as being of a certain ESI type. Furthermore, a patient can be given a host of attributes, which drive what happens to the patient, where they go, how long processes take, which resources are involved, etc. As the patient moves through the system, the model might direct different patients to different process steps based on their various attributes. So, a patient attributed as ESI level 3 might have a higher probability of receiving a CT scan or a second round of lab tests. Each process step could even have a different process time for each patient type, such as level 3 patients take longer for disposition than level 5 patients. This further allows the models to replicate complex realities for the purpose of analysis. Thus, models can be made to replicate even the most complex systems. That said, keep in mind that there is often great value in confirming one's suspicions. In the process of getting to an "ah hah" or two, models often confirm what might seem like "well, duhs." This does not necessarily make your model less valuable. Indeed, confirming one's suspicions, assumptions, and gut feel can lend credence to arguments and offer some "science" to back up one's intuition. Furthermore, even the best of intuition and gut feel cannot accurate *quantify* the results of future change, as models can. It's one thing to say LOS will go up if we see an increase in volume. It's entirely another thing to accurately quantify *by how much* LOS will increase. Models are often the only tools capable of this feat when analyzing these complex systems.

When it comes to "Ah-hah!" analysis, models are particularly good at offering strategic answers about the future function of dynamic systems. This can include answers to questions on staffing, outliers, and the proper responses to the system's dynamism based on future parameter changes and alterations to system components. If your model doesn't deliver an appropriate amount of "Ah-hah!" via good predictive analytics, you might want to reconsider your strategy and how it was developed.

Therefore it is important to remember to use models for those questions and issues for which easy (and accurate) answers are unavailable. Building a model to analyze a single process might not make sense. However, analysis of hospital-wide capacity cannot be achieved without a model. Just as a builder chooses the right tool for each job, combining PI methodologies, data analytics, and simulation will allow for a complete toolset with which to achieve your goals.

Fortunately, if you follow the recommendations herein, you are almost certain to receive ample ah-hahs for the effort. The DCAMM methodology is all about getting to the strategic, important answers that are otherwise difficult to attain and foresee.

In the next sections of this chapter, we will begin to pull together the dynamic analysis of an entire hospital's flow such that DCAMM can be achieved. One key to the effective use of models is to ensure that, as variables change, realistic adjustments are made to the rest of the model, as needed. For instance, in our sample ED model, we could test the impact of large arrival volume increases. This would show the impact on LOS and wait times quite readily. However, to truly gauge the expected impact, we would need to adjust staffing in the model, as we might in real life. This would likely reduce the overall impact of the increase, since the larger volume would be met with more resources. Still, even without these additional alterations, the model would deliver far more useful and realistic answers than could be derived otherwise using static tools. Nonetheless, those answers will enjoy greater confidence and accuracy if they are based on realistic alterations in any necessary assumptions. Fortunately, one of the benefits of these kinds of models is the ability to alter multiple variables at once while maintaining overall model accuracy and legitimacy. This multi-parameter analysis is very handy for large system predictive analytics where multiple changes are commonly made simultaneously.

The second part of the modeler's creed—some models are useful—speaks more to the skill of the modeler and the deliverables from a modeling effort. Again, models tend to be *directionally correct*. Meaning, they offer the right direction and magnitude of change, while perhaps not hitting the exact numbers to the second decimal point of accuracy (which is not really the goal). So, if we are seeking information on the LOS of our ED based on a general 15-percent increase in volume, we might get an answer from the model that shows a range around a forty-five-minute average LOS increase. Although the actual results may be different, the general direction and degree of the change should be accurate enough to warrant any actions derived from the model analytics. The greater the specificity of the question and the altered inputs, the greater the accuracy of the answer. So, a 15-percent increase in volume of level 3 patients will yield a different result than a more generalized 15-percent increase in volume of all patients.

Furthermore, models can deliver two types of information: "Well, duhs!" and "Ah-hahs!" "Well, duhs!" are those answers that could be derived through a little extra thought, have already been discovered, or could otherwise be more easily derived.

Models should be focused on delivering information that cannot be attained elsewhere or by traditional analytics means. Models have great analytical capabilities, but those capabilities are only brought forth by answering questions that otherwise would remain unanswered or nebulous. I have seen many "Well, duh!" models built. These models, while well constructed and functionally accurate and based on proper assumptions and data, offer little more than confirmation of the existing knowledge of the client or user. Commonly they were the pride of the modeler, who used great feats of logic and programming skill to achieve his or her replication.

However, when push came to shove, the model failed to offer the end user the necessary strategic value and answer critical questions about the future state. That said, keep in mind that there is often great value in confirming one's suspicions. In the process of getting to an "Ah-hah!" or two, models often confirm what might seem like "well, duhs."

A Word about Modeling Assumptions

Simulation models have been used for years to seek information on complex system performance, at both the process and systems levels. Models have been used in nearly every industry under an enormous variety of circumstances, from manufacturing to military operations to airport security. Users often swear by the ability of simulation models to create the means for dramatic improvements and creativity. However, there are a few caveats that are critical to their effective use. This includes what is commonly called the "modeler's creed," which reads: (1) All models are wrong. (2) Some models are useful.

Before you throw out the idea of modeling based on the first statement, consider its context. All models, however well constructed, are inherently based on assumptions, the underlying data, and the skills of the modeler. The assumptions we build into our models often have as much to do with model accuracy as any of the data we might put in. Change the model's underlying assumptions, and you can get a different result, either slight or significant.

For instance, if we assume that all patients entering an ED are of only three patients types (e.g., levels 1, 2, and 3), then our answers will be different than if we assume a higher degree of granularity. So, if we break down categories into seven or ten patient classifications, we might get some different answers out of our models on LOS and other key metrics. The ranges of our answers might be similar but the added granularity will enhance our understanding.

Resources

Real life has more than processes flows, of course. Our work environments include the constraints of limitations to the number of staff, equipment, and space. In order to replicate the environments, the precise replication of the resources that do the work are required. Though our little sample model (from Chapter 2 and

Figure 2.5a) does not include them, it is common for models to include resources, such as staff, beds, and equipment, such that capacity constraints can be mimicked based on resource availability and capability. (Indeed, an excellent use of models is the analysis of resource requirements for a given set of process and demand criteria.) And, just as in real life, resources can be limited such that there are only a certain number of nurses and techs on a given unit at any given point in time. Similarly, actual staffing patterns can be used as model inputs and thus become variables for testing and analysis. Our model would thereby only use the number of resources as would be present in a real-life shift, thus constraining the system if there are not enough resources for the workload.

When a process needs to be completed, there a number of ways in which a resource is assigned to the task, including prioritization, queues, and the availability of other capable resources. Interestingly, "resourceless resource models" can be created to demonstrate the number of a given resource required to exactly match the work in the system at any given point in time. This is done by programming the model to create a new resource to complete a task whenever one is not available, such that there is never a wait for that resource. The model keeps track of the number of resources it uses to service the demand throughout the model run. Data and graphs can then show how many resources were needed to completely meet any and all demand, regardless of how many might actually be available. This is a handy analysis for a facility trying to determine staffing patterns based on demand and workload rather than traditional shift constructs. This is also handy for isolating and examining the impact of other constraints in the system by eliminating any constraints generated by a particular resource.

All this detail is readily programmed into modern discrete-event software programs, such that resource constraints can be accurately replicated and thereby analyzed. Therefore, as with process times and the predictive analytics of demand patterns, staff requirements and resource utilizations can be accurately predicted based on both of the current parameters and alterations to those parameters.

As we will see later, we can use these models to also test our resource allocation and various configurations and resource mixes under a variety of possible circumstances and scenarios, such that we can eliminate as much of the resource capacity constraints as possible.

So What?

Since simulation models have been used for decades to improve processes and systems in nearly every industry, there must be something more to them than replication of current systems. Indeed, if all our model achieved were an accurate and sophisticated replication of current reality, we would merely become masters of the obvious—hardly the goal. Instead, the ability to replicate each individual discrete event gives models the power to analyze changes to individual components within the context of system performance, and thereby predict the outcomes of those changes.

Assuming that the models we create are relatively accurate, and assuming we have captured all the relevant and important variability, interdependencies, and key parameters of the system, we can assume that changing those elements will yield changes to the model that will mimic real life. This leap of faith can be made because (a) each event in the model occurs discretely and (b) we have accounted for dynamism. This allows the unaltered processes in the system to occur and function as they normally would, while changes made to others are studied. Thus changes to one component of the system only impacts the other components, and thus the system, to the extent of its own influence and the impacts of the dynamism it generates. This is what would typically happen in real life.

Furthermore, because we have captured the dynamism of the system, we have accounted for the variability in each component and the system, which makes our analysis far more realistic and accurate. We would simply not have the same degree of confidence in the model's outcomes if the sum of the averages were being used, since the outliers (and any process results other than the average) have such a tremendous impact on component and system performance. Since the models takes all possible results into account (using statistical distributions to represent process times) we can have confidence that the outcomes of the changes we make in the model will be replicated upon actual implementation. And because we have also captured the outliers in the component inputs, the impacts of those outliers will show up in the system's future performance just as they will in real life. This concept holds true, regardless of the granularity and scale of the model. Rather than offering the simple sum of our averages, as would a value stream map or spreadsheet, our models will output the full range of possible outcomes such that the dynamism of the system can be effectively studied, tested, and repaired as necessary. Therefore, when using dynamic analysis of system performance, we can see how the outliers of the components and inputs will impact the system at large, allowing us to determine where, when, and to what extent to attempt to control the various inputs. The only limitations are the ability to correctly ascertain and mimic the flow, interdependencies, and variability of the environment and correctly model our assumptions.

What-Ifs and Model Outputs

The real value of simulation, then, lies in the ability to alter the system parameters to predict future system performance rather than merely replicating the current system. Due to the way in which models work, accounting for the dynamism of the system, internal and external parameters, and so forth, models can be good predictors of future performance based on historical data. By tweaking the system parameters, demand patterns, and components, models can create a realistic replication of the future state, allowing for the study of causality and impact of system and component change. The results and outputs of modeling can be data similar to that we have studied heretofore. That is, the demonstration of the dynamism in the future state via the same histograms, candlestick charts, and other analytics. This gives a much more realistic, robust and believable assessment of our system and expectations for the future.

But because models offer this full range of results, inclusive of all the outliers and everything in between, models don't offer a single answer. Models are given distributions as inputs, rather than averages; the inputs vary based on the variability of the analyzed system. In fact, there may be millions of discrete, individual inputs as the model runs over days, weeks, or years of elapsed time. The process time inputs representing a component process are therefore essentially all the possibilities for a given component's process time, input as a statistical formula. Similarly, the outputs can show each occurrence of each event or, more important, each systemic reaction to the various model inputs. Modeling software typically turns this information into graphs, charts, and data sets for each analysis (see Figure 5.1). So, rather than a single average result, we receive the full scope of possibilities of results. This lets us begin to ask and answer questions differently than before. For instance, the question no longer needs to be "What is the average wait time for a patient at triage?" The question can be "What is the range of wait times, and how often will a patient wait longer than five minutes if we change X, Y, and Z?" Or, we might ask "If our volumes go to X this winter, on what days and during what hours will we mostly likely need to add physician staff based on an LOS exceeded Y hours?" This means that our questions can be accurately reflect the true condition and dynamism of the system rather than a single, average state. Thus our answers can be much more specific, quantified, and meaningful.

When trying to understand the implications of any changes to the system parameters (inclusive of components, demand, staffing and resources, etc.), it is important to gauge the results in terms of the future dynamism of the system, such that the variability and, more important, the outliers do not surprise us when we go to implement changes in real life. So, in order to assess future potential system performance, we must do so in the context of the dynamism and ranges of that future performance. Simulation models are typically capable of analyzing a variety of "what if?" scenarios to ascertain the impacts of change to one or more of the system parameters. These "what-if?" scenarios are more than merely exercises in the hypothetical. They provide valuable analytical capability. More specifically, models quantify expected outcomes within the context of the dynamic system and the assumptions made. So, rather than stating "the results should improve," we can say, "The results will be a X percent change, plus or minus Y, based on A, B, and C assumptions." This is a far more valuable answer, which elicits confidence in the actions taken and yields realistic and quantifiable expectations of future system performance.

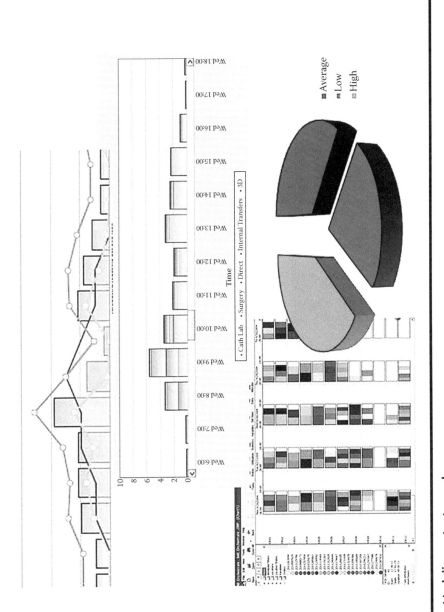

Figure 5.1 Modeling output samples.

To demonstrate this further, go back to our little sample ED model and think about wait times. The prephysician wait time output will vary, as does the inputs, depending on HODDOW WOMSOY and other input variables. However, there may be a broad range of wait-time outputs, the individual results of which depend on the particular parameters for a specific patient in the system. The wait times we are willing to tolerate may require a specific mix of input variables, parameters, and conditions. The model's predictive capability can be used to test the various parameters for impact on this key output, stress test assumptions and the robustness of our solution, and thus determine, with greater specificity, the exact parameters that make up an acceptable solution for patients. As those parameters veer away from their targets of acceptable performance, we can proactively intervene as necessary to avoid constraints, knowing in advance which input parameters will offer the proper corrective action. This, of course, is based on repeated use and analysis of the simulation environment under a variety of what-if scenarios. Additionally, since some patient types are known to have a greater impact on the system than others, we can specify and analyze certain processes for specific patient types. Examples of these might include impacting outlier wait times for a particular patient category. So, the care and processing of mental health patients, who might have a greater impact on the system or be more heavily influenced by the parameters of the system than other populations, might require special attention.

This means the models can be used iteratively to replicate a number of scenarios and develop expectations of future performance under a variety of conditions. *This simply cannot be done using Lean or other static tools.* Such analysis allows for, at the very least, understanding of the parameters that cause systems to function or fail, and where and to what degree changes take place. If all this can be done as part of learning the dynamism of the system, the ability to manage inherently becomes better. *Our answers and expectations can now reflect the range of possible outcomes rather than that of the single, average condition, making analysis and the resulting answers more complete, accurate, and actionable.* Furthermore, the accurate replication of the created future state allows us to foresee the impacts of multiple possible changes to and within systems, such that we can both learn and proactively manage these changes before and as they happen.

This opens up an entirely new management capability allowing us to proactively and quantitatively study the dynamism of the system and take bold steps to precisely strike at the heart of our issues. Out actions can now be based on precise ranges of expected performance by which we can gauge the effectiveness of the implementation of our solutions and the accuracy of our assumptions. This knowledge, applied strategically, is the dynamic predictive analytics upon which DCAMM relies. DPA provides the visioning necessary to plan for staffing, process changes, facilities, and demographic trends and, importantly, manage to the inevitable variability and evolution that dominate complex healthcare systems.

Effective Model Use and Learning from DPA

As we have seen, models do not give a single, end-all-be-all answer, nor does current modeling technology contain artificial intelligence which would allow for such an answer to be automatically derived. Therefore, they will not prescribe the exact solution required to optimize a given situation.[2] Nor should we want them to, since it is the ranges, dynamism, and outliers with which we are concerned. Only our best judgment can take proposed solutions and decide which will offer a legitimate and realistic solution.

Clients will often ask for a model that tells them exactly what to do. They want a model to look at the data and prescribe the perfect solution. However, no such technology exists. Such a comment is most often voiced by clients whose creativity and enthusiasm for problem solving long since left them. It is in the iterations that learning and education lies. And it is through these iterative experiments with future scenario parameters that teach us the most about our system's performance.

Models, then, are best used to help direct users to the appropriate correct answer via iterative learning. As some have put it, models are directionally correct. Meaning, they give the direction in which change will tend to go, offering "signs along the highway" to guide our future questions and changes. By repeatedly altering the parameters and inputs, models begin to teach the system responses to change. This gives a view of the system performance as it relates to both internal and external variables. Using a model in this way helps in learning the system and its nuances, interdependencies, and HODDOW WOMSOY constraints and issues. In doing so, we can actually learn to manage the system more effectively and begin to learn how the pieces of the complex puzzle fit together to form dynamic healthcare systems. We can begin to learn how the dynamism of the system impacts performance and constraints, and, in doing so, better understand how we might proactively deal with those issues as and even before they arise. This latter benefit is perhaps the most critical, since it is the interdependencies that drive many of the key patient flow constraints. Understanding and predicting them, as well as outlier-based constraints, allow us to proactively manage and react more effectively to situations before and as they arise.

Time Frames

We need to discuss the issue of time. This is important as we look into predictive analytics, since the distance into the future will determine the kind of data needed, the analytics to be expected, and the granularity of any models that might be built. As we look further out, the parameters, models, and analytics will all need to change.

The first question is "What time frames do we need for our particular analysis: hours, days, months, or even years?" This question might yield a variety of answers. Depending on the needs of the analysis, the answer may vary from days to years. If we are trying to analyze the impacts of future demographic trends on a new hospital's total capacity, years might be appropriate. If we are trying to analyze staffing or equipment requirements for an existing or future facility during a particular season or other scenario, then intraweek days would be sufficient. Alternatively, the C-suite might use DCAMM to determine future budgetary requirements for a new unit or new construction project based on the capacity available under a variety of utilization circumstances. Or, the operating room (OR) management team might use DCAMM to determine staffing levels for the coming winter schedule. On a more granular basis, a given process flow might need to be analyzed for robustness under a variety of daily demand scenarios. Or, an individual process may need to be analyzed based on a variety of ways of completing a given task. This highly granular process analysis will obviously contribute to the larger departmental and system analysis as the results are rolled upward into the bigger picture. The time lines for analysis, then, depend on the questions to be answered and the needs of the inquisitor. Determination of the time lines for analysis will determine several other factors of the DCAMM process and tools. We will go into these as we get further into the methodology itself.

Keep in mind that completing one time-based analysis can help analyze other time frames. For instance, daily analysis helps determine the patterns of arrivals and resource requirements over the course of a twenty-four-hour period. Taken to the next step, this helps us detect the day-to-day variation that might exist throughout a week, now or in a future scenario. Weekly analysis will show us the intramonth dynamism, caused by variations in the surgical schedule and direct admit volumes. We might then go to a seasonal DCAMM analysis, with which we can foresee the impact of seasonal variations in patient acuity, case mix, volumes, and outliers.

Additionally, to effectively determine the impacts on a given process (e.g., triage), we might study the results during different seasons, with different volumes and acuities. Thus, we will need to know the process-level dynamism that might impact a given day's operations, as well as seasonal variation in demand such that we can test the robustness of the developed solution. Thus, while we needn't necessarily start with the hourly analysis to achieve our analytical goals, thorough DCAMM analysis will often require that level of granularity.

Simulation and the Creation of Creativity

Perhaps one of my favorite books is Michael Schrage's *Serious Play*, a fascinating exposé on the development and use of creativity within organizations. Some of the concepts Schrage purports are embedded herein, and he is owed due recognition.

Schrage posits that some companies and organizations are simply more creative than others. This can readily be seen in the business world, where some companies are known as innovators, as others seem to live by the mantra "We put the NO in innovation." (Do you know any hospitals like that?) Schrage attributes much of the difference to the relative use of prototypes.

Prototypes can be many things, such as a clay automobile model, a mock-up of a new building, or a computer simulation, and are visual and/or physical representations and replications. The use of prototypes helps people create by giving them a venue in which to use their imaginations. In other words, they provide something onto which to project creativity rather than relying solely on abstract thinking and imagination.

Schrage's premise is that the prototypes, not our own creativity, drive innovation and creativity. We tend to believe that our creativity drives the creation of prototypes and that we, through our own innovative spirit, create the new designs and ideas of tomorrow. To the contrary, Schrage claims (accurately, I think) that the prototypes drive our creativity by giving us a venue in which to "play." This "serious play" with prototypes lets us place big fins on the rear fenders of our clay automobile model to see how we like the new look. The use of 3-D computer graphics to replicate the inside of a proposed building lets the viewer conduct a virtual walk-through. Or, it allows us to visualize changes to a new process in a computer simulation. This serious play with prototypes is the source of much of our creativity. By opening our creativity through the venue of the prototype, we can go well beyond where we would have if using our creativity alone. Schrage posits that organizations that regularly use prototypes are inherently more creative and innovative, and more successful, than those that do not.

I find this makes logical and historical sense. I have worked in hospitals where new physical layouts were being designed for new units, departments, and entire facilities. It is not uncommon to see a patient room created entirely in Styrofoam and cardboard to allow for nurses, techs, and physicians to play in the new workspace. These mock-ups allow workers to "feel" the new space that will ultimately be their home and make adjustments before the steel is ordered. Furthermore, many architects now regularly use 3-D computer renderings of their designs, allowing the user to walk through a lifelike layout, complete with lighting, shadows, and architectural details. This might be seen as bells and whistles just to impress the CEO and make the board happy. But used correctly, these tools can aid staff and management in determining how the layout will flow, look, and feel as patients and staff interact with their environments.

As another example, process improvement methodologies have their own versions of prototypes in the form of trial runs of process change, small Kaizen events, and other tests of new ideas before going live and full-scale with a systemic change. All of these prototypes enable creativity to be deployed more effectively, such that new systems can be better designed. Of course prototypes, as with any tool, must be applied properly and within the right context. As long as the prototypical worlds in which we play are relatively stable, and as long as the prototypes change as they might in the future, prototypes are extremely useful to create creativity.

Applied to the world of DPA and DCAMM, Schrage's prototypes come in handy as we seek solutions to the complex problems faced in improving hospital capacity. Our prototypes are the DCAMM models that we will use to experiment with various solutions, test for results, and try new ideas, and thereby derive the all-important DPA.

These prototypes are especially important for healthcare, since (though Schrage did not say it explicitly) the larger and more complex the problem, the more prototypes help. As the problems become more complex, the human brain loses the capacity to create. This is particularly true of dynamic and interdependent problems, such as ED or perioperative patient flow. We simply don't think in dynamism the way we can think in averages. In the case of hospital-wide dynamic capacity analysis, our brains are simply not wired to account for the degree of interdependencies that are influenced by the HODDOW WOMSOY variance of communal demand. Thus asking us to be creative without a means by which to focus our creative efforts is asking the impossible. With DCAMM, we are dealing with the dynamism of the entire hospital's flow, as it changes based on HODDOW WOMSOY, evolution, and other parameters. The complexity and dynamism begs for the use of the right kind of prototypes, since grasping the complexities, let alone creating within them, is nearly impossible.

So our DCAMM models and DPA, as a component of DCAMM, are essentially Schrage prototypes. The models should serve as fertile testing grounds for new ideas and concepts. Indeed, some of the new ideas and concepts that will drive healthcare to the next level of performance can only be derived using DCAMM's DPA and simulation methodologies. Without them, will we never be able to effectively understand, predict, and manage the complex systems we want to optimize.

Strategic Analysis Using DCAMM

The main capellini diagram in Figure 5.2 has the major components of hospital-wide flow at a strategic level. These components make up the significant sources of hospital-wide demand patterns as well as the significant opportunities for improvements. Using the DCAMM methodology, tools, and simulation models, we can now understand and predict, and therefore proactively manage, complex healthcare systems.

The arrows in the capellini show us the direction of patient flow, from the demand source areas to the recipient(s) of the demand. The demand, of course,

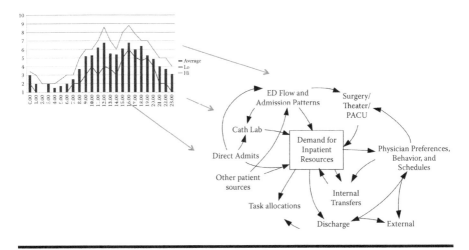

Figure 5.2   Hospital-wide capellini diagram.

begins in the community (Figure 5.3) and presents on the front end of the system in the ED, surgical services, direct admissions, and so forth. Notice that demand enters the system and may then proceed in a variety of directions. As patients flow throughout the system, their paths diverge, depending on their requirements and disposition. In the next sections, we will examine the various sources of patients, discuss some best demonstrated practices (BDPs) for flow enhancement in each, and how demand plays into the bigger DCAMM methodology structure.

Beginning with the community demand, DCAMM accounts for the variability and interdependencies in the flow of patients and demand throughout the system and back into the community.[3] This allows the DCAMM methodology to more accurately and effectively evaluate a system's function as it changes in the model and will change in real life. We can now analyze the entire system, complete with its dynamism, from the community through the healthcare facility and back into the community, and evaluate the impacts of changes throughout the system on our key metrics. In doing so, we learn the interworkings of the system better and are thereby able to more proactively manage the system's dynamism. Furthermore, we know that we can now drill down into the components, using our PI tools such as Lean, Lean Six Sigma, simulation, as well as DCAMM, and analyze a variety of component opportunities. Then, of course, we will want to analyze those results within the context of the higher level DCAMM analytics to attain optimization of the system and not just an individual component(s). This is what we will call an "up–down–up" approach to the use of DCAMM tools, as we will see in a moment.

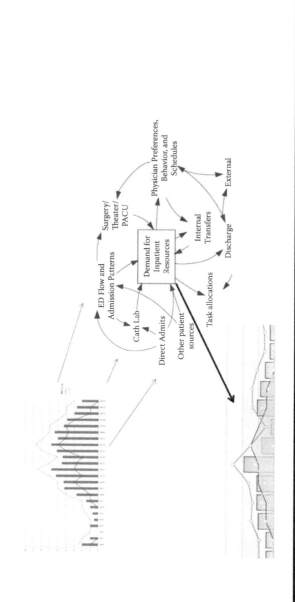

Figure 5.3 Variable community demand patterns create variable, internal downstream resource demand patterns throughout the hospital and the community of care (e.g. Nursing homes, LTAC's).

Model Scale

The scale and scope of the DCAMM model shown herein starts with the communal demand for the various hospital services shown in our capellini diagram (Figure 5.3). However, there are obviously a great deal more that might be included. For instance, the outpatient demand for inpatient radiology services has been known to cause bottlenecks throughout the patient stay as priorities cause backups on the inpatient side. This in turn can delay inpatient discharges, increase ED LOS, and other interdependency-driven constraints. Additionally, the increasing use of the "medical home" may have significant impacts on the resource demands, particularly physicians, in the hospital setting. So, we might want to move the scope beyond the four walls of our hospital to examine the entirety of the patient healthcare experience (this will be the subject of the second book in this series, to be published in the winter of 2011).

The Community Demand

The community demand, from which all hospital demand derives, is often ignored outside public policy wonks and strategic facilities planners. However, this communal demand is what keeps our doors open and is our raison d'être each and every day. Indeed, it is our calling as providers of acute care to service this demand to the best of our abilities to ensure the health of our communities. Understanding this demand, and being able to manage it, is critical to our mission.[4]

Communal demand begins in the top left-hand corner of the capellini (Figure 5.3), with variable demand and patterns coming into the system at various entry points, including the ED, surgical services, and direct admissions. Clearly, the upstream community demand impacts downstream capacity requirements throughout the system. As the starting point for all system demand, it is easy to see that as the community demand patterns change, the downstream demand patterns within the healthcare system is also altered (i.e., hospitals, clinics, physician offices, etc.). Changes to the upstream community demand may have a significant impact on at least some of the downstream capacity requirements within our facilities and beyond into the postacute health systems. Our systems are therefore either able or relatively unable to effectively care for our communities, depending on this demand and our ability to effectively meet it with dynamic capacity.

Community demand is evaluated in the short and long term. Both have their places in the grander scheme of strategic management, being intertwined, as they are, in the results of the business decisions we make. To gauge long-term trends, there are a number of "futurists," consulting firms, and strategic planners who use a variety of analytics tools, techniques, and brain trusts to predict trends in healthcare. Strategy consultants and others seem to constantly crank out information, theories, and predictions on the future world of healthcare, including annual summaries and ten-year projections. These analyses commonly start with demographic trends, budding technologies, and political machinations and lead to an assessment of health needs of the population writ large and possible systemic obstacles to the optimization of the provision of general population healthcare. These analyses are valuable, if for no other reason than to take our minds off the mundane, day-to-day hospital management allowing us to color outside the lines as we think about the future work of providing for our communities, consider new facility and care-system designs, and so forth. Models, then, help "operationalize" change, bringing policy down a "practical use" level.

Indeed, more healthcare providers, employers, and governments are trying to drive real change into this critical portion of system demand via health education, lifestyle, and preventative incentives, and service offerings.[5] Since the services provided by a typical community hospital run the gamut from emergency departments to elective surgery, our interest in community health spans the many facets of communal lifestyle, employment, leisure activities, and income. Managing to, or at least predicting, communal demand is the difference between reactive, suboptimal service levels and DCAMM's proactive, predictive capacity management optimization. Therefore, accurately predicting short- and long-term trends and systemic changes will mean the difference between a misguided strategic plan and a solid one. When combined with these business and trend forecasts, the DCAMM toolset helps ascertain a more realistic approach to multiple possible future-state scenarios. Thus while strategic planners and demographics analysts strive to reveal the possible future of communal demands, dynamic system capacity analytics is required to tackle the actual day-to-day challenges of care.

Trends of concern should include variation in daily, weekly, and seasonal volumes, arrival patterns, and acuity patterns, as well as the HODDOW WOMSOY variations that can plague improvement efforts. These must be balanced dynamically against the capacity we bring forth as providers. So, as ACOs (Accountable Care Organizations) and other business/care models take hold, we can better gauge the actual operational impact on our hospitals, resources, and systems, so as to better align capacity with changing demand. This may mean optimizing either a reduced or expanded capacity. Regardless, as the demand–capacity continuum is altered for one component, the systemic impact can now be foretold.

For instance, if we can begin to address the five main disease categories that drive 70-plus percent of all the healthcare costs in the system, we can significantly alter the overall capacity demand in our facilities. Take, for example, obesity. Americans are significantly more obese today than just 20 years ago.[6] Based on Centers for Disease Control (CDC) and other government estimates, obesity increased dramatically between the 1960s and the early 2000s. Although there was no significant increase in obesity between 2004 and 2006, the "bun is in the oven" as it relates to the current population, meaning obesity rates are likely with us to stay, particularly for the age groups for which healthcare will be increasingly required. Obesity, once it infests a population and individuals, is difficult to extricate. Weight-loss miracles "as seen on TV" are few and far between, with any dramatically lowered body mass index (BMI) difficult to maintain. And while we do not know the exact correlations between a given excessive BMI and the resulting health status, we do know some general trends and correlations that should lead us to be concerned.

Although a laudable goal, a community cannot immediately reduce overall obesity rates, particularly for the over-50 population. Solutions may take many years to work through the population. Nonetheless, long-term implications of these trends are important for decision making in facilities design, workload and staffing, and equipment and technology planning. We know from previous chapters that small, outlier patient populations can have a significant impact on the opportunities for optimization of care, since they can significantly impact the total load on the system at large.

Of course, many short-term questions arise. For instance, how will we deal with this patient population as the nursing staff ages and space constrains specialized equipment and resources? A quick look downstream in our hospital capellini might help give you a way to consider what you might expect.

First, the structure of the demand for service might change. Think more specifically about the over 65 and obese patient population. What services do they currently require? Diabetes, bariatrics, cardiology, interventional radiology, and orthopedics might immediately come to mind. In the current population, what impact will obesity have on the demand in a facility? How has that demand been manifested thus far? How will this demand begin to evolve over time?

Furthermore, how will we manage the spatial requirements of additional, specialized equipment; additions to the surgical schedule and rehab; growth of physician referrals; and so forth? Are we prepared to adequately manage comorbidities common to this population, which might result in longer LOS? Solutions to these issues at a component level might include better interphysician and care-team communication and coordination, and greater access to patient medical records across multiple facilities and offices. At a DCAMM level, simultaneous management of multiple conditions, home-health and rehabilitation coordination, and lifestyle training might be considered. All this is part of the overall DCAMM flow and capellini, and reflected in both the strategic level model and the component drill downs. And, this can now be analyzed and tested dynamically to give us a necessary and quantified predictive vision.

Clearly, the answers that can lead to the efficient inclusion of this and other groups in our overall patient population will require both detailed process analysis and high-level DCAMM analytics. For instance, at the more granular process level, heavier patients can require greater time and workload than other patients. This in turn will impact all other work on the unit in which these patients reside. At the component level, processes take longer and therefore the workload is magnified, potentially impacting wait times for services, LOS, upstream admission rates, and downstream discharge times. Solutions might include segmenting this population to special units, or having specialized resources roaming to specific patient rooms to prevent pressure ulcers and complete other tasks. If the capacity is impacted vis-à-vis outlier LOS, or if special needs of specific patients delay discharge times, the upstream demand might be negatively impacted. Specifically, how will we prevent these patients from remaining outliers and reduce their systemic impacts? (Need I add that the dynamism will significantly impact the answers to these and other questions?)

Therefore at the component (unit) and process level, these patients may require different resources (human and equipment), such as physically stronger nurses and "big boy" toilets. At a DCAMM analytical level, we may also want to include downstream lifestyle training and monitoring to prevent, to the extent possible, readmission and advancement of existing comorbidities. This may require adjustments to staffing levels and specific, dynamic processes for these particular patients. It may require different spatial considerations, as unique equipment requires doubling up on storage space to accommodate both outlier and in-range patients, or more nurse travel to and from special supply areas. Remember, these patients must be effectively integrated into our overall patient population without disruption of the system's flow and efficiencies. So, understanding the community demand patterns of the obese subset of the overall population will aid us in the short- and long-term analysis of the system's capabilities to take care of the total community population. This is particularly true to the extent that these patients create outlier conditions in workflows.

As you can see from thinking through this example, answers to specific, process-related questions will invariably roll up to the system-wide levels where DCAMM plays a role in evaluating the impacts of these changes. The DCAMM analysis, as visualized via our capellini (Figure 5.2), will help demonstrate where and to what degree specific system changes need to be made to accommodate the alterations to communal demand patterns. So, looking downstream at resource requirements might cause us to work with local community colleges to create specialized resource pools for future resource requirements. Or, reworking processes and task allocations to accommodate special-needs patients may require both physical plant and process changes to continue to optimize performance. Also, segmenting patient populations based on special needs and specific comorbidities may result in spatial constraints that will need to be managed (e.g., special beds or units may be outgrown by the patient population, thus requiring process and operational redesign to accommodate the communal demand pattern changes). Last, how much will technology and surgical advancements influence what can be provided via outpatient services (which in turn will influence both our systems [in the larger facilities context] and our individual hospitals and service lines)?

The answers to all these questions, in some way or another, are impacted by the original community demand. This demand, when broken down into smaller groupings such as bariatric patients, can be analyzed within the larger context of total demand and capacity management and thus evaluated for systemic impact. Importantly, this methodology allows one to analyze the creation of outlier populations, which inevitably will drive performance issues and system constraints. Recall from the previous chapters how much influence outliers have on the system's performance. These outliers, in this case in the form of specific patients within the total community demand, have their influence on system performance and optimization. Outliers in the total population heavily influence the total demand and therefore must be considered. Thus, simulation and DCAMM analysis, with its inclusion of interdependencies and variability, is vital to managing in the face of inevitable changes in the communal demand patterns and within the context of the total system performance, capacity, and demand.

A Word on Real-Time Data and Patient Tracking Systems

Is real-time data needed? It depends. Let's narrow the discussion to patient flow and patient/bed tracking systems rather than all real-time systems. Obviously, real-time locations of equipment and even staff can add tremendous value and reduce significant amounts of waste. Several radio-frequency identification (RFID) systems exist, which can track the locations of everything from IV poles to patients, to reduce time spent hunting and gathering and increase nurse–patient care time.

Although the specific capabilities will vary, the major patient tracking system vendors should all have the ability to take the existing patient volume and current patient placement to predict where the patients will be, or perhaps will need to be, in the coming several hours. This is relatively easy logic, some of which is likely already in the head of an experienced nurse supervisor or bed control manager. In the case of patient and bed tracking software, this output can be based on information as to the status (current disposition and diagnoses) of patients in the ED, completed surgeries in the OR, expected direct admissions, and so forth. This information can simply be added together to form a view of the pending inpatient bed needs, such that "bed huddles" and intrastaff communications can reflect the most up-to-date information. This data would obviously be based on assumptions about patient LOS, bed placement parameters, current patient placement, exclusion of flow bottlenecks and constraints, timely data entry, proper actions taken, and so forth. These assumptions, if correct, should yield the summed short-term demand. Furthermore, patient and bed tracking systems could easily provide predictive information as to anticipated resource needs and send alerts when specific capacity thresholds are crossed such that action might be taken. Therefore, this information can be helpful in the hour-to-hour management of patient flow, which is what these systems typically purport.

But, although the real-time location of all the patients in a hospital can be very handy information, the current condition is too late to illicit anything other than a reaction. Real-time data offers real-time analysis, which only gives us the ability to react—in real time. In fact, once an event takes place or a certain critical condition is reached or threshold crossed, we have already lost the opportunity to act proactively to stop it from happening. We must now react to the existing circumstances. *Real time, then, is actually too late.*

Furthermore, as we have seen in the previous chapters, there may be a host of variables that impact, in one way or another, the system's performance. Isolating one or even several contributing factors may still require additional analytics to account for all relevant influences. Furthermore, isolating root causes on the fly, based on our real-time data, may seem futile since it is already too late to act. Additionally, if our real-time data systems only collect information on a few elements (e.g., ED flow and PACU census), we may still lose sight of the other factors that influence demand patterns and capacity requirements. A piece of the system may indeed be in an outlier status while other parts of the system are not. These interdependencies might alleviate some of the pressures to act or change a response or its magnitude. Lastly, since the real-time systems might only capture specific data elements related to patient status, they might be ineffective at providing enough data for the DPA necessary in this DCAMM methodology.

Additionally, real-time tracking systems commonly offer data on the current condition with little or no information on what must be done to alleviate the current or near-current condition. Certainly, long-term solutions are not available from most. A current outlier condition must be managed with a systems perspective in mind, within the context of the dynamism of the system, such that we do not create or exacerbate upstream or downstream constraints and capacity. Knowing what to do, the extent of the response, and when to do it necessarily requires the depth and breadth of knowledge that can only come from the kind of predictive analysis and serious play of DCAMM, DPA, and simulation models.

Additionally, we can now employ "workflow engines," which can prescribe specific actions based on specific input circumstances. Workflow engines take existing parameters, such as current volume in the ED, the current case load in the OR, and volumes of Direct Admits, and prescribe the exact tasks and responsibilities required to manage the flow of patients and other portions of the operations. It can also recommend staffing and resource allocations based on the tasks required. If set up correctly, these are based on multiple inputs, including the outcomes of modeled "what if?" scenarios, parameters specific to the hospital, such as staffing patterns, and even BDPs (Best Demonstrated Practices) and government regulations. These workflow engines are commonly customized to each hospital, so as to capture the nuances and details of specific operational models. When deployed, workflow engines can assist staff with being more efficient and getting the right tasks completed, in the correct order, at the right time.

A few, lesser patient tracking systems are built with preset notions of potential solutions in mind. One such system emphasizes nursing and housekeeping as bottlenecks in the discharge flow of patients (which, according to the proponents of that software, cause upstream delays and constraints throughout the system). Thus that system is geared toward solutions that provide better real-time data from housekeeping and nursing staffs in an effort to improve overall flow. While this might be true in some or even many situations, there are, again, multiple variables constantly in play. We have seen that one variable might offset another, mitigating, eliminating, or exacerbating others. Thus, we need more holistic systems responses that are not geared toward a few solutions, but rather offer the system data needed for better analytics of future trends, such as (1) model input and (2) outlier management.

Last, real time might not mean real time. Keep in mind how any data is collected, and the relative accuracy or inaccuracy of its input. Depending on how the real-time data is input into the patient/bed tracking system and whether reliable processes are in place to achieve the input timeliness required the data might be skewed. If the data is erroneous enough or if its reliability is questionable its usefulness drops dramatically.

This might be the case if retroactive data entry is common or even possible, or if processes are not designed to make the data-entry process and timing errorproof.

Bad data might yield incorrect responses or misguided perceptions of the current condition. So, for example, delayed or incorrect input of discharge data might misrepresent the availability of beds. Thus, technologies such as RFID, sonar, and other "passive tracking" systems are preferred to ensure constant and process-free updating. Yet, there is still great potential value for real-time data. Real-time and passive tracking systems can serve a valuable purpose in our efforts to maintain efficiencies, especially if used with the appropriate analytical tools and methodologies. RTLS which properly feeds simulation models is a sort of a "holy grail" of true ongoing system optimization.

Coupled properly, these tools can offer the data needed to detect outliers and evolution within the system, give faster clues of the occurrence of seasonal shifts and demand abnormalities, analyze variations within patterns on a more regular and systemic basis, and aid us in better monitoring the dynamism that can plague us. Of course, we first need to understand that dynamism and its impacts within the system using DCAMM. Once we have this knowledge, real-time data helps us in the ongoing monitoring of the key elements of our dynamic systems. Thus if RTLS data is incorporated into our use of DCAMM, predictive analytics, and simulation toolsets, true, ongoing dynamic demand–capacity optimization becomes possible.

Summary

DCAMM is all about the strategic use of specific tools to capture the dynamism (defined as variability mixed with interdependencies) of complex systems in order to better understand them, predict their behavior, and proactively manage them.

Notes

1. Models can be quite complex, accounting for far more interdependencies than are depicted here. Furthermore, models commonly account for resources (e.g., staff, beds, equipment) as well as other variables in the replication of system performance. For the purpose of explanation, we assume that each process step is programmed simply to process each patient in a given amount of time. However, simulations offer an enormous range of options for replicating even the most nuanced of systems. Thus, with some additional effort and expertise, interdependencies that are not based strictly on process times can likely be replicated as well.

2. "Optimization engines" have been used in the past to offer up the optimal combination of a limited number of parameters (usually, just one or two) to achieve a given performance metric (e.g., length of stay and total resource cost). These are normally sold with simulation packages, though not often used by modelers. In practice, optimization engines tend only to offer directional advice rather than precise and legitimate solutions. This is because the solutions developed may be truly optimal, but yet impractical to implement. For instance, optimizing for length of stay may yield an unrealistic number of resources.

3. As of the time of publication, I have not yet delved into the specific interdependencies of the so-called medical home. This will no doubt be part of additional analysis and perhaps an updated version of this text and concept.

4. As of the time of this writing, US healthcare "reform" passed and will slowly be implemented. However, despite the promises of politicians, demand for services and costs will likely continue to increase over time if nothing is done to dramatically alter the system. This will mean something far different than even the pilot and demonstration projects in ACOs and Medical Homes will produce. Even if the current reform legislation proceeds unscathed, it does not have within it the elements needed for the kind of radical change necessary to sustain the system.

5. I remain skeptical of most of the incentives currently used and proposed. Having worked with "troubled patients" in the past, I know that these patients do not, or cannot, respond to wellness initiatives, smoking cessation, weight control, and other programs, regardless of the incentives we put in place. Some, though certainly not all, might respond better to negative incentives. That is, sticks rather than carrots. I am not proposing to remove any more freedoms from society than have already been removed. Rather, I propose that lifestyle choices should come with clear consequences. For this I am not proposing simple taxation (a ploy to increase revenues with minimal impact on actual behavior). Instead, I suggest that those who choose to smoke, or remain or become obese, and so forth, should be asked to pay for their own decisions if and when the time comes for behavior-related illness. Smokers should not be offered a lung transplant paid for through public or private insurers. Those who choose to smoke would

be left to their own devices, likely hoping for charity care or generous civic or church groups. These negative incentives make the lifestyle choices that seem so easy to justify more difficult to accept. Risk increases, and with increased risk comes some behavior modification. As a nation, we would necessarily need to come to grips with the concept of personal responsibility, and the often horrible results of certain lifestyle choices. Nonetheless, an under twenty-five-year-old overweight smoker has few if any excuses for the choices he or she makes. Why should the rest of the population be forced to pay for those choices?

6. Some of the best data on American obesity rates comes from the CDC and other US Federal Government sources. http://www.cdc.gov/obesity/data/index.html. Additionally, there are websites devoted to obesity tracking, such as obesity.org. http://www.obesity.org/statistics/.

Chapter 6

Demand Components: The Emergency Department

We will now briefly examine one of the major recipients of communal demand and the subsequent demand it creates for downstream capacity (remember, *capacity* herein refers to space, resources, equipment, and other requirements for patient care). The emergency department (ED) and surgical services are two of the largest sources of inpatient capacity demand, followed by the other, smaller sources such as direct admissions, cath lab, and external and internal transfers. In this chapter, we will begin to discuss the discernable patterns of demand generated from these departments, what it means for dynamic capacity requirements, and how dynamic capacity analysis, matching, and management (DCAMM) analytics can help in ongoing system and component management.

Communal Demand Recipients: ED as a Source of Downstream Demand

In many hospitals, the ED is the largest single source of inpatient capacity demand. Admissions from the ED make up the largest percentage of total admissions, sometimes up to 60 percent or more of the total. Although patternable and somewhat predictable, admissions routinely frustrate nursing units as the demand often exceeds capacity and requests commonly come at precisely the worst time. For this reason, it makes sense to gauge and predict any discernable patterns of ED admissions such that the demand and capacity might be more precisely and proactively matched and managed. To do this, we must start at the initial upstream demand patterns: arrivals to the ED. These will dictate all downstream demand patterns throughout the patient visit.

The general arrival patterns into an ED from the community are said to be similar across the country. It is common for arrival volumes to grow from 9 a.m. to noon, remain high and relatively steady throughout the afternoon, and slowly drop off after 5 p.m. and into the night. A basic pattern resembles that in Figure 6.1. This general pattern (though not the volume) can be roughly the same each day, with variations on the weekends, outlier days, and certain seasons. Of course, volume and acuity patterns can change dramatically by day of week (DOW) and season of year (SOY). And there will inevitably be deviations from this general pattern, as individual hospitals see different demand based on current overall community capacity, competition from other facilities, acuity and demographics, patient and physician preferences, and even community economics. These latter variations are based on everything from the neighborhoods we serve to the reputation of the facility in the community. For now, we will use the pattern in Figure 6.1 to reflect arrival patterns for the following discussion. As we discuss this and all demand patterns, keep in mind that this arrival pattern reflects only one DOW and may reflect only one SOY.

Diving into the Patterns

Notice the variation in the pattern of demand, represented by the lines on the graph in Figure 6.1. The lines represent 80 percent of the variation in each hour. (For Six Sigma aficionados, these charts are similar in concept to control charts.) This is, as we have discussed, critical to understanding the system itself. Without this, we would simply rely on an average demand per hour (or worse, an average for the day) to discern any patterns, and would fail to realize the degree to which in-range variation and outliers impact demand, flow, and downstream components.

The variation demonstrates what might be seen now and in the future. Gauging the degree of variability gives a distinct sense of the degree to which the downstream systems might be tightly controlled. High variation and significant numbers and degree of outliers tell us that our systems will be less controllable. Low variation and only occasional outliers allow for more downstream control and management of patient streams. The latter, surprisingly, is more commonplace than we might suspect.

Breaking our patterns into subcomponents is critical to understanding the eventual inpatient and other downstream demand patterns. The breakdown of patient types can be based on a number of characteristics but should, in some way,

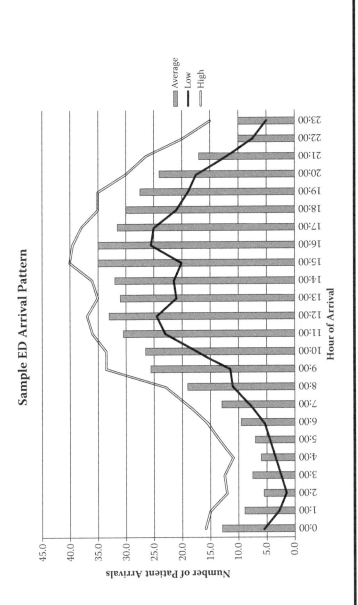

Figure 6.1   Sample ED arrival patterns.

reflect differences in either ED workload or admission likelihood. The arrivals of high-acuity patients needs to be analyzed separately from low-acuity patients, so as to discern any relevant differences that might influence decision making about workload, task, and resource allocation, downstream capacity requirements, and upstream controls. Furthermore, the arrival of emergent patients (level 1, 3, or 5, depending on the ranking system) should be analyzed for unique patterns that might indicate OR or admission patterns, such that they exist. Additionally, mid-acuity patients (e.g., abdominal pain) may require greater testing and radiology exams than other patient types, so their arrival patterns should not be lumped into the averages so as to avoid missing opportunities to develop downstream analytics for ancillary services.

Depending on the volumes of a given patient subcategory, arrival and down-stream demand patterns may be more, or less, easily discerned. Remember, though, that the lower the volumes, the more "random" the arrivals will seem within the day and week. For example, arrival patterns of mental health patients may follow a pattern of daily total volume (e.g., four per day during 85 percent of weekdays, six per day 80 percent of weekend days). But the actual pattern of arrival by hour of day is far less discernable. Since there are so few, it is difficult to assume a consistent arrival every six hours or that one patient arrives during the 1 p.m. to 2 p.m. hour each day. More likely, their arrivals are nearly randomized throughout the after-noon and evening. Therefore, depending on the volumes and the patterns gathered from our data, we will need to adjust the expectations for the analysis. This also requires a change in the way data is used for decision making. So, for those low-volume mental health patients, it might be appropriate to use blocks of four or five hours, during which a patient is expected to arrive. This will aid in using resources more wisely, allowing for the expectation of a given number of arrivals within a given time frame. This in turn helps us better anticipate what seems to be random-ized work.

This may also help to determine any historical patterns of outlier arrivals or those patients arriving with some degree of consistency within a typical time range but in higher percentages of unexpected volumes. Essentially, this means looking for patterns in the outliers. For instance, arrivals of mental health patients might be higher after external community resources close at the end of the business day, but lower after 11 p.m. So, from 5 p.m. to 11 p.m., we might expect to see larger numbers of arrivals but also a higher likelihood of outlier volumes as both volumes and variations ramp up.

Arrivals and the Debates on Predictability

Some contend that the arrival patterns of ED patients are indeed so predictable that they needn't be modeled or studied in great detail. They argue that the arrival pat-terns of patients into a given ED is relatively steady, predictable, and furthermore uncontrollable, thus needn't be deeply considered when trying to optimize hospital-wide flow. Rather, "surgical smoothing" uses the elective surgical schedule as the primary/sole source of managing inpatient demand, with which proponents claim to smooth a hospital's entire flow. Using simple, nondynamic queuing models (a.k.a fancy Excel spreadsheets) as analytical tools, they maintain that controlling and managing hospital-wide flow is merely an exercise in the control of the elective surgical caseload. By smoothing the elective surgical caseload across the week, and preventing spikes in demand for particular beds on particular days, they thereby smooth the total demand for beds across the week, steadying the demand for resources. This, it is said, eliminates capacity constraints and conflicts caused by boluses of surgical case types on particular days. For instance, smoothing ortho cases across the week prevent a large number of ortho cases on, say, Tuesdays. This decompresses the ortho units by eliminating the single day's bolus of patients.

By contrast, ED-generated demand variability (and that of the other sources of downstream demand) is considered by surgical smoothing proponents to be both largely uncontrollable and yet forgivingly consistent. Therefore, averages are sufficient to represent demand since the demand is both steady and relatively predictable. Since the arrival of patients into the ED is also largely uncontrollable (e.g., we cannot stop the car accident from happening) the downstream response can only be, at best, reactive. Thus these surgical smoothing *queuing models* account for some, though not all, of the total inpatient demand variation.[1] The theory thereby suggests that the nonelective surgical demand variation is of little consequence if the elective surgical schedule can be effectively managed.

While I would agree that the arrival and subsequent admission patterns of ED patients is discernable, I respectfully disagree that they should not be considered within the context of overall inpatient and downstream demand. Additionally, I would suggest that the smoothing approach and its use of averages discounts the true HODDOW WOMSOY variances in ED and other source demand patterns. Such an approach also belies the importance of the granularity of intraday variation, evolution, seasonality, and other important issues for which ED patients (and others) are a significant source. As one, if not the, largest source of downstream demand, ED admissions can and should be analyzed and indeed controlled to the extent possible.

Furthermore, since ED patients make up a great deal of the lab and radiology demand, especially during peak arrival and demand times, discerning any patterns and variations therein should aid in capacity matching in ancillary services and elsewhere in the system. This of course impacts resource availability as demand is generated elsewhere in the facility, such as inpatient units or the OR. One only needs to look at the alterations in ED admission and downstream demand patterns brought on by a bad flu season to see that these patterns change enough from the average to warrant serious consideration.

Day-of-week variation in arrival and downstream demand patterns are cause enough for concern. Mondays can be significantly different from Thursdays, and weekends are certainly different from midweek. Thus unless one's analysis accounts for multiple simultaneous patterns of variation, one will lose a great deal of analytical granularity. So, we immediately lose the nuance of the variation and instead take the gross average, which will rarely actually happen on any given day. Those who use queuing models often rely on the same, average number since queuing models are not themselves dynamic enough to manage any better inputs.

Then there is the seasonality of these patterns to be taken into account. Seasonality in both the ED and the OR can have a significant impact on total demand. Furthermore, there is the evolution of the community demand that inevitably takes place, as well as marketplace changes such as the increasing use of "minute clinics" and urgent care centers in lieu of EDs. There may also be ongoing efforts to improve ED flow within and downstream from the ED. These variations and changes to the patterns of upstream and subsequent downstream demand are enough to cause significant disruption in downstream flow, and therefore must be considered as they relate to the total system capacity. Importantly, although arrivals may be out of our control (to the extent that we do not divert ambulance traffic), controlling the flow through and out of EDs is in large part in our hands. Therefore, to disregard the downstream demand as uncontrollable belies the control we have of internal processes and our ability to predict arrivals and manage flow to, through, and from our units.

And although certainly not the only source of demand (as shown in the capellini), it is certainly worthy of consideration as a significant source of both demand and HODDOW WOMSOY variation. This is NOT to say that the surgical smoothing concept is complete bunk. Indeed, applied properly it has value. However, it has far less value if taken as a singular solution. By incorporating this concept into a more holistic approach to DCAMM, we can attain far more effective and sustainable results. There is no single magic bullet…we must bring an arsenal of tools to achieve the goals of ongoing system optimization.

The ED and DCAMM: Using Patterns to Manage the System

We need a solid understanding of the arrival patterns into the ED to understand the admission patterns generated by the ED. The former impacts the latter. As we analyze the arrival patterns by patient type and HODDOW WOMSOY, we can begin to see the correlation between arrivals and inpatient demand generation. This correlation should help to discern any patterns generated. More important, we should analyze how those patterns might be influenced or managed.

For instance, let's use Figure 6.2 to represent the demand pattern from the ED to a given inpatient unit. Each of the patients in this particular inpatient demand

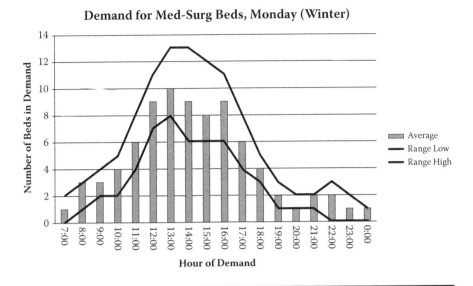

Figure 6.2 Sample demand pattern for med-surg beds, Mondays, and winter season.

pattern came to the ED within some arrival pattern. Correlating the initial demand together with the inpatient demand will reveal a great deal about the function of the ED, the consistency of the disposition time, and any significant variations. This analysis might even be conducted by shift, so as to determine practice patterns of various combinations of staff and a variety of physicians. Further, as we conduct this exercise by patient type and for select time frames, we may begin to see patterns in the length of stay (LOS) by which these patients are admitted. This might lead to some intra-ED process change, regimentation, and waste-reduction efforts.

Without an understanding of the variability, however, we will fail to understand the degree to which a given capacity will solve for the problems. So, even if we make a set amount of capacity available (usually, if anything, the average), we do so without understanding the extent to which it does or does not solve our problems. We also fail to understand the percentage of time higher or lower volumes can be expected, and what demand might constitute a true outlier. Additionally, we fail to understand the extent to which any excess above or below our provision impacts the upstream processes.

Furthermore, looking at the chart in Figure 6.2, we see that the variability changes throughout the day. We not only use averages far too often, we sometimes fail to realize that any variability and outliers, recognized or not, are inconsistent throughout the DOW, and even WOM and SOY. Through this recognition, we can see how our systems might need to dynamically adjust to the varying conditions such that we stay abreast of and proactively manage to the dynamism. This might be done by creating additional capacity buffers, altering processes, changing resource and task allocations, and other dynamic solutions. These dynamic solutions might become less important as the downstream demand wanes or becomes more predictable and manageable.

We also need to ascertain this same variability information for the various patient and bed types. For example, we see that the chart in Figure 6.2 specifically refers to med-surg beds. Without effectively discerning the differences in patient type metrics as they arrive, it will be more difficult to change the processes that will impact the flow on the back end. For instance, if we lump in belly pain with chest pain patients, we lose a great deal of the analytical granularity that might aid the creation of flow solutions for each. We might also miss opportunities to regulate the streaming of patients. Therefore, any differentiation we need to make that will guide us to more effective solutions should be attained. Deep dives into the data must reveal which patient types, bed types, and other parameters require the most attention. As we start to understand the arrival patterns, juxtaposed against the inpatient demand patterns created, we begin to see how flows within the ED might be more effectively managed to impact the entire stream. If we can discern either a reasonable pattern for inpatient admissions (by admitting unit or patient type), or a reasonably steady pattern for LOS (by patient type), we can begin to understand if we might manipulate the patterns of admission into a steadier downstream flow. As both "ends" of the admission process realize the patterns that drive much of the system's demand, they can work together to create and manage as much capacity as possible when it is needed.

Taking this concept one step further: If admission volumes are high enough, it makes sense to actually schedule some of the admissions to specific units based on the historical patterns of demand, still recognizing that variability will have its usual impact. As we look to managing to the variation in the system rather than being managed by it, there may be opportunities to engage the inpatient units in dynamic demand–capacity matching discussions. These discussions should focus on the patterns and variations of arrivals, the subsequent downstream demand, the in-range versus outliers demand, and when and how much downstream capacity is required, by HODDOW WOMSOY. Then, we can begin to have specific discussions about the concept of scheduling at least some of the admissions each day, such that the expectations of admission are more set and specific rather than seen as random events (we will see more of this in later chapters). The concept of scheduled admissions is similar to that of Capacity Entitlement and Acceptance Patterns mentioned earlier. As we begin to learn the patterns of demand [and capacity], and further how to control and manipulate them on both "ends" of the admission process, we can begin to see how we can plan for the patterns to the point of scheduling at least some of the admissions for each given day. This concept is especially true in busy EDs, wherein the flow of patients is heavier and, in many ways, steadier. In these situations, we can effectively predict the range of demand generated by HODDOW, and thereby better plan for a certain volume of admissions during each hour of each day. Knowing that there is variability, we cannot plan to always schedule *all* the admissions on any given day. However, we can schedule *some* such that there is an expectation of performance in the "receiving end" of the admission process. This scheduling concept allows for both the ED and the receiving units to better anticipate workload and workflow, by HODDOW, even if all the admissions will not be accommodated this way, or if there are no admissions for a scheduled slot due to low admission volumes. Recall from the earlier descriptions of Capacity Entitlement and Acceptance Patterns that we can do a great deal with the various patterns once we see and understand them, even when we are over capacity. Even in an over-capacity scenario, we can begin to see how we might schedule admissions from the ED, based on a total Capacity Entitlement for that component and the Acceptance Patterns of a given unit. So, regardless of our volumes and capacity scenarios, it is possible to know and control the variation to the extent that we can schedule what used to be considered chaotic.

That said, we are not so unrealistic and fanciful to assume that scheduling of all admissions from the ED will work in every situation. Nonetheless, it is critical for both "ends" of the demand to understand the concept of the demand–capacity continuum, and identify and, to the extent possible, manage to the patterns such that both can impact the system's flow. To the extent this can be achieved, both ends of the continuum will recognize benefits in anticipating and better managing workload, resource and task allocations, and workflow. Importantly, to the extent that either end of the continuum recognizes and controls any discernable patterns, the system's optimization will be enhanced.

Other Demand Patterns

Of course, we all know that the demand patterns from the ED make up only part of the overall demand. The rest comes from the other feeder components such as OR and direct admissions. As we will see in later chapters, DCAMM and the up–down–up (UDU) methodology will aid in determining the overall demand patterns and what part of the demand–capacity continuum we might influence. Next, we will see some examples of how the flow through and out of the ED can be influenced through process change. These changes should always be taken within the context of the demand of the other feeder sources, such that the entire demand pattern is understood and its variability accounted for. This is key to the DCAMM concept and requires the kind of simulation modeling already discussed. Without that, we will simply be executing changes in one component without an understanding of the impact on the system.

Case Studies and Sample Outputs: Possible Solutions for ED Flow Issues

To some extent, EDs are alike around the world, certainly within the United States. The volume, acuity, and types of patients who arrive might be different, but the processes are remarkably similar. At a high level, these include at least triage, registration, workup, physician disposition decision, and departure. There are a number of concepts, ideas, and best demonstrated practices (BDPs) that have been tried and used to alleviate the many bottlenecks in ED flow. Some will have downstream impacts to the extent that they influence the time, volume, and workload of an inpatient admission. Following are a few ideas that can be tested in your facility.

Eyeball Disposition

It has been well-documented that physicians and many experienced nurses can peg a patient as an admission within seconds of laying eyes upon them. Studies have shown that physicians can disposition a patient as either an admission or discharge 95 percent of the time within thirty seconds of the first evaluation. Experienced nurses get it right over 80 percent of the time, and even relatively inexperienced nurses are better than 50 percent correct. If true, then, why do we wait for hours for lab results, specialist opinions, and radiology reads to make a "final" disposition and admission decision? We may not know precisely the diagnosis and treatment plan, but really what is an ED for? Diagnosis and treatment planning, or disposition? In the formal sense of a true ED, it is the latter. If taken to a logical conclusion, the purpose of an ED physician is to stabilize the highly acute patient, perform necessary diagnostics, and disposition the patient. In the case of the admit, this means placing the patient in the care of the inpatient staff who can then spend the time and attention necessary to see the patient through to a healthier status. So, again, why do we wait hours before "officially" admitting a patient, knowing within the first minute that our patient is "going upstairs"? There are several reasons why this delay has been allowed.

Often, the cause is the preferences of other physicians in the system. Having the burdens of practice and care already on them, attending physicians would prefer to have all necessary diagnostics available prior to taking the patient and making their official admit decision. Thus they demand multiple sets of diagnostics until a precise treatment plan can be developed prior to the patient leaving the ED.

Furthermore, the final admission decision is often left to hospitalists or specialists who must "lay hands" before they will allow an admission. This requires numerous, often repetitive communications between ED and physician, or a wait for a physician to arrive and see the patient. All too often, this results in more tests and longer delays. To be fair, these specialists may want all necessary information available to them prior to their arrival on the scene, such that their workload and time requirements are reduced, so they can speed through their own processes.

This might be due to previous frustration with inappropriate admissions. True, there will always be those patients for whom the initial disposition was incorrect and who were inappropriately admitted. But statistically, this is a very small percentage. The natural tendency to recall the hassles and frustrations of those errors yield an unwillingness to allow for these mistakes by denying the ED physician decision control.

Last, there may be some debate as to where the patient will ultimately reside. It is not uncommon for a belly-pain or lower-back-pain patient to have several potential destinations upon admission, depending on the diagnostics, segmentation of units and beds, and physician preferences. This, however, can be merely an excuse that slows the admission process.

Regardless of the intra-ED circumstances, politics, policies, and procedures, the ED is often clogged with patients waiting to be admitted. The diagnostic and decisioning processes often contribute mightily to the issue by slowing the admission processes until an "official" disposition is made.

The alternative is to allow for the true meaning of *triage* (i.e., the definition from the French word, meaning "to pick" or "to sort") and a more focused purpose of the ED staff: to disposition patients to their proper caretakers. Physicians and skilled nursing staff in the front-end processes, as early in the patient visit as possible, will allow for an immediate understanding of the probable disposition of the presenting patient. Notification is then immediately sent to the probable unit of admission, such that expectations can be set and preparations made. Time limits and expectations should be set forth and strictly followed. For instance, if it takes two and a half hours to complete the required workup, then the expectation should be that the floor will receive the patient in no more than three hours (allowing for some variability). A scheduled admission time could even be set up such that transport and nurse assistance can be scheduled for the admission event. At the very least, the unit nurses and director will know of the impending arrival of the patient and when that patient is to be expected.

This eliminates much of the mystery around admissions. Allowing for preparation time encourages staff and physicians to communicate and schedule events in the admission process, such as nurse-to-nurse reporting and physician-to-physician communication. The more that these events can be melded into the process (or "hard-wired," to borrow a phrase from Quint Studer[2]), the more they can be actually scheduled into an otherwise seemingly randomized series of process steps. Thus, pushing the admission/disposition decision as far upstream in the ED flow as possible will allow for much more freedom, flexibility, and proactive work.

Impact on DCAMM Analytics

This is the "down" part of the DCAMM UDU methodology, wherein processes are analyzed on a granular, departmental level, with the changes rolled up to the strategic level for analysis of systemic impact. The speed and timing of an admission from the ED obviously impacts the demand patterns and workloads within the inpatient components. Of course, if we've done the proper due diligence using the DCAMM methodology described herein, we should already know the ranges and variability of ED admissions by HOD DOW WOM SOY. These ranges have already shown what is to be expected and what might be considered outliers. Thus, our nursing staff is knowledgeable and anticipates the expected workload as patients come in and out of their units. Therefore, the call from the ED stating "expect an admit to your unit between 2:30 and 3:00" should come as no surprise. Nor should it then be a surprise when that patient actually arrives from the ED, with necessary information gathered and ready for the unit staff and admitting physician, attending, hospitalist, or specialist.

If we speed admissions to the point of changing the demand patterns by HOD and DOW, we should consider how this might conflict with existing demand patterns, especially by DOW. So, for instance, moving a series of patients forward in the day from 4:30 to 2:30 might create demand conflicts with the PACU's downstream flows. Thus, decisions will need to be made such that proper prioritization and sequencing of admissions can be achieved. Furthermore, conflicts that create significant bottlenecks in flow or constraints in inpatient resources (including nurses, techs, and even transporters) should be worked out in advance such that demand conflict resolution and contingency planning can occur.

Of course, the entire DCAMM capellini needs to be considered. As demand and capacity is altered upstream, *all* downstream capacity should be analyzed for potential issues. This means that altering the upstream demand for inpatient beds should result in any necessary corresponding changes in inpatient workflow to make capacity available at the right time via the right resources. Further downstream, changes to patterns of admission may alter the downstream physician rounding requirements days later, which might alter office schedules. Or, nursing homes and LTAC's may need to alter their intake processes such that new and returning patients can be accommodated based on potential new arrival times and days. Essentially, the entire capellini should be analyzed any time a significant change to the demand–capacity continuum is made.

Physician on the Front End

ED flow is heavily influenced by the front-end processes. Failure to cycle patients efficiently through the triage, registration, and initial assessment phases of their visit can significantly increase the overall LOS. Furthermore, many patients need only minor care and treatment, and should be cycled quickly.

New concepts for faster and more efficient front-end systems are being developed across the country. These normally include some sort of physician or physician "extender" to quickly disposition and even treat low-acuity patients. Dubbed super fast track, ultra fast track, or physician triage, these flow concepts all involve the use of physician expertise to triage and immediately treat low-acuity patients in the triage or front-end areas. These patients are discharged without ever seeing the main ED or crossing over into "the back." Commonly staffed with physician assistants (PAs), or nurse-practitioners (NPs), or physicians, these expanded front-end systems help to reduce the number of process steps and the staff with which the patient must interact.

There are significant operational issues to overcome here, however. These systems normally require special staffing patterns and process flows. Some proponents of these concepts heavily staff these front-end systems with, for example, a physician, two nurses, and a tech covering ten rooms or less. Volumes and throughput must justify such expense, obviously. Thus, the HODDOW WOMSOY community demand patterns must be analyzed to avoid overstaffing and excessive costs.

Process issues can also arise as the speed of the treatment process overwhelms the parallel and downstream processes, such as registration. It is not uncommon for a patient to be treated and ready to leave before Registration can complete their tasks. The speed of the registration process should necessarily be addressed, such that Health Insurance Portability and Accountability Act (HIPAA) regulations can be managed while information is gathered in a nonclinical area. The latter is important to avoid tying up the clinical areas with nonclinical tasks. However, care should also be taken to ensure that patients do not exit the system without first going through the necessary steps, to avoid possible legal and accounting issues.

The use of physicians in the process can, in some cases, actually slow the process. For example, one Midwestern US hospital instituted a physician-at-triage at the suggestion of an external consultant. The physician was placed in a four-room triage area in the lobby area of the ED, to compliment the triage nurse, registrar, and PA. However, the physician functioned at the tail end of a serial process flow, being behind the three other major process steps. These other process steps also happened in serial, such that there was a very regimented and inefficient patient flow. Combined with the physician interaction, this new process actually added to the overall process time and LOS, since this regimented process was repeated on each patient. Ironically, in the same ED, low-acuity patients who went to the "main side" were allowed to be seen and dispositioned by properly trained and accredited, nonphysician staff. Clinical oversight of those patients by physician staff was given through physician signoffs and chart reviews rather than direct physician involvement in the care process. Thus, the physician served to slow the process rather the increase throughput.

A more successful example involves physicians at triage merely listening in and making recommendations on treatment paths rather than becoming directly involved in the treatment of every patient. Arriving patients who clearly needed immediate physician attention avoided delays in treatment by having a physician immediately available at triage. Space near the triage area was made available specifically for this physician intervention. This relieved the triage nurse from overstepping his or her decision authority and speeding the process care, reducing rework, extra testing, and other redundancies in the process. Furthermore, this process allowed for a physician to use eyeball triage to immediately assess the need for admission, which would allow for the admission process described earlier in the "Eyeball Disposition" section to be readily instituted.

Result Waiting Area

Patients awaiting lab results and radiology reads can take up critical clinical space during busy times. To avoid this, a "results waiting area" is recommended as a means to free up clinical space for more patients. Depending on the patient population, these spaces may be curtained or open, with comfortable chairs or stretchers, depending on the patient need. The space would need to be nearby to clinical resources, such that visual monitoring can be done. Regardless of your particular setup, the concept is a place wherein patients awaiting test results can wait for those results to come back. Rather than waiting in an ED bed, patients who might need a yes or no, or who are waiting for clearance to leave can wait in a comfortable, nonclinical space. A private consult space is used so that physicians can share information with patients while avoiding HIPAA violations.

Used effectively, this allows for quicker bed turns. Even minor time savings (i.e. ten to fifteen minutes) add up over the course of a busy day. This can be especially important during busy times when clinical space is at a premium. This space might also be important for high-volume, low-acuity patient populations who need labs and testing for diagnostics but who do not necessarily need a private ED bed.

Use of Cardiac Markers

Makers of cardiac markers tout savings in both time and unnecessary admissions. BioSite™, now part of Inverness Medical, and others make markers that speed the analysis of specific patient diagnostics through the use of clinical markers in the blood. Markers eliminate much of the time associated with clinical decisioning, testing, and waiting for results. The manufacturer claims the use of cardiac markers in combination with a panel approach to diagnose acute myocardial infarction eliminates serial testing that normally takes six to eight hours.

Some EDs have used these tests with their "frequent flyers,"[3] holding these patients in the waiting room or results waiting area to prevent the use of clinical space while awaiting marker test results.

In addition to the per-patient time savings, markers are said to reduce unnecessary admissions by adding quick clinical assurance to a normally extensive workup. Some hospitals are known to admit patients on strong suspicion of, for example, acute myocardial infarction (AMI) to eliminate long ED boarding time and reduce liability. Quicker test and clinical feedback might eliminate admissions that otherwise might occur.

Of course, the financial and clinical viability of such systems much be gauged by each facility. In some facilities, wherein throughput trumps cost considerations, or insufficient capacity requires a reduction in LOS at any cost, these systems can be adopted without consideration of the financial implications. In others, physician preference will dictate a traditional approach. We make no judgment about the clinical efficacy of the systems, and only offer them as a suggestion to elicit creativity in the development of an appropriate set of solutions for your system.

Summary

The ED is one of the largest sources of inpatient bed demand. It can account for well over 50 percent of the admissions to a busy hospital on any given day. The variability coming in and out of the ED can therefore have a significant impact of the rest of the hospital's capacity and resource requirements. If not studied properly, these downstream demand patterns can lead to a sense of chaos and randomness. In fact, as we have seen, demand falls within typical ranges, depending on HODDOW WOMSOY, which are discernable to a great degree. And while other elements of system demand, such as the elective surgical schedule, can have a significant impact on downstream demand, the EDs demand patterns and variances should not be discounted.

The demand that falls outside those ranges can be deemed outlier or possibly evolution. These outliers are what often cause the system's flow to begin to break down, with ripple effects throughout the downstream interdependent components. As we will see in the coming chapters, outlier management is a key element of the new approach to hospital management.

Notes

1. Queuing models were developed for use in the 1950s as a means to analyze variable systems. Because of their construction (often done through spreadsheets or simple modeling software) they account only for a limited number of variables and a limited amount of variation. They are quite good and perfectly sufficient for rudimentary analysis of queuing systems and their wait times, bottlenecks, and constraints. However, they are not, in my mind, sophisticated enough to account for the true dynamism of hospital-wide demand and capacity.
2. Quint Studer, *Hardwiring Excellence: Purpose, Worthwhile Work, Making a Difference*, Fire Starter Publishing, Gulf Breeze, FL, 2003.
3. The term *frequent flyer* refers to patients who used the ED regularly and often, sometimes for nonclinical reasons, such as a warm place to rest.

Chapter 7

Surgical Services and DCAMM Analytics

Surgical Services and Downstream Demand Analysis

Surgical services is a complex beast in and of itself, aside from its impact on down-stream demand patterns. For clarification's sake, we refer to *surgical services* as the in-hospital services and not outpatient surgery. And for the sake of this text, surgical services includes more than the OR or surgical suite, encompassing processes from the initial scheduling of a procedure all the way through to post-PACU discharge or admission. This broader perspective is necessary to analyze processes as they relate to the operations and flow within the surgical services component and the entire system.

As seen from our hospital-wide capellini,[1] (See Figure 7.1) surgical services is driven by a number of factors and components, not the least of which is physician preferences, rounding patterns, and office schedules, which in turn drive the pre-ferred surgical schedule. Physicians tend to drive the utilization of surgical services through their use of the OR and scheduling demands and needs.

The performance of surgical services is also influenced by the ED and, to a certain extent, the other sources of interdependencies, conflicts, and overlaps. If we are to manage the entire hospital system, a solid and deep understanding of all the component demands must be fully understood, including that of surgical services. Without a "root-cause" focus and mindset, we may miss the up- and downstream interdependencies that complicate surgical services and inpatient flows.

Patient arrivals into surgical services are more or less controlled except for emergent cases popping in from the ED, the occasional emergent referral from a physician office or clinic, and external transfers from other facilities. Furthermore,

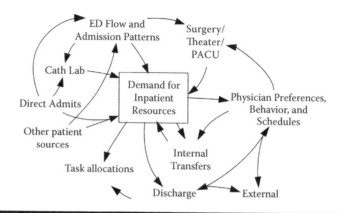

Figure 7.1   Hospital-wide capellini diagram, depicting the interdependencies of patient flow and resource requirements.

patients utilize preoperative testing based on scheduling for procedures. The surgical schedule drives many internal resource demands, from day-of-surgery radiology procedures to later discharge and rounding requirements.

Indeed, the surgical schedule essentially drives all other surgical services demand patterns, both upstream and downstream. Once a case is scheduled, other upstream demand patterns are generated, including pre-surgical testing, insurance verification and preapproval, anesthesiologist–patient communication, and pre-op on the day of surgery (DOS). As the patient arrives and after the case begins, there are multiple downstream processes generated, from PACU to inpatient beds to radiology, physical therapy, and discharge. Therefore, we want to examine the surgical schedule as the source, or root cause, of up- and downstream demand patterns. Individual OR processes are commonly analyzed via common PI methodologies, such as Six Sigma. Processes may need to be improved to the extent that they reduce costs, eliminate waste, and prevent process errors on DOS. Such errors and wastes might include lack of proper paperwork, lack of history and physicals, failure to properly document preoperative testing results, rework of paperwork, excess transportation and patent movement, and canceled cases. For instance, lack of proper communications is a key constraint to effective OR flow on DOS. To the extent this issue cause delays on DOS, the impact of improvement can be rolled up to the system's dynamic capacity analysis, matching, and management (DCAMM) analysis to test for possible systemic throughput, flow, or cost improvements. The results of any process changes made within a subcomponent stream should always be rolled up into the larger surgical services flow, since there may be an impact on the larger system. Here, changes to the schedule or subcomponent processes might be analyzed within the greater context of system capacity if those changes might have significant or perhaps hidden downstream impacts. (If the entire stream of preoperative flow is analyzed, potentially encompassing everything from the scheduling process through to the history and physical signature, a discrete-event simulation model will likely be required to account for the dynamism. Of course, the hospital-wide simulation models described herein are necessary to study the system dynamism and impact of component change.)

OR TATs and First-Case Starts

Delays in first-case starts are an all-too-common problem. Issues from late arrivals of surgeons and anesthesiologists to missing paperwork to lack of equipment and testing supplies can cause a delayed start. These can ripple throughout the day, particularly for quick-turn cases. Before starting a project to improve first-case starts, however, it is always a good idea to understand to what degree you need to improve, what the expected outcome of change will be, and where the next bottleneck will emerge. This is where both simulation and our DCAMM methodologies can come into play.

Before embarking on a first-case start improvement journey, and to ensure buy-in for any change recommendations, you should begin with an analysis of the impacts of late starts on both the surgical services flow and the entire system. The impacts may not be what you think, given that the variability in case lengths, or intra-operative delays, may have an even larger impact. Our simulation model of flow interdependencies will gauge the impact of changes to key components and help us to prescribe appropriate solutions. Should you decide to proceed, based on the decision that first-case start delay reduction will impact key performance metrics, you may want to concurrently look to the padding you give the surgeon's blocks or OR turnaround time (TAT) to guarantee that you are not encouraging, or at least accommodating, bad behavior in late arrivals. *The project should therefore focus on the process as you keep an eye on the system.*

Look, too, at how the next case or follow-on case is scheduled. Is a single surgeon in the same room for multiple cases? Contrary to popular opinion, simulation analysis often demonstrates that, in some situations, same-room surgeon utilization can mean better throughput and productivity, despite what seems like an eternal delay between cases for the surgeon. Why? Because delays between cases in different rooms can lead to the "magical disappearing surgeon" and reduce overall productivity. Take a surgeon who is working in two different ORs on the same day, mixing in cases with other surgeons within the schedule. So, for example, let's say surgeon A is to go from her first case, case 1, to case 2 in another OR where another, surgeon B, also has a first case, case 3. If case 1 with surgeon A ends prior to case 3, surgeon A is delayed starting her next case. So, wanting to utilize time optimally, surgeon A uses the downtime caused by the case 3 delay to check in with the office, return calls, check e-mails, or even perhaps round on the inpatient units. Although these are all valuable uses of a surgeon's time, they can in turn delay the next-case start in the second OR once it becomes available. Instead, a set and prescribed TAT in the same OR allows the surgeon to know exactly when the next patient will be ready and waiting, reducing lost time and AWOL surgeons. Of course, depending on the situation, the case length may dictate differently, since it is often feasible to alternate OR's for faster cases.

Additionally, process improvements around TAT such as parallel processing, use of induction processes, and scheduling case end times so as to allow for staff efficiency all have an impact on the productivity, throughput, and downstream demand patterns. Again, the variability in case time will be a significant issue here and may not allow for some of the otherwise achievable solutions.

Chasing the Rabbit in the OR

In the OR, we often chase and improve bottlenecks only to find they move upstream or downstream in the flow, or have little or no impact on the overall system. This is a common issue in complex systems in which there are multiple serial processes. In the OR, the serial nature of many of the processes makes it easier to shift a bottleneck up- or downstream to other processes. In a parallel process flow, in which multiple processes occur at once, one process can "make up" for degradation of another, helping to keep the system moving. In a serial or single-stream flow, this is more difficult. For instance, speeding up the registration process might improve initial patient satisfaction but might overburden pre-op staff attempting to manage the pre-op processes and patient preparation. Improving OR housekeeping turnaround times might impress the surgeons, but only insofar as there are no other delays in prepping the patient for surgery and starting the next case. It doesn't help if to have a clean and ready room with no anesthesiologist, a surgeon who has disappeared, or an incorrect case setup or incomplete supplies. Serial processes must be well managed and deeply understood to prevent potential bottlenecks from erupting. This includes a solid understanding of the upstream and downstream flows and the variability at each process step, such that effective flow can be maintained in the face of real-life circumstances. Since, as we have seen, the variability at each step can heavily impact the overall flow, we need a level of granularity in our analysis that allows us to study our processes with variability included, so as to more repair the system. Assuming that variability in certain processes cannot be eliminated, it needs to be accounted for in the scheduling of resources and the assumptions of throughput, so as to avoid inevitable delays. Or, in some cases, resource and task allocation should be such that resources can be quickly reassigned as needed to pick up process slack when the system falls behind.

There may be obvious variance in the process itself based on patient type. For instance, there is a slightly different set of processes for our lumbar surgery than for a coronary artery bypass graft (CABG). Each must be analyzed for its own nuances and standardized such that the potential for errors and delays are eliminated. The PPI methodologies (e.g., Lean, total quality management [TQM], and LSS) can be excellent for achieving an appropriate degree of operational regimen to avoid both. To the extent that variance has an impact or interdependencies are complex and impactful, the use of simulation in the analysis of the process and value stream maps should be considered.

Furthermore, the physical plant may not be effective for the process improvements we wish to implement. For instance, mixing pre- and post-op space works well under the correct scheduling algorithms, which prevent conflicts from erupting. However, it requires a physical space conducive to that alignment of patients and resources. Such a space is able to smoothly transition from one role to the other without interruption of services to either, and without delays in care or undue errors. This requires excellent coordination of resources (particularly staff) and the surgical schedule, and demands an integration of variability into the analysis. We must consider these variables when attempting to create solutions to increase capacity, throughput, and so forth for both processes and the system.

Keep in mind that chasing variability can itself be a fool's game if the process has no impact on the system itself. Even reducing variation in the long, highly variable cases will only impact performance to the extent that there are to-follow cases or worked hours are impacted. *Always look up- and downstream to determine the possible benefits of change before marching into battle.*

We may also need to come to grips with why we need improvement. For instance, a few minutes shaved off TATs might not impact total length of stay (LOS) or throughput. However, it might build surgeon loyalty such that other changes might be implemented, such as surgeon arrival times. Although the former may not impact the system at large, the latter might. So, with one eye on the goals of greater system capacity, we must avoid the creation of bottlenecks when we endeavor to improve our components or subcomponents. Merely improving one component or subcomponent may have benefits, but should only be attempted if there is clear indication that we will create no up- or downstream constraints, errors, quality issues, or waste. This is how we create bottlenecks and work for ourselves in constantly reanalyzing the same systems. To prevent this from happening, we must have the greater system in mind, such that we understand the patterns of downstream demand we create.

If the OR schedule and the related rate and pattern at which we demand downstream resources creates downstream conflicts with the ED in the demand for a specific type of inpatient resources or bed, whether on day of admission or day of discharge, either or both components must make accommodations such that flow is improved. This brings us to the issues of surgical smoothing and takt time matching.

Surgical Smoothing and Systems Thinking

Surgical smoothing is an idea that has been around since the early 1990s. Its proponents have advocated a variety of similar theories around changing the surgical schedule in order to control the downstream demand patterns for resources coming from surgical services. However, although the many throughput improvement efforts and concepts may have an impact if implemented well and maintained properly, much of the difficulty lies in physician preferences and an inability to force changes in the surgical schedule. As mentioned in Chapter 6, many hospitals find the surgical smoothing approach limiting in its impact since few, if any, of their surgeons were willing to upend their practice patterns (part of the downstream capellini diagram), surgical schedules, and lifestyles to accommodate inpatient bed smoothing. Furthermore, caveats exist in the implementation of such systems, which can alter its effectiveness, even assuming physician buy-in.

The theory is relatively simple and intuitive: According to proponents, we know that there is variability throughout our systems (as shown in this text). We also know that there are demand patterns that we can control and those we cannot. Furthermore, smoothing proponents say that we cannot control demand patterns generated in the ED because we cannot control the events and illnesses in the community that lead to ED arrivals. Likewise, we cannot control emergent communal demand for the cath lab, since, again, we cannot control the emergent nature of cardiac diseases. Nor can we control emergent surgical cases, since, again, we cannot control the emergencies that generate them. However, we generate our own elective surgical schedule (it has been suggested that nearly all cases are elective in some sense). To the extent that the elective surgical schedule generates downstream constraints and excess demand, it should be controlled to smooth the demand for those resources and minimize or eliminate excess demand.

Some proponents of smoothing believe that the variability in the elective surgical schedule creates most if not all of the excess demand generated in a given facility's (hospital-wide) flow. For instance, because orthopedists tend to work on certain days of the week and during specific hours, the flow from the OR to the ortho units is high on some days and minimal on others. These spikes and lulls in demand generate extremes downstream, which flow throughout the downstream processes, from PACU to hospital discharge. This, according to proponents, creates much if not all of the conflicts for inpatient bed demand with the other components such as the ED, as the spike in surgical demand overwhelms the system and thus prevents all components from smoothly flowing. As new patients attempt to come into the system from the ED or other components on certain days, they are blocked due to the boluses of patients created by the peaks of surgical demand. Or, surgical flow is blocked due to the peaks of demand, which overwhelm the system's capacity. Cases on these days or later in the week might be canceled due to this demand, which overwhelm specific inpatient units. Thus, anything we can do to prevent the spikes and lulls in inpatient bed demand should be done so as to prevent these and other excesses. This smoothing of downstream inpatient bed demand, driven by the smoothing of the surgical schedule, is what this theory is all about.

Keep in mind that, in order to implement this approach effectively, there must be certain specific parameters and conditions to allow for the effective implementation of surgical smoothing. For instance, there must be enough excess capacity in the OR and the schedule to allow for the designation of one (or more) rooms for only emergent cases. This prevents the bumping of elective cases, allowing for emergent patients to be seen without delay or consideration of the current surgical schedule. Additionally, the OR utilization must be relatively low, else otherwise there is no wiggle room in the surgical schedule to allow for the movement of cases within the schedule. In a Northeast hospital where surgical smoothing was initially touted, the OR utilization was approximately 50 percent (not bad by some standards but still low). This allowed for the necessary changes to both the surgical schedule and the OR assignment such that smoothing could be implemented. (Ironically, more work on patient flow was needed at that facility in subsequent years and external consultants continued to be hired to fix problems, new and old.) Most obviously, the physician staff must be on board to the extent that the changes impact their schedules.

A few thoughts: First, this bolsters our notion that the surgical schedule drives everything else in the surgical services system. Clearly, the surgical smoothing concept relies heavily on the notion that, if effectively managed, the surgical schedule can become a powerful tool in increasing capacity in systems. And indeed, this is not entirely incorrect. The surgical schedule, having such a strong influence over downstream resource demands, can indeed have implications if altered. Indeed, as we have already pointed out, before the schedule is altered at all, the up- and downstream impacts should be thoroughly analyzed for both negative and positive impacts. Based on any ability to better manage downstream demand patterns, and improve overall system throughput, cost, or other key metrics, alterations to the surgical schedule can and should be made.

Second, the general focus of smoothing is the peaks and valleys of inpatient bed demand generated by the surgical schedule, and not the downstream issues associated with them. This belies the other downstream operations that might accommodate and even benefit from these demand peaks. Furthermore, there may be much that can be done to achieve higher capacity with or without altering the surgical schedule. Consider how impactful discharge patterns are on the front end of the demand–capacity continuum. As we change the discharge processes (hopefully, for the better), we alter the demand–capacity continuum for the initial admission of patients.

Or, for instance, physical therapy (PT) might be very busy on certain days due to a high number of requests for service in the days after a bolus of ortho patients hits the unit. This, however, might be preferred so as to limit the spread of PT work within the week, allowing for more flexible PT scheduling. True, multiple orthopedists working in the OR on a certain day will generate a bolus of patients to the ortho units. Whether this initial demand surge can be managed is a very real question. However, the downstream care patterns might actually benefit from this surge. What if, for instance, the efficiency and productivity of physical therapy and other care specialists benefited from having a higher concentration of ortho patients on subsequent days? What if their schedules might actually become more hectic, rather than less, by smoothing the demand across the week and requiring more trips to the unit or weekend hours? Assuming they were not overwhelmed already, they, along with other care providers, may find that these boluses make for more efficient workflows and reduced overall cost of care due to the concentration of patients. If we are solely focused on the demand for beds, we may miss other resource allocations and issues that might be used to offset, accommodate, or perhaps exacerbate the boluses of patient demand.

Obviously, one of the benefits to the surgeons is rounding patterns. By creating a "slug" of patients on a single day, they focus their downstream work demands on specific days, matching the other work throughout their week. This may have other benefits such as increasing the volume of patients these physicians can actually manage, both in their offices and within your facility.

If your facility employs some or all of its physicians, consider the impact of changing the surgical schedule on the office schedule and the capacity of physicians to see patients. One would want to analyze whether altering the surgical schedule might impact office capacity due to required changes in rounding patterns, additional travel time, or office staffing constraints. The left side of the main capellini diagram shows that a strong consideration of physician work outside the OR is critical to this change.

Think, too, of the far-downstream demand patterns you might generate for small segments of your population. It might be fine for your hospital to alter the surgical schedule to move (as in the aforementioned example) ortho cases from Monday until later in the week, until you discover that your local long-term acute care (LTAC) facilities, nursing homes, and medical home providers won't take new patients on the weekends. You might actually increase your LOS and increase costs for a small segment of the population if all these considerations are not taken into account. Indeed, if we cannot smooth the surgical schedule, for whatever reason (e.g., physician defiance, logistics, lack of available capacity, etc.) we may need to adapt our internal systems to better accommodate the existing schedule and its demand patterns.

Furthermore, and important, we would need to consider by how much various components of the system needed to be altered to accommodate the surgical schedule (as is or altered) including the schedule itself. Some combination of small changes may be able to achieve the same goals as one large change. Therefore, we would want to consider all aspects of the resource demands, not just the demand for inpatient beds so as to determine (1) when, where, and by how much change is needed; and (2) to what extent changing existing operations will accommodate any current or new schedule or demand structure.

Third, failing to account for the system and its dynamism can lead to the same issues as failing to account for process variability at the process level. Indeed, the proponents of smoothing tend to use queuing models as analytical tools. Although handy for some uses, queuing models (most often extensive spreadsheets) fail to accurately account for the variability and interdependencies of the system and the surgical schedule. Indeed, as we have already seen, queuing models are only good for system analytics where there is low interdependency and low variability. That certainly is not the case in hospital-wide flow, or the surgical schedule, where extremes of variability and system interdependencies make system analysis difficult, at best.

Last, the variation in surgical procedures themselves may cause downstream issues. By taking into account only the average case time, we might make assumptions about the demand patterns that could be largely false. The greater the variation in case length, the greater the likelihood that some downstream component will be thrown off by the postsurgical demand. So, trying surgical smoothing without understanding the case length variability can result in frustrating performance.

Do not misunderstand the message here. Just as I have stated that Lean is not the end-all-be-all methodology, surgical smoothing is not the end-all-be-all answer to hospital capacity. But let me be very clear: nor is DCAMM alone! So while I would agree that the surgical schedule is an input ripe for capacity analysis, I would not agree with smoothing proponents that it is a panacea for all our woes. Yet, there may well be circumstances in which it might help. Certainly, if parameters are correctly aligned, smoothing can have a significant impact on inpatient bed demand patterns. But this is not so simple as it may seem at first. Consideration must be given to all downstream processes and components, not just the initial demand for inpatient beds. Although the aforementioned hypothetical examples may or may not have relevance in your facility, such downstream analysis is certainly worthy of consideration. Thus, to truly address capacity at both the surgical services and the hospital-wide levels, it is imperative that the *entire system be considered, complete with its dynamism, when considering smoothing as a solution.* Indeed, the history of the degree of successful smoothing implementations varies between hospitals. This is due to a number of problems with the approach, not the least of which is the availability of excess capacity in the OR, surgeon willingness to realign surgical schedules, and other issues mentioned earlier. Since these many stars don't always align, smoothing has seen failures as well as successes. Nonetheless, the surgical schedule is indeed a source of potential improvement such that capacity can be maximized if properly managed based on systems thinking.

Case Length Variation and Analysis

The complexity of the parameters of this utilization improvement concept suggests that managing the variability of case time is another significant root cause of surgical services issues. A good use of analysis would therefore be to analyze the variability of case length, by case type, by surgeon, to eliminate the underutilization of blocks, the time between cases for the same surgeon in different ORs, and improve overall OR utilization. All too often averages are used to represent the case length, with little or no understanding of the actual variance that creates the average, and the extent to which the variance impacts our downstream processes. The question that should be asked is: "What percentage of the time does this case, with this surgeon, fit into this block time?" And, "What percentage of overage and excess are we comfortable with?" Comfort levels vary, of course. So, a surgeon for which a case fits into the block 100 percent of the time may actually have too much block time, especially if the case length is relatively variable. In case types for which the variance and case length are both relatively low, a higher percentage of in-block percentage should be expected. In contrast, a lower lumbar spinal fusion case may have tremendous variance and thus a lower in-block percentage. This means that more cushion will be required to ensure case starts are properly managed.

As we'll see, schedule modeling is a great tool for these analytical applications. Of course, models are great tools for analyzing many alternatives to the current state. "What if?" scenarios can be conducted with our model(s) to analyze block schedule optimization, resource allocations, turn-around processes, the impact of additional ORs on throughput and downstream capacity constraints, the possible constraints to combining pre- and post-op areas into one, etc. As with any process improvement, unless we take the system's dynamism into account, we risk simply moving a bottleneck at best, and causing significant capacity disruptions and cost escalations at worst.

Remember, the longer the case and the higher its variability, typically the greater the opportunity to effect changes that will impact total procedure time. Since there may be multiple causes of delays, it is wise to examine all issues for possible impacts. For instance, having properly equipped case carts, and ready and proximal supplies, can mean reduced hunting and gathering during the procedure. These are excellent Lean Six Sigma (LSS) projects and can significantly improve costs, surgeon satisfaction, and procedure time variation reduction. These are also helped by instant communications, which allow for staff and physicians to keep up with the movement of patients and the progress of cases. Such an analysis will lead to a far better utilization of the ORs than using averages for analysis and scheduling. Always keep the system in mind as you examine which problem to tackle, to eliminate waste in your projects and quantify the expectations of future performance.

Schedule Analytics, the DCAMM Way

Scheduling analytics is an excellent starting point to any alterations of the OR flow, since it is the engine of the surgical systems operations. Commonly, when managing the surgical schedule, we typically examine block times and allocations within the block schedule. Block schedules may be full, but those blocks aren't necessarily filled with cases. In an effort to manage capacity or improve overall efficiency, OR managers will commonly address an individual surgeon's or group's block allocation based on utilization patterns and any unused time. In doing so, the utilization of the block is most often based on average case lengths over some time period, normally the past five to ten cases. However, by using averages, both these methods leave off the critical issue of variability and the potential to gauge utilization or case length in a more productive way. Achieving better analysis of the surgical schedule holds the potential to increase efficiency, reduce staff and supply costs, increase volume without adding physical capacity, and increase total throughput and revenues.

The following discussion will focus on actual case time rather than blocks. This is because a large block, which might encompass several cases for a group or a particular physician, can mask the intra-block variability that can lead to lower utilization. Rather than using average case time to determine case length, block allocation and utilization, and the expected performance of the system, we should begin to look at case length variance by case type, by physician, as it relates to the percentage of time a case fits within a given blocked time. The image in Figure 7.2 is a highly simplified, explanatory interface designed for use in this text. It shows the use of variability in determining a correct surgical block.[2]

Now, Figure 7.2 shows several important aspects of this sort of schedule analysis. First, it shows the range of process times for each case, set to a preferred maximum and minimum.[3] This range is represented both by the "wheels in to wheels out" time, as well as "cut to close" time. The total range is the expanse of both. As with other demand, this is set to 80 percent to 90 percent, if we remove the outliers to tighten the range. Low-variability case types can use 100 percent. High-variability case types might also use 100 percent of the variation, so as to capture more of the probabilities of downstream patterns. However you choose to input the information, the analysis helps you to understand (through visual cues) the relative variance within each case type, and compare the variance of case types across physicians. The variance of each case, in a visual display such as this, helps us to quickly ascertain the relative need for accommodation of a particular surgeon or case type. It also informs us, again visually, of the relative need to account for the proximity of next-case starts.

Second, since it shows us the wheels-in and wheels-out time, it offers a good visual and quantitative indication of the efficiency of room turnover as well as the relative amount of surgeon downtime.[4] This can also help us understand the relative efficacy of various scheduling methods, such as back-to-back surgeons (or same-room) scheduling. Here, we also see the potential for overloading housekeeping and nursing staff when multiple cases end during the same short period. This is not uncommon, requiring nurses and housekeeping to scramble to keep the day on schedule. Additionally, if specific nurse shift leaders have an overly large role in the turnover process, as can be the case, we can see a degradation of the turnover time brought about purely by excess simultaneous demand. So, we want to analyze when and to what extent this overlap occurs, and what it means for any delays in flow. (Of course, this is where we would want to drill down into the processes using our process improvement methodologies such as Lean and LSS.)

Third, it shows the percentage of time a case fits within its allocated time. This is a much different metric than average block utilization. Rather than comparing the average of the previous several cases of a given block period as a determinant,

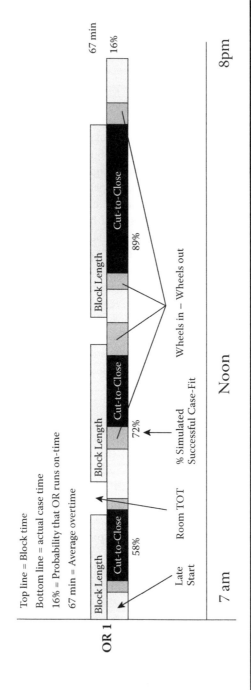

Figure 7.2 Simple surgical block schedule and variability analysis.

this tool uses a percentage of occurrences *within block* or *percent case fit*. The percentage of case fit allows for several bits of additional and potentially important information:

1. It tells us the degree to which variability impacts the block utilization. Take, for instance, the difference between an eye case with Dr. Jones and a spinal fusion with Dr. Smith. The eye case has very limited variability, due to the nature of the case, so its process times can more readily and tightly fit within a given allocated period. The percentage of time this case fits within its given block is naturally expected to be higher. However, the spinal case length is highly variable. It is less likely to fit within a given block, particularly if the block time deviates from the longer end of the range. It also will have a much longer block allocation, perhaps the better part of a given day. Of course, if the block is long enough such that it compensates for the high end of the variability, even highly variable cases will always fit. This, however, is how inefficient blocks are created.

   Thus, this percentage gives a much better means by which to gauge whether the block is actually working as it should, offering surgeons sufficient time to complete their work without creating unused capacity. This helps us address possible intra-OR process issues.

2. Using the percentage of case fit offers us a specific metric by which block times can be judged. To say a block is too long or too short is a relative measure. Using a percentage by case type, blocks can be compared for relative efficiency. Even blocks of different case types can be easily compared for relative efficiency. Used as a probability of a given case fitting within a given block, we can quantify the viability and appropriateness of a particular block length.

   Furthermore, it would also be helpful to understand as a measure of the distribution of case length around the average. Since it is common that the length of a given case of any given surgeon is something other than a nice, steady bell curve, the degree to which there are outliers in case time will aid us in understanding the degree to which the variance might impact us. The analysis will also help us target our improvement efforts to specific cases, physicians, and blocks.

   One way to measure the relative effectiveness across different case types is to group degrees of variability and case fit into categories. Admittedly, this analysis will most likely require your management/performance engineering group or other process improvement (PI) professionals. But grouping cases into categories based on their degree of variability and case fit allows for several benefits. First, it allows you to understand the relative variability of all the cases in the system, as judged by individual scores as well as by the number of case types in each category. When applied to case fit, this in turn helps you assess the degree to which you might improve your system. A relatively low case-fit percentage with low variability would indicate excess capacity as well as the potential for additional case volume, reduced staff cost, reduced numbers of available suites, schedule smoothing, and so forth. By contrast, high case fit would likely indicate a more efficient schedule, with less opportunity for capacity creation.

Case-Fit Scoring

With this data in hand, it is possible to develop a case-fit scoring system which objectively ranks blocks by their efficiency relative to their variability. So, a block that allowed for low-variability cases to fit 50 percent of the time might score poorly. A high case-fit percentage for a relatively variable case might score very well. Such a scoring system would, of course, need to be developed on an individual basis, since the relative degree of comfort with case fits and excessively large blocks will vary between hospitals, physician staffs, scheduling preferences, and case types. However, with some parameterization of a few key variables, an automated ranking system could be developed.

Look at Figure 7.3, a duplicate of Figure 7.2. It shows us:

The percentage of time the entire day's schedule fits into a given period: This allows for some obvious predictive analytics.

The range of overtime expected (if any) based on the variance in the total day's schedule: This can be quite handy for staff scheduling purposes, as it lets us ascertain what might be expected on outlier days. Without a good understanding of the possibility of high variation, as it accumulates and exacerbates throughout the day, we cannot predict what an outlier day might look like or how we might react to it. This may cause us to consider altering the schedule to reduce excess and eliminate, to the extent possible, staff overtime.

An interface that allows for the analysis of late starts: In this visualization of the proposed interface, we could see how late starts (regardless of their reason) would impact the rest of the schedule and flow. Late starts can have significant impacts on the day's later activities, depending on the length of the delay, the to-follow case volume, and the time gap to the next case start. To the extent that it impacts the productivity, throughput, and/or capacity of the OR, it should be eliminated.

This simple visual and analytical method simply allows for a better and more sophisticated understanding of the variability within the surgical schedule, and the viability of change. Importantly, such an interface allows for the kind of serious play necessary to test solutions and resolve issues.

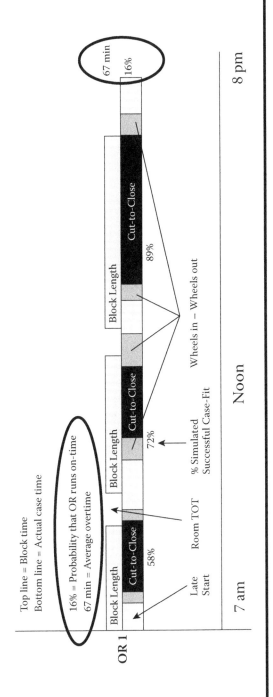

Figure 7.3 Impact of variation: Percentage on-time OR finishes and overtime hours.

So What? We Get by Just Fine Doing What We Are Doing

There will be a number of retorts against this detailed analysis. For instance, many will quickly say that a good manager or scheduler will know this information intuitively…they would be correct. However, quantification of percentages will help even the best of schedulers and OR managers make the case for change and examine how the block schedule might be squeezed for more case capacity, or to justify reduced capacity.

Some will say that other factors, such as late starts, patient tardiness, and nurse call-ins are more an issue than the block schedule itself. However, without a starting point for an efficient system there is no way to improve these other critical elements such that the entire system is impacted. We need the schedule developed such that it can offer the best possible results if and when the rest of the system becomes more optimized. Perhaps most important, the other, critical elements of surgical services' functionality may not see the full impact if the schedule doesn't first allow for improvement. For example, room turnover is obviously critical, but the need for resources will in part depend on the schedule and the likelihood of simultaneous case completions.

Lastly, others will say that in the final analysis it is PACU and the downstream components that cause issues in the OR, not the OR schedule. Perhaps a valid concern. However, to better ascertain and manage those downstream demands, a better understanding of the variability of case length and the probabilities of downstream demand, by individual cases, throughout the day and week will allow for better planning and analysis of potential bottlenecks. Without a solid understanding of predictable downstream demand patterns, we cannot expect to ward off capacity issues and manage the system's flow of patients and demand. Thus, the schedule is used to help study the back end of the OR and the interdependencies that can drive bottlenecks and constraints throughout surgical services and downstream.

All this points to the need for a dynamic scheduling model, which will allow for the analysis of the various governance fixes that might be put in place. With such a model, we can study the downstream impacts of higher percentages of on-time starts, reduced case-length variation, and more optimal resource allocations. As we make improvements to the surgical services systems, we can study the downstream impacts to look at constraints and conflicts using the up–down–up methodology and DCAMM models (see Chapter 8).

Downstream Demand and Scheduling

This leads to the next, very obvious step downstream: inpatient resources. Even if your current surgical scheduling system is refined and humming like a well-oiled machine with properly allocated and highly efficient blocks and an optimized capacity, the downstream demand patterns generated from surgical services has a potentially large impact on performance throughout the system. Therefore, as with the rest of the DCAMM methodology, it makes sense to look downstream to the demand–capacity continuum for bottlenecks and potential capacity issues that might disrupt flow. This will, at the very least, allow you to foresee any issues with the current and future-state schedule as it relates to the other feeder departments in the hospital.

The outcome of the surgical schedule is obviously felt far downstream in the system, into PACU and inpatient beds. As we look downstream, we want to roll the OR demand up into the rest of the system, so as to evaluate its impact on inpatient bed and resource demands, physician scheduling, and external resources. This "serious play" with the schedule and the resulting downstream demand patterns underlying this interface will allow us to envision the outcomes of any schedule changes we might make.

The downstream demand patterns generated by a given surgical schedule must include:

- The time of demand for resources: Depending on the issues we face, we may look simply at inpatient beds. We might also look to transporters and nursing staff functions, and even further downstream to discharge processing and physician rounding, labs, and radiology exams. Recall that demand time, in its pure form, does not reflect when a service is actually provided. Demand time should reflect the actual time of service need. So, our analysis should predict the demand patterns generated as early as the patient's "wheels out" time, followed throughout their inpatient visit and back out into the community. Based on our capellinis, this would include the "back end" of the care system such as nursing homes and acute rehab facilities. Through the downstream demand analysis, we should be able to establish care requirements of a given patient type, and the associated workload, categorized by day of patient stay. This workload should be grouped into time "buckets," so as to allow for an aggregation of total workload on a given unit so as to better allow for workflow and task allocation analytics (see Chapter 10 for more on this concept).
- Patient type or bed type for the case: This is relatively easily discernable, though there may be bed-type alternatives. We simply want to study volumes as they relate to the unit to which the patient is being placed. In later chapters, we will group patient care into prioritized tasks and align the critical determinants of capacity and flow with the routine tasks required.
- Appropriate and secondary placements: A nursing executive friend once commented that today's med-surg patients are the intensive care unit (ICU) patients of the 1960s. Placement criteria changes over time, and

may depend on physician preference (whether clinically justifiable or not), available resources, etc., as well as actual clinical need. The unit to which a patient is assigned may or may not be the ideal, either from a clinical or a capacity standpoint. Our historical data may therefore be somewhat tainted by inappropriate placements. Therefore, it is wise to study the appropriate location for a patient, not just where they are historically placed.

We need to analyze both where a patient goes, and where the patient should or could go if circumstances were altered in our favor. We can then better determine the actual clinical capacity required, not just that which might be currently made available. Otherwise, it will be difficult to ascertain the actual demand patterns and the capacity requirements.

Furthermore, without this placement analysis, another component of inpatient demand, internal transfers, will become less clear as inappropriate placements lead to inappropriate internal transfers later in the patient visit. A deep study of the initial patient placement and internal transfer processes and policies, which will necessitate the inclusion of physicians and various department and unit managers is necessary. Such a study may be "politically sensitive," depending on the situation, the extent of the issue, and the openness of the physicians to change.

■ PACU LOS by case type: Commonly, this data is aggregated and not necessarily precise to the minute. More precise information might be helpful if a higher degree of PACU LOS precision is desired, as might be the case as flow moves closer to optimization. In this instance, historical PACU LOS by patient or case type would offer information as to the distribution of LOS and the relative impact on downstream demand.

As we aggregate the demand from the OR, the ED, and the other feeder components into system demand patterns, we can begin to ascertain by HODDOW WOMSOY, where, when, and to what extent any demand conflicts occur. As we look upstream to the various components for cause and effect, we can begin to determine the following important information:

1. The range of variability of the demand patterns and the feeder components that make up this demand and variability
   a. Ideally, we would use the range of demand from each component by HODDOW WOMSOY as well as the total demand range, so as to ascertain which component might be generating unusual variability in demand, which in turn contributes to higher total variability. The HODDOW WOMSOY analysis will aid in dissecting the demand sufficiently such that unusual patterns or breaks from patterns can be detected, at both the component and total demand levels.
2. The extent of any capacity gaps, by unit, bed, or resource type

3. The HODDOW WOMSOY of the conflict(s), and the components and volumes that cause it
4. The extent to which mediation is required, by component, bed type, resource type, and so forth

Altering the surgical schedule, whether via smoothing, altering case and block times or block allocations, redistributing post-PACU patient populations, or otherwise significantly altering the outflow of patients from surgery should be analyzed within the context of the entire system. Failure to do so could lead to creating conflicts with other components, such as the ED or internal transfers, which could in turn reduce the throughput and increase wait times within the OR and PACU. Severe conflicts have even resulted in the cancellation of cases and the reduction of the total production and capacity of the system.

As part of the DCAMM analysis, we dynamically and systemically analyze the flow of the entire system so as to optimize the performance of each component relative to the whole. It is important to note: *Optimization of the system may require suboptimization of a component(s), at least during some HODDOW WOMSOY periods or under specific circumstances.* Thus, optimizing any component's performance relative to itself may not yield a more optimized system.

Capacity Entitlement and Surgical Services

The concept of capacity entitlement was introduced in previous chapters. The same entitlement concepts that applied to the ED apply here to surgical services. Surgical services, often referred to as the financial life's blood of the hospital, often gets first dibs on open beds, leaving other components to wait for available slots. This is not true "entitlement," as we'll define it herein, since it might be based more on politics and finances than a deep understanding of the system's demand–capacity continuum and effective use of predictive analytics.

Common approaches to bed availability belie the predictability of the demand in the system and other management concepts purported herein, including *capacity entitlement* for all components. Since, as we have discovered, 80 percent or more of the total demand in the system is predictable, and since this predictability can be shown to vary based on HODDOW WOMSOY, we should be able to proactively divvy up the capacity in the system based on the predicted demand patterns from the various components during most circumstances. Constraints typically come if we fail to see the predictability of demand, assume demand is chaotic and that daily bed boards are the only solution to capacity problems, and essentially refuse to take proactive control over the demand–capacity continuum.

Some assume that since they are "overfull" or "running at 100 percent-plus census," there is nothing they can do to alleviate the pressure. Chaos becomes the norm for bed huddles. Indeed, there are hospitals that are indeed at or beyond their capacity to take more patients. Their flow systems, regardless of how optimized they might become with DCAMM and other methodologies, are simply overtaxed. Yet, even in these situations, the aforementioned acceptance patterns and capacity entitlement will enable some predictable control over what available capacity there may be. Capacity will be made available, to some degree, as patients are discharged and resources are freed.

Therefore, we should take advantage of any predictability and our HODDOW WOMSOY analysis to enhance the ability to optimize flow and available capacity, even in capacity-constrained systems. This is done, as before, through analyzing the demand patterns and variability, managing those patterns and controlling the demand to the extent possible, predicting the inpatient resource needs of the various feeder components, by HODDOW, and allocating some reasonable amount of capacity to be expected during each time period. For instance, though fifteen med-surg beds may be needed on 30 percent of Tuesday afternoons, it is reasonable and feasible to "guarantee" the availability of twelve. The remaining demand can be managed differently, on a week to week basis as demand fluctuates. This approach will eliminate at least some of the chaotic feel, and allow for a focus on specific and smaller volumes of excess demand.

In less-constrained environments, capacity entitlements can serve a slightly different purpose. No, there may be no crunch for beds and no chaotic bed huddles each morning and afternoon. Nonetheless, knowing the capacity entitlement enables the feeder departments to plan for their appropriate admission slots while respecting the unit staff. The scheduled approach also allows for nursing units to anticipate workload and workflow around what are expected admission patterns. Furthermore, such a system can help reduce excess capacity (as defined as nurses, beds, and even entire units) while accounting for the inevitable variances of demand and capacity.

Surgical services often has more predictable patterns, based on the surgical schedule, case variability, and physician preferences. These patterns can and should be matched with the often more variable demand patterns from other feeder components (along with their requisite variability) to determine the total demand for resources. By analyzing the total demand and the variances therein, we can do a much better job of proactively assessing the resources, tasks, and processes required for making necessary capacity available when it is required. Otherwise, there is tremendous waste in our systems, including common Lean wastes such as overproduction and waiting.

Surgical Services Demand and Workload Analytics

It is not uncommon for a patient to arrive on the unit more or less prepared, depending on the originating component. Patients from the OR may be "completely prepped, ready, and wrapped up in bow" (to quote a nurse exec friend) relative to patients from the ED. Patients from the OR may see their physicians more readily and may have more treatment prescribed than patients from the ED or direct admissions. Thus, the admission workload for these patients is altered to the point that task allocation might relieve some nursing functions. It is therefore important, perhaps critical, to keep in mind the source of patients, predicatively and by HODDOW so as to allocate the necessary resources to the work expected. This, of course, requires the DCAMM analysis across the feeder components and the predictive analytics of admissions and discharges described in this chapter. With this predictive, systems-level analysis in place, the work of patient care becomes more strategic, less randomized, and far more productive. As we will see in future chapters, workload and workflow analysis will be important to the DCAMM methodology. Both are predicted by the combination of HODDOW WOMSOY demand and capacity analysis and the general understanding of the workload on a given unit.

Summary

The surgical schedule is one of the most important drivers of hospital flow. With it and an understanding of its inherent variability, one can analyze a great deal of the downstream demand patterns such that the total demand–capacity continuum can be studied in depth. Conflicts can be reduced and perhaps eliminated. By combining the surgical demand patterns with that of other feeder components, we can ascertain (1) the degree and extent to which conflicts exist by HODDOW WOMSOY, (2) the degree to which solutions need to be provided, (3) the extent to which those solutions provide relief under various conditions, and (4) the extent to which an excess demand impacts the upstream components. We can then go about the process of allocating entitlements as required.

As we reach the understanding that our systems are, at least to a certain extent, manageable within the context of their inherent dynamism, we can then develop solutions to optimally impact the systems writ large rather than reacting to the dynamism a single department or unit.

Notes

1. This capellini isn't as detailed as it could be if surgical services were the main focus of an improvement effort. One might add OR TAT and PACU processing to this mix if the focus was more directly related to this area.
2. Simulation tools for the analysis of block schedules already exist. One, developed by researchers at GE Healthcare, aids in the optimization of block scheduling. Called the Block Optimizer (mental note: never let your developers name your products), it can take an entire block schedule, and, by physician and case type, optimize the correct block allocations. Alternatively, a simulation interface called Orchestrate was developed by the British firm, Production Modeling, LLC. Originally developed to

improve "job shop" scheduling, it uses a sophisticated VBA interface hooked to a simulation model (of any vendor, thankfully) and allows for the dynamic serious play with the entire schedule. Neither of these tools shows well in black and white due to the need for color to represent cases and physicians. And since I try to avoid advocacy of a particular firm or product, it did not make sense to use them in this text.

3. With some creativity one could develop a chart to show the variability within the range. I have traditionally used something similar to a "heat map," wherein the depth and intensity of color represents the degree of variance from a given point. But these are not appropriate for a black-and-white text. The ability to show, easily and succinctly, complex data is as much as art as a science. A great read for those interested in how to display quantitative information are the works of Edward Tufte. These include *Visual Explanations* (Graphics Press, 2001).

4. While this is not an immediate issue for us here, it certainly is an issue for many facilities and physicians. If TAT is not on pace with the rest of the system, it can and does slow flow and increase wait times and frustration.

Chapter 8

Up–Down–Up: Creating a Systems View from a Component Perspective

As you have already surmised, the effective analysis, matching, and management of hospital demand and capacity requires both process-level analysis and improvement coupled with systems-level interdependency and flow considerations. One without the other inevitably fails to offer the correct solutions. (Note: The term *process level* is used here to generally describe an analytical granularity and level at the individual process, process set, or department level. Essentially, any analysis within the larger system components is termed process level. By contrast *systems* level refers to the analysis of the interactions between the major component groups as their variability impacts their interdependencies within the system and the system's performance writ large.)

Many process improvement methodologies improve only processes and not the system. As described in previous chapters, there has been a dearth of effective analysis of the interdependencies of complex systems flow and resources such that system optimization can be attained. In the past, we have been so focused on fixing the ED or surgical services that we lose sight of the upstream and downstream impacts of the decisions we make. Or, perhaps more frustrating, we know those interdependencies exist but have no way to effectively capture, analyze, and predict their performance. Lean and Six Sigma, and all the iterations thereof, are fine process improvement methodologies. However, they fail to effectively account for the systems level and all the interdependencies and complex interactions beyond the process level. Even when advocates and users purport to consider the higher-level issues (which Lean and Six Sigma advocates will), their tools and thus their analysis and the resulting answers remain quite static. Without a systems perspective, PPI often just moves the bottlenecks around within the system. Like chasing a gopher in a field full of tunnels, the bottlenecks simply move from one place to the next, leaving us to chase them as they pop somewhere other than where we are focused.

Another reason methodologies fail is a lack of understanding of precise and quantifiable expectations. "We got better" is not a metric, and "we want/need to improve" is not a sound and solid goal. Departmental metrics may not reflect the strategic goals of the organization. Reducing triage turnaround time (TAT) means little if the bottleneck (and the patient wait) is simply moved to an ED bed and a wait for a physician. Similarly, improving TAT in the OR is good for physicians and can reduce schedule bottlenecks but might not improve overall throughput as much as reducing other time wastes, such as late first-case starts and hunting and gathering during cases. Furthermore, reducing TAT might have very little impact on total throughput volume or staff overtime pay.

Of course, there are the HODDOW WOMSOY (hour of day, day of week, week of month, season of year) variables that can cause a solution to both work and fail under different conditions. What is required is a precise understanding the system's needs for improvement, such that the necessary steps can be taken to achieve those goals. Of course, improvement efforts that do not contribute to overall system flow and capacity goals should be considered for their relative value. Efforts focused on reducing nurse workload or improving patient satisfaction, as the voice of the customer dictates, are still very worthy goals even though they might not move the needle on capacity enhancement. Certainly, improvements which might create downstream or upstream conflicts need to be dynamically evaluated for these impacts. This might occur if a process-level effort in the ED reduces admission processing time but inadvertently creates a conflict with PACU for certain inpatient bed types. Ironically, excess improvement might be a form of waste if the excess fails to improve the system's metrics (which of course would include financial, logistical, and patient-related numbers) and only improves process-level performance.

Similarly, systems analytics without PI methodologies can be stuck in "lala land," with only vague ideas and concepts of system optimization, and without the process-level analysis and improvements required to achieve the results. Systems-level analysis, alone, is an excellent resource for strategic planning, future- and current-state optimization, facilities planning, and understanding the dynamic demand–capacity continuum. However, the implementation rubber meets the operations road at the process level. If changes to processes, surgical schedules, or demand management cannot be made, the systems level goals cannot be attained.

Process improvement methodologies therefore need additional analytical power to achieve true system-wide optimization and vice versa.

The result of the blending of the two through this DCAMM methodology is an *up–down–up* (UDU) approach in which process- and department-level related changes are "rolled up" into a higher level analysis to test for validity, impact, and efficacy. The DCAMM analysis is then rolled down to both guide the PI goals, and prescribe actions and results needed to achieve systemic improvement(s). The results of actual changes made, whether on target or not, are then rolled back up to determine the relative impact on the system's performance. This is made possible and much more effective by the use of simulation tools described herein. Simulation can capture the detailed outputs of process changes which act as inputs to systems-level models of hospital-wide interdependencies, flow, and capacity. In the simulation world, this is sometimes known as "hierarchical modeling."

As an example, if changes to ED flow include reducing the current length of stay for admitted patients, there will be a downstream impact as inpatient beds are required earlier than they might have been otherwise. This is typically considered a positive outcome since such a result will help decompress the ED and improve flow. However, if such changes result in conflicts with inpatient discharge processing, or compound demand patterns for inpatient beds from the OR, the positive results in the ED can become negative results for the system. Thus, the actual results of the implemented changes to ED flow may fall short of expectations or fail to be realized at all due to the newly created downstream constraints.

As another example, smoothing the surgical schedule can work if the coordination with all downstream components as well as other feeder components (e.g., the ED and direct admissions) is achieved. Smoothing the schedule in a highly constrained environment may not have the impact expected. The coordination of care activities and resources throughout the patient visit should be accounted for, from the admission time through to transportation home. Without such considerations, we risk creating bottlenecks somewhere in the system when we are actually trying to alleviate them. For instance, moving some ortho cases to Thursday might require physical therapy to be available over the weekend when there may be none.

Lastly, we need to use the UDU approach on an ongoing basis, as the parameters both within and external to systems change. Whether it is demand patterns altered by demographic changes, expansions of our facility components, or additional surgeons added to the schedule, a dynamic UDU approach will be necessary to ensure that any optimization achieved is maintained. UDU thereby engages both the process and systems approaches, and should be a part of your ongoing analytical effort.

UDU, Processes, and Design Parameters

DCAMM and UDU let us study critical issues about patient mix and volumes as we look to new facilities. Of course, there are architects, planners, and consultants expert in demographic analysis for facilities planning. However, projecting the impacts of demographic changes onto and into a new facility design can be difficult at best. This is particularly true as design elements evolve, government regulations change, and old facilities are gradually remodeled. Again, the same dynamism that plagues static analysis of the current and future state systems naturally impacts static efforts to forecast spatial, resource, and equipment needs for a new or remodeled facility. Thus, again, the need for DCAMM simulation analytics arises.

To effectively plan for a new facility or remodeling/expansion, a similar effort using DCAMM capellini can and should be undertaken (Figure 8.1). Using DCAMM and capellini diagrams similar to the one we are using now, accurate analysis of the patterns of demand, by patient type, and the resulting demand for staff and other resources, as well as downstream demand generation for community services, can be made. This will allow for experimentation with a variety of volumes of a given patient type to foresee how possible variation yields new requirements for various downstream capacities. These downstream capacity requirements can be altered in our DCAMM simulation model such that experimentation with the components related to the upstream demand can be achieved. Furthermore we can then begin to analyze how the various components and the system itself might be pushed into outlier status.

"What ifs?" can then be run to demonstrate the effects of various combinations of capacity, including beds, staff, internal and external treatments, space, and the use of various technologies. So, if a given volume of cancer patients tips the capacity of oncology beds into an outlier status, such that demand significantly exceeds capacity to the point of denying services, we can understand the patient-specific system breaking point. In other words, volume, arrival pattern, and surgical schedule combine to push the system into outlier status based on specific demand

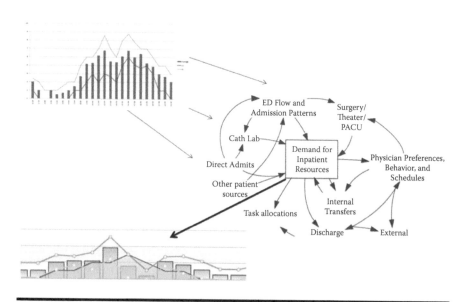

Figure 8.1 Hospital-wide capellini diagram showing system interdependencies.

patterns, LOSs, and hypothetical capacity. We can look at all aspects of the care patterns and resulting resource and task requirements to analyze where and under what circumstances additional resources will be required, and to what extend any breaking points impact overall system performance. This lets us foresee any capacity constraints anywhere in the system, upstream and downstream, so as to avoid mismatching the capacity of one component with others and the system at large.

The differences in design-related constraints within differing layouts beg for such analysis. Three different designs for a given unit, all legitimate in their own rights, might require three very different process flows to be optimally functional. The design of a facility is, in fact, nothing more than an additional operational constraint. Walls, hallways, and other spatial restrictions to flow inherently reduce the efficiencies of flow. Additionally, processes, technologies, communication systems, schedules, and so forth add to the fixed spatial constraint to the extent that these elements do not reduce its constraining influence. Our new patient-centered design criteria do not necessarily create an optimal working environment. This is revealed in larger, single-patient rooms which make travel distances longer and communications more difficult. Thus the design of the facility must be optimized within the context of the processes and operations within it. Failure to do so can lead to a system that is even more suboptimal than it should be.

Take the examples in Figure 8.2 from a layout analysis. The layouts represent possible configurations of the same unit. Each is perfectly legitimate as a concept in that it allows for care of patients and meets design standards and mandated criteria.

Furthermore, each has nuances that can make it relatively better, in some way, than the others. However, as the chart associated with Figure 8.2 illustrates, optimizing the capacity and efficiency of each design requires a different set of processes, technologies, and perhaps staffing. One operational design might work well in one space but yield a different outcome in a slightly different space. This means that the capacity and output of one design is either greater or smaller than that in the others, depending on the design of the operations and systems in each. The three layouts in Figure 8.2 were simulated (Linear, "T", and Square), using a variety of parameters and "what if?" scenarios. The results of some of the simulation analysis can be seen in the nearby chart. In the "baseline" scenario, the "old" processes and staffing patterns were laid into the new space. From the results, we can clearly see that this was *not* an acceptable solution. Old processes laid into a new space, with new technologies, reduced patient density, and larger spaces, are typically not robust enough to adapt to the new surroundings. Indeed, it is very common for old processes to become quite "broken" in a new space, despite how efficient they might have been in the old space. As we can see in the chart, the current process with current staffing in the new space results in *greater cost and more patient waits for care*, even if supplemented with new technologies.

However, the third option (the Linear layout with new processes, technology, and staffing algorithms) shows only minor positive results. In this case, we could

SCENARIO				MODEL RESULTS	
Config	Staffing	Technology	Trans	# Delays/PT Day	% Change in FTE Cost/PT Day
ASIS - CURRENT STATE MODEL				9.1	
Linear	baseline	redesign	current	8.7	23.4%
Linear	redesign	redesign	redesign	4.6	9.2%
Linear	redesign	redesign	redesign	6.3	-6.7%
Square	redesign	redesign	redesign	5.9	-8.5%
T	redesign	redesign	redesign	5.2	-19.7%

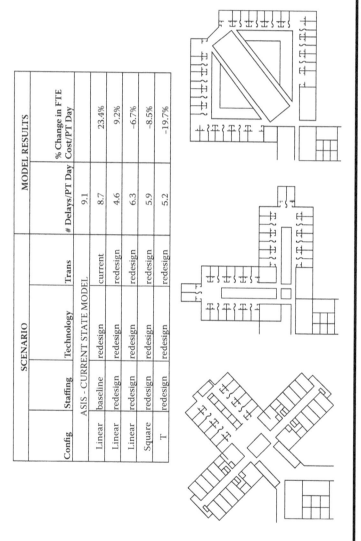

Figure 8.2   Different layouts require different operational models to be more effective.

hope that our current system is *so* efficient that only minor improvement could be expected, and that this would be considered an excellent outcome. Clearly, however, further analysis reveals that the physical plant can have a significant impact on the performance.

If we use the same scenario (new processes, technology, and staffing algorithms) in a different layout, however, the results are dramatically different. The "T" design clearly works the best with these specific parameters and processes in place. The differences might include subtle but important details, such as:

- Proximity and density of supplies, meds, and information
- Areas for nurse-nurse and nurse-physician interaction
- Relative distance between tasks, patients/rooms
- Distance traveled to complete a given task
- Patient types and care requirements
- Staffing patterns, task and resource allocations, and available resources
- Process-enhancing technologies
- Access to information, patient records, other staff and physicians

These nuances can drive up the workload for a given workflow. Meaning, they make work harder to do. The specific reasons for the "T" design's superior performance are likely a combination of these and other factors.

Study of physical plant within the context of the dynamism of care processes is critical to achieving an operationally sustainable facility. The above factors, particularly communications and resource/task allocations, can significantly impact the functionality of any space and must be considered, preferably *before the design is completed.*

While many architects worry more about the "greenness" of a facility than its ultimate functionality, it should be noted that only 5 percent or less of the total cost of the facility over its lifetime is in construction. The rest is in the staff, supplies, and other operational costs over the 30-plus years of its use. While a $500 million-plus construction price tag is a big number to worry about, it is still a pittance compared with the its total operational cost. That $500 million facility will cost some $10 billion to operate over its lifetime, of which some $6 billion is staff cost. It is therefore the latter which should be of the most importance.

Design and Component Optimization

Remember that when combined with the optimization of other components, the suboptimization of one component can reduce the overall system capacity. Yet interestingly, optimization of capacity of each component, in isolation, does not necessarily yield the optimization of the entire system. This is due to both the dynamism of the components and the need for system balance within and between the components. Therefore, it is critical that component and system optimization be studied together as an integral part of the design–build process.

It is worth noting that any good hospital-wide systems-level model should always include capacity variables at the community level at the back end of hospital flow. The demand patterns created by our hospitals can be effectively modeled, analyzed, predicted, and tweaked to look for potential downstream impacts and hidden constraints. This is particularly critical if we are to address long-term systemic demand for physical plant development. With this we can examine any systemic and component repercussions of public policy initiatives, regulatory schemes, new care models, reimbursement incentives, and technological advancements.

The suboptimization of any design is quite possible if the right processes are not injected. Indeed, it was long ago discovered that building a new space does not necessarily improve flow. Stories of new EDs with higher LOS are far too common. This happens for myriad reasons, including:

- Old processes were transplanted, neither assessed nor changed, into the new space. This is just a bad idea regardless of the size or scale of the new space.
- The new or remodeled component was immediately imbalanced relative to the system. So the new 40-bed ED that replaced the old 20-bed unit now puts out far more downstream demand than before. Yet, neither ancillary services nor transportation nor inpatient capacity or processes were simultaneously matched. Thus, the system (regardless of the new design) is immediately out of balance and suboptimized as it becomes constrained by the components of flow. Obviously, we don't want to build in systemic imbalances. This can happen if the ED is expanded without expanding inpatient capacity, such that admissions overwhelm the system's capacity and turn new beds in holding beds. In the postdesign reality check, it is not at all unusual to see administrators struggle to ascertain the system's new balancing point, having just built in systemic suboptimization.
- Processes, if they were studied at all, were examined statically and failed to account for the new patterns and dynamism of communal demand. So, an ED in a new, green-field hospital absorbs some of the volume of the local urgent care clinic, thus dramatically altering the demand patterns for component and system resources without accounting for the new process requirements.
- HODDOW WOMSOY variation wasn't accounted for, such that the robustness of the new facility was not ascertained. So, the facility may work well under certain conditions and processes, but not as well under others. (As we will see, *dynamic standardization* of operations may alleviate some of these issues if studied during the design phases.)

These examples could go on for pages, but you see the point. Failure to effectively analyze the operations of a new space as or before the design is created will invariably yield a much higher risk of systemic and component suboptimization.

Facilities, Communities of Care, ACOs, and Capellinis

Healthcare is rapidly beginning to understand the need for the systemic analysis of resources outside the four walls of the acute care hospital. In order to bring to total cost of care into line, and prevent a complete meltdown in the access to healthcare and the U.S. economy via onerous taxation, we are beginning to analyze care delivery and resource options throughout our communities. ACOs (Accountable Care Organizations) have been legislated by Congress as an option to bring hospitals and physicians into closer harmony and cooperation. Other business models, such as that of Kaiser Permanente, Geisinger, MultiCare of Washington State, and Montefiore of New York, are being examined as possible U.S.-based models for care delivery for rest of the nation.

Expanding on this notion is the concept of the "Community of Care" (CoC). The CoC is a holistic and in many ways radical approach to the delivery of care for a given population. CoCs tear apart the traditional business models of healthcare delivery, rather than merely tinkering with payment models and limited changes to delivery mechanisms. A CoC differs from the traditional ACOs and similar models in that it is more focused on the redesign of the delivery of care throughout a given community, from the home through to hospice, and is not limited to physician-hospital alignment. A CoC actually invents new resource types, locations, and technologies so as to reduce the cost of care while increasing the quality and access by more appropriately allocating the 4WF ("who does what where when and how frequently") for specific patient types, rather than the population at large. This will allow for a different analytical perspective on high-cost patient types, the 1 percent which chews up 70 percent of healthcare expenditures. In doing so, we can develop specific care streams for specific patient types, and use these to prevent erosion of population health. This systemic look at the entire resource pool will enable the analysis of alternatives not currently considered, customized to specific communities, their demographics and care requirements, and resource availability. (CoCs are the subject of an upcoming book by this author, to be published in the winter of 2011.)

True "communities of care" can be effectively represented through similar capellini diagrams and models such that the downstream community resources can be analyzed, by HODDOW WOMSOY, based on the far-upstream demand pattern alterations and the UDU approach. Obviously, these sorts of changes have impacts for facilities and strategic planning as well. If, for instance, a high rate of obesity in the community requires greater capacity in dietary, mental health counseling, and rehabilitation services, these resources will have to be placed into current and future considerations of space, process flows, and resource planning. Importantly, the far downstream community resources in nursing homes, long-term acute care (LTAC) facilities, rehabilitation, and other services will need to be considered such that bottlenecks are not created upstream in hospitals, constraining discharge planning and flow throughout the CoC. Technologies and changes to the surgical care of patients will impact future spatial requirements and resource demands. Already, what was once a five-day hospital stay for a full knee replacement is now a minimally invasive procedure requiring only a short stay of less than a day. A CoC will result in a monitored and controlled flow of patients from the community into acute care settings and back into the community, without intervening bottlenecks and misallocation of resources within the clinical pathways.

Thus a community capellini has been created that models the far-downstream impacts of the flow from several hospitals (now upstream components of the even larger system) into the community as well as the coordination of multiple providers in the care of a given patient population. Granularity of the data could point to the relative capacity requirements for a variety of up- and downstream resources, including medical homes and physician offices. Further study might reveal the demand patterns for clinic and office visits, checkups and vaccinations, and general community wellness. Such capellini would aid policy makers in developing the right number and scale of resource components to meet the community demand rather than merely chasing the "demand gopher" around in the community's healthcare capacity "field."

Summary

A systems approach is not enough to optimize performance, because many of the changes necessary to impact system performance occur at the process level. However, process level analytics are not sufficient to optimize performance either, because the dynamism and HODDOW WOMSOY variability play such a huge role. Thus, a combination of dynamic analytics of the dynamic demand–capacity continuum requires both process- and systems-level analysis. The latter will tell us what is required for optimization and the impacts the changes made at the process level. The process analysis will tell us what can be achieved and when, such that we can determine the actual impacts on the system writ large. Thus a dynamic up–down–up analytical approach, complete with HODDOW WOMSOY variability and ongoing analysis, will ultimately aid us in determining the right combinations of parameters, flows, resources, and other inputs that will optimize performance under a variety of circumstances. This will be a significant key to the ability to dynamically manage these dynamic systems.

Chapter 9

Capacity Patterns and Analytics for DCAMM

Thus far our discussions have been focused primarily on demand. We have surmised in that there are patterns to the demand within healthcare facilities, and that these patterns in turn generate downstream demand for services throughout the patient visit. Some of the communal demand is more volatile and variable (e.g., into the ED). Some is more controlled or at least controllable (e.g., surgical services, wherein the surgical schedule initiates patterns of demand and thus creates its own downstream patterns). Regardless of the source, the arrival of the patient into a facility triggers various downstream demands that are generated throughout the length of the patient visit. Of course, in order to study the demand–capacity continuum, we must also consider the availability of capacity throughout the system. Many falsely assume that capacity can be viewed either as a constant, or, worse, as an uncontrollable variable. Neither are true.

Capacity in this text refers to the available capacity rather than the total theoretical capacity, which would be obtained if all resources were fully and optimally utilized 100 percent of the time. The latter might be a relatively fixed number, though largely unattainable. Additionally, keep in mind capacity refers to both the general and specific ability to service incoming demand. As an analogy, think of a restaurant. When you arrive to have dinner you generate demand for a number of services and resources, not just food. You create demand for waitresses, dishwashers, and managers, as well as food, plates, utensils, paper products, and downstream external resources such as garbage pickup, credit card processing, and accounting services. Similarly, the demand created as a patient arrives into a hospital generates a number of immediate and downstream demands, from staff to supplies to services.

Perhaps unfortunately, capacity is variable, as we know from our day-to-day experiences. HODDOW WOMSOY (hour of day, day of week, week of month, season of year) again rears its ugly head in the form of capacity variance. From a DOW (day of week) perspective, the capacity available on, say, unit 4-West may be greater or lesser today than it will be tomorrow. This DOW variance will depend on a number of interrelated factors, not the least of which are the demand patterns in previous days which influence the currently available bed capacity and downstream resources. So capacity for incoming patients is dependent upon, for example, the surgical schedule that determines which patients go home on which days, as well as the availability of nursing home beds in the community. The HOD (hour of day) capacity variation is influenced by factors such as physician behavior, rounding patterns, workload patterns, information availability, transportation, and shift change, to name a few. HOD capacity variation can also be influenced by external factors such as the availability of downstream resources, including family, transportation and nursing home beds.

This is, in part, why the dynamic nature of our analytics is so important here. The human brain is incapable of thinking in complex interdependencies, variable lengths of stay (LOS), and predictive analysis. Of course, the issues of capacity variance involve just that and more as it intertwines with demand. In order to study the variability of capacity as it relates to our variable demand, it is necessary to look into the future from the point of time of demand to all the significant demands and processes along the way. Capacity at the component level (e.g. the ED or the OR), has its own constraints. These would include numbers of care spaces, staffing and resources of various types (e.g., techs and equipment), and total patient processing times. Capacity at this level is thus the sum of the space, resources, and process capability available, impacted and constrained by the variability and interdependencies of the operations and interrelated systems. Thus, capacity varies. Think of the inpatient nursing unit. The capacity made available via discharges and open beds is not always steady. Staffing patterns, workload, workflow, and patient-related variables such as acuity and co-morbidities can influence the patterns by which capacity-creating work is done. Take, also, lab throughput and the available capacity to complete testing. While the same number of machines and staff may be available at different times of day and days of week, the volume of demand, or specific types of testing required may reduce the overall capacity for additional work. Furthermore, staffing changes in radiology may mean capacity on some hours of some days but not others. Hence, capacity is not steady.

Of course, just like demand variability has finite and largely discernable patterns, so too does capacity. Indeed, capacity likely has more discernable patterns, since capacity is rarely randomly made available, and since a given amount of capacity can be relatively quickly estimated based on the simply math of arrival patterns, length of stay, and staff assigned to discharge processes. Matching this variable capacity to the inevitably variable demand is, of course, the subject of this book. What we must do is understand the variability of *both* the capacity and the demand so as to see how, when, and to what extent capacity should intentionally vary to achieve a match to variable demand. Thus, the same HODDOW WOMSOY and other dynamic analytics will be similarly employed, as we will see shortly. Any capacity variation must be accounted for as we try to synchronize the demand–capacity continuum at multiple levels, both process-level and systems-level. To the extent the upstream capacity constrains the downstream systems or vice versa, we need to understand the interdependencies of the capacities of the various components as we look to create and manage a well-synchronized, dynamic demand–capacity continuum whether at the component level or the system level.

A good example of the continuum issue is the construction of a larger ED while failing to expand capacity in inpatient beds, radiology, or other related components and elements within the workflow. It is not uncommon to see a focus on ED flow, wait times, and patient satisfaction lead to the construction of additional space, only to see that space occupied by patients awaiting admission. Indeed, many hospitals have found themselves building million-dollar holding beds rather than ED beds to allow additional capacity and throughput. This is because the system simply is or becomes out of balance, and the addition of a larger feeder into the inpatient side only exacerbates that problem. The dynamic demand–capacity continuum must be respected.

In the case of inpatient units, capacity is the beds, staff, and other resources, as well as the processes and space. Each inpatient unit, of course, has its own unique capacity based on staffing, number of beds, LOS and LOS variability of the patient population, process efficiency, and so forth. Unit capacity on any given day is also influenced by previous days' admission patterns, outlier status of patients and operations, LOS, physician practice patterns, and the general flow of patients in and out. Capacity, at both the unit and hospital-wide levels, is therefore fluid, depending on the current status of patients in the system and the communal demand coming to the facility.

All this means that capacity is influenced by both controllable and seemingly uncontrollable factors. Yet, capacity, constrained and variable as it is, must be specifically synchronized to the variable demand patterns to optimize performance. To effectively assess the capacity in systems, go through the following analytical steps:

1. Analyze the HODDOW WOMSOY capacity. How much capacity, and in which service areas, do we make available on a daily basis, by hour of day? Is there flexibility in this and, if so, to what extent?
2. Determine the capacity requirements, by HODDOW WOMSOY, by analyzing the various demand patterns. How much additional capacity is required, if any, to effectively match demand? Is there seasonality or daily variation that might impact capacity requirements? Does capacity dynamically match the variable demand?

3. Understand where and how additional capacity might be made available, if necessary.
4. Determine controllable and uncontrollable elements of capacity and its variability.

How Much Is Enough?

If capacity is variable, how much should be made available given the variable demand? Excellent question. And of course, the ever-magical answer is: it depends. Because demand is variable, the required capacity depends on the variance in the demand. Furthermore, since capacity is variable, some range of capacity must be available to meet the patterns in incoming demand.

Examine the graph in Figure 9.1, similar to the model outputs seen in the past. The bars and two lines represent the demand and its variability. The shaded area graph represents capacity. Notice the addition of the two dashed lines, which represent the variability of the capacity made available. The area graph can represent capacity made available 80 percent to 90 percent of the time or all capacity variation, depending on your analytical needs and the degree of the outliers. This one graphic gives a much better feel for the current state and the relative need for additional capacity at any given point during this DOW (keep in mind that much more visually appealing and informative graphs can be colorful!). Furthermore, this graph quickly shows how the current state operations are and are not able to meet demand on a regular basis.

The ranges of capacity can be analyzed the same way as demand. That is, we should look at the "in-range" capacity which encompasses 80 percent or more of the capacity made available, by HODDOW WOMSOY. These patterns would, of course, be based historical data for the purpose of current state analysis, and altered as we look at scenarios for system change. Using ranges allows to account for the outlier days in the performance as well as the relative variability on in-range capacity. This will allow us to do the necessary root-cause analysis, and determine when, where, and if additional capacity needs to be made available. Charts like that in Figure 9.1 will quickly allow us to see when and by how much capacity is made available, and when and by how much we fall short. Furthermore, because we are now using ranges instead of averages, we can more precisely determine the percentage of time that capacity meets demand, as they both vary. If we do this by HOD, DOW, and SOY, as we should, we will begin to see patterns (and gaps) in the demand–capacity continuum. We can then home in on when, where, and to what extent we need to increase capacity and/ or adjust demand.

Ideally, in-range demand should be met with in-range capacity, else you essentially create an outlier on one side or the other of the demand–capacity continuum. This might require different capacities depending on the variability of the demand

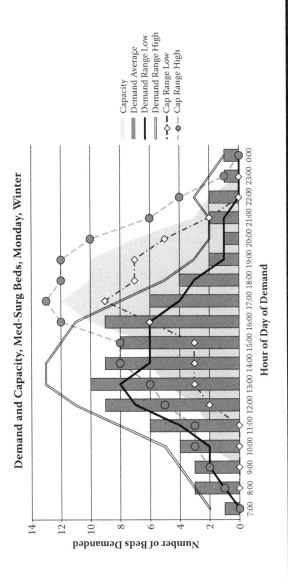

Figure 9.1 Variable capacity related to variable demand patterns.

at any given point and the status of specific demand parameters. So, on days when the OR can be particularly busy, driving higher numbers of patients to the inpatient side, we might need different resource allocations to accommodate the unique demand. However, matching capacity at the high end of a high-variability demand pattern may elicit extremes in resource allocations, as we try to manage to what might be an outlier or close to it. To avoid this, we need to ensure that as much variability as possible is removed from the demand patterns and rely on a comfortable percentage of success in meeting that demand.

Therefore, one key element of your analytics will be the *percentage of time (variable) capacity meets variable demand, based on in-range demand and capacity patterns*. This metric adds far more meaning than a simple average, which tells us nothing about the relative ability to match to the ranges of demand. Since both sides of the equation vary, this metric is far more telling about the actual ability of the system to create a functional and ongoing demand–capacity continuum.

In the more common, low-variability scenarios, the capacity needed to meet 80 percent to 90 percent of the demand would be inherently closer to the average or median. Here, the demand is a little more constant and consistent, meaning that our capacity can be a little steadier and tightly patterned. Needless to say, the less variability there is, the more likely we are to nail the demand–capacity continuum with ease. Indeed, early in your analysis, you may find that the demand variability is such that capacity can be a single number for a given HODDOW due to the relative control exerted over demand or the relative steadiness of the patterns.

Capacity as a Single Number

Importantly, from a planning perspective, capacity may need to be seen as an expected single number. For an ED manager, the expectation of admitting, say, a total of six patients to 4-West between the hours of noon and 4 p.m. may be critical to the operational and staffing planning for the ED. This might be the goal of the unit in order to match as much of the demand as possible of a given in-range hour or day. As long as the capacity requirements have been sufficiently analyzed based on HOWDOW WOMSOY variability, such that a sufficient percentage of in-range demand is met and a comfort level with any excesses is set, we can use a single number. Indeed, using a single number may be required, given that planning requires some degree of consistency day to day. *Still, the knowledge of the range will help both sides of the continuum understand the potential for failure and the degree to which performance expectations should be met.* Furthermore, the range will help staff on both sides to understand the degree to which variances away from the single number will impact performance, workload, and workflow.

Tips on Making Capacity Available

Matching variable capacity with variable demand is made easier by the fact that, in large part, capacity is in our control. Here are a few simple yet effective tips for dealing with the variability of capacity:

- Discharge upon admission—The concept of getting out in front of the workload is common in many planning environments. In building a new hospital, one doesn't wait until the CON (Certificate of Need) is approved before seeking out an architect. More simply, we don't wait till dinnertime before thinking about what's in the fridge. *Discharge upon admission* simply means that the patient LOS is calculated upon arrival and discharge time is assigned. This time is communicated to the family, if any, and all efforts are made, as early as possible in the patient visit, to alleviate any possible delays from nonclinical sources. In truth, this might actually happen at the ED level; upon an eyeball disposition from an ED physician, we can often nail the patient's diagnosis in mere seconds.

  Physicians, including hospitalists, of course have the right to alter these plans as needed, based on the patient's clinical needs. However, it should (again) only be the outlier whose LOS exceeds a standard for a given patient type. If physicians object to this notion, is it because they may sense some loss of control over their patients and their care. However, this should never be the case, nor should this ever be implied. Instead, physicians are encouraged to aid the hospital in the maximization of capacity by removing all their own bottlenecks in the flow, being a critical resource for proper flow functionality.

- Scheduling predischarge testing such that discharge is not delayed—It is common for testing to delay a discharge, because results are not submitted in time for the physician's rounding patterns. Testing might be ordered too late to allow for compliance or too late to allow for a timely discharge. Therefore, any critical day-of-discharge testing should be scheduled and completed prior to the need for the information.

- Managing hospitalists' time and efficiency—It is not uncommon for the hospitalist to take many of the more clinically difficult patients. This puts a strain on an already hectic job. Effectively focusing on the potential bottlenecks specifically in a hospitalist capacity means pushing information to them rather than waiting for them to do rounds or asking for support staff and coordination of patient care with the nursing staff.

- Coordination with external resources (e.g., nursing homes) using DCAMM and predictive analytics, to the extent possible—At the very least, begin the coordination of care prior to discharge, preferably upon arrival. If DCAMM is well utilized, patterns of external resource requirements might be assessed and made available. Again, if the volumes and patient types are predictable enough, scheduling the discharge and transfer of specific patients to these facilities can be done ahead of time, even predicted before patients arrive.

■ Focus on the outliers—The high-variability LOS patient populations are those that often frustrate our efforts to create capacity. These outlier patients create much more confusion and uncertainty in the system than do patients with more predictable, less volatile stays. Focusing on the outlier patients and those diagnosis-related groups (DRGs) with the highest variability will allow for a greater impact on LOS variability, adding to our ability to control capacity. This is similar to the concept of outlier demand days 20 percent or less of the time.

■ Understand that outlier days will occur—There will be outlier days in which capacity simply falls significantly short of expectations, entitlements are failed, and patients wait in feeder components longer than normal. These outlier days should occur only on a limited number of days though they may have a significant impact on key performance metrics. These should be the focus of our management attention, such that use of predictive analytics are used to help understand and manage these situations.

Acceptance Patterns and Capacity Entitlement

We need to manage outlier days as outliers, rather than reacting to each day as if it's an outlier. If you are like many, you've repeatedly tried to impact the flow from the feeder components, such as the OR, to inpatient units, only to be frustrated by demand that exceeds capacity. Even in facilities with flow choreographed as a Cirque du Soleil performance, there may be too many patients for too few spaces. Depending on the situation, bed rationing may result as allocations must be made. You may have simply given up and thus deal with excessive wait times caused by the seemingly inevitable constraints by canceling surgeries and turning away ambulances. Needless to say, however, we should always strive to improve quality, patient care, flow, and resource optimization, regardless of the situation. This can be especially challenging in healthcare's increasingly overwhelmed systems as capital dries up and spatial expansions become more expensive and difficult. In the highly constrained hospital, continuing improvement will require new ways of thinking about patient flow, some of which are only now being developed. In these situations, the analysis needs to expand from a focus on demand patterns to include acceptance patterns and capacity entitlement, two new concepts in the DCAMM methodology.

Acceptance patterns are those by which specific inpatient units take patients, regardless of what the demand in the system might be. Acceptance patterns focus attention on the capacity that is made available, by HODDOW WOMSOY, even if that capacity in no way matches the patterns or volumes of demand.

Capacity entitlement is the amount of capacity a given feeder component should expect from a given unit (by HODDOW WOMSOY). This concept is derived from the acceptance pattern concept, since it may reflect either the acceptance pattern that a unit is willing and able to create (Note: *Ability* should never be constrained by lack of willingness), and the amount that should be created given a certain set of conditions. Allocations of capacity can be made by whatever prioritization may be deemed necessary. For example, the ED is often lower on the proverbial totem pole than the OR, whose patients generate the revenue that keeps the hospital's doors open. Regardless, the entitlement should be known and understood, by HODDOW WOMSOY, so that each end of the continuum can know what to expect from the other end.

These concepts focus attention on what should be happening and what should be expected, regardless of the excuses. Treating entitlements and acceptance patterns as laws to live by creates a new mentality of ownership[1] on the part of both sides of the demand–capacity continuum and removes the sense of randomness of available capacity. For instance, if capacity entitlements are created, deviation should be seen as defects and a failure of the system's optimization.

Important, however, if we begin discussing acceptance and entitlement, it should only be because all available options for the optimization of capacity are not sufficient to create the necessary balance of the continuum. This might occur only on certain units, or only on certain hours or days during certain seasons (based on HODDOW WOMSOY). But these terms should be reserved for demand–capacity continuums that are truly, unchangeably out of sync. We should only use them if and only if we have mastered the dynamic demand–capacity continuum and enabled as much throughput as DCAMM makes possible. Unless the continuum is perfected to the extent it can be, discussion of acceptance patterns (especially) should be avoided so as to prevent giving up on potential improvements.

The Highly Constrained Environment

Acceptance patterns will vary to the extent that processes, patient recovery, overall unit acuity, external resources (such as nursing homes), patient transportation, and so forth varies. Patterns for a particular unit might also vary depending on any prioritization of admission given to specific feeder components. Efforts to improve the entire discharge operation will also yield changes to the available capacity. And as we start to think in terms of the continuum, patterns might be able to be created where they are less obvious.

In a highly constrained environment, we tend to view the constraints as altogether unacceptable yet often irreparable. Indeed, capacity is thought of as being almost as chaotic as demand. In these situations, we view discharges as almost randomized, offered only at the whim and fancy of circumstances, unit managers, physicians, and operations beyond our immediate control. However, regardless of the capacity situation in the inpatient units, there are patterns by which patients are discharged and new patients accepted. So, in the highly constrained environment, we need to change the definitions and ways of thinking about the capacity.

Once the demand patterns are determined, capacity allocations can be developed and standardized. The capacity patterns should be studied both for variability and the possibility of alterations. The current capacity patterns may well be more randomized than would be appropriate, since the thought of directly matching demand with capacity may never have been considered. To change the existing patterns to something more regimented, we need to begin creating a potential demand–capacity continuum.

By relating the clear and present patterns of demand, we begin to bring the inpatient side of the equation into an understanding of what is required. Understanding the patterned nature of the demand and the realization that the demand can, to a certain extent, be managed if capacity is better managed begins to bring about the creation of what could and should be patterns of capacity (Figure 9.2). Without starting with demand, and developing an understanding of the patterns therein, the capacity side of the equation will have difficulty dealing with how to make the right amount available.

To study this, we should strip down the demand patterns to look for elements which could lead us to specific solutions. Patient type and the associated workload requirements, spatial requirements, and resource qualification requirements may point us to solutions outside the standard streaming of patient flow.

We have already discussed the control of demand for the sake of limiting the impact on downstream capacity. There are a number of ways to manage demand, particularly for a highly constrained environment. These included scheduling admissions from certain feeder components, and developing staff algorithms to better address workload. Similarly, we need to consider more creative ways to control capacity, other than simply calling in additional staff and opening shuttered units. This might include the use of non-nurse resources to care for specific patients, e.g. discharging patients, expanded use of ED observation and holding beds using a reduced nurse-patient ratio, increased use of discharge holding areas, cohorting some patient types in specific holding areas, etc. Importantly, as we will see in Chapter 10, the use of workload and workflow analysis may assist us in developing less expensive resource pooling based on the type of work and staff qualifications required. Of course, space in which to place patients may simply be unavailable, making options limited. To the extent that we can expand existing capacity without a direct increase in our most expensive labor source, we should consider our available options.

Measured approaches to various scenarios can be created from the serious play with predictive analysis of DCAMM simulation tools, thereby ascertaining the impacts of a variety of combinations of parameters and variances. These scenarios and the subsequent outcomes allow for better learning of the system's complexities and patterns, which will yield the proactive management of a variety of circumstances, both in-range and outlier. Whether caused within or

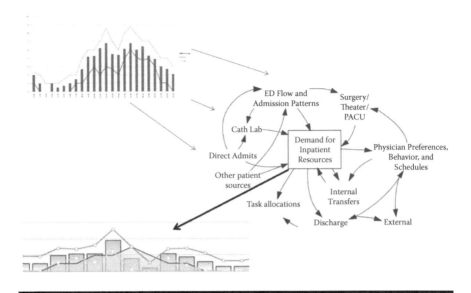

Figure 9.2   Hospital-wide demand–capacity continuum.

outside the department, or whether due to outliers or in-range variation, we can and should analyze the consequences under a variety of conditions to predict future behavior. The predictive analytics we used in previous chapters will again aid us in quantifying the upstream constraints created by limited acceptance/capacity. Thus, to effectively manage these variable systems, we again use the DCAMM up–down–up approach to determine the correct course of action under a variety of in-range and outlier capacity situations. (Models are very handy, eh?)

Furthermore, since in the highly constrained environment we seek only a certain percentage of matching, the requirements for capacity are more reasonable yet still able to elicit ownership of the issue. As the concepts are developed and engendered on both ends, the reality of the limitations of capacity to meet the demand becomes quantified, yielding a much better understanding of the realities of what might be left over. Thus both ends of the continuum understand what is available and when, and how to deal with the quantifiable overload. The simple quantification of the overage and the understanding of the acceptance and entitlement expectations will yield a far different inter-department conversation, and allow for the kind of ownership and accountability that will drive at least some efficiency. Thus, the "scientific" and quantified analysis of the patterns by which a given inpatient unit can and should accept new patients from a feeder department, by HODDOW WOMSOY, then becomes both a planning and communicative tool. If there seems to be a chaotic and random allocation of capacity, more should be done to ascertain any actual, perhaps hidden, patterns of capacity variability such that the appropriate predictable percentiles can be determined. This may require a change in thinking from siloed to systemic on the part of unit managers and administrators. From this information, and an understanding of the demand patterns by HODDOW WOMSOY, managers can more precisely determine the gaps in downstream capacity and what these gaps will mean for the components' ability to flow patients, both internally and externally/downstream.

Discharge by X

Many consultants tout a "discharge by X p.m." concept. *X* is usually noon or 2 p.m. Some have gone a step further and tout an "80 percent by X p.m." solution, acknowledging the fact that getting all patients discharged by the early afternoon is nearly impossible. While simple and somewhat statistically valid, the concept fails to account for the variability we've discussed. It fails to account for variability in the demand patterns by HOD and DOW; the workload patterns created by admissions and discharges; the inevitable outliers of demand and capacity; and the need for beds later in the day and the bolus of activity they create for nurses and staff. Furthermore, it only endeavors to control one end of the continuum with a very "blunt instrument". I have actually known consultants with major consulting firms to say that nurses can't understand a discharge target more complex than a single hour.

Instead, we need to dive deeper into the stats, the patterns, the variability, and the demand to better structure a continuum that works throughout the day. As you look throughout the entire system, at all the processes, flows, and patterns, you will begin to see the continuum to which you must strive and all its nuances and variability. Then you can use more precision to develop the necessary capacity while understanding the extent to which demand can be controlled and managed. This will become particularly true of highly constrained environments. And from this comes the wherewithal to schedule discharges by HODDOW based on the knowledge of the variable demand patterns. Rather than working to what might be an unrealistic goal, we can now work towards a goal that will specifically and precisely address any issues in the demand–capacity continuum.

Therefore, while "discharge by 2 p.m." is a valuable, albeit simple, goal, it may not be precise enough, especially for highly constrained hospitals. Greater precision may be necessary to discern both the variability of demand and specificity of capacity required.

Outliers within Outliers

In highly constrained hospitals, the tendency is to view every day as if it's an outlier. This is obviously a bad idea regardless of the circumstances. Thus, we need to home in on the differences that might drive significant performance changes in the system. Even within these highly constrained systems, where long ED waits and even canceled surgeries occur, *outliers exist within the seemingly constant outlier conditions.* They might be thought of as outliers within the outliers. What needs to be determined, therefore, is 1) the demand patterns (as before), and 2) the capacity which can regularly and consistently be made available, even if that capacity is not sufficient to meet demand. This offers us a quantification of the capacity that can be attained, relative to the excess demand.

Think of this as an outlier within the already constrained acceptance patterns. We call these outliers because they are outside the normal (80 percent-plus) ranges of system behavior. They are caused by the same issues that lead to all capacity variability and outliers. Yet, we must still understand them as outliers and not assume that they are more common than they are. Rather, we should learn how to manage those 10 percent to 20 percent of the days that truly reflect out-of-range available capacity, and analyze where and when these outliers occur such that we can detect any evolutionary trends or failures of our management systems, just as we do for the outliers in unconstrained environments. The same principles apply whether in an outlier or an in-range scenario. We must manage outlier days as outliers, rather than treating every day as if it's an outlier. This new way of thinking helps us to standardize work in what might be a more chaotic world of highly constrained systems.

So, for instance, an ED becomes constrained on Monday winter afternoons, as both the OR, the ED, and direct admissions simultaneously admit large volumes of patients to inpatient units. The hospital is in a highly constrained situation, and its available capacity is inherently too low due to a lack of available [staffed] inpatient beds. Then, as if that were not enough, on a particular winter Monday afternoon, we get an unusually high number of admissions due to flu season. However, there is some available capacity during these specific hours, as determined through our acceptance patterns analysis. We need to differentiate between this circumstance and the more common demand scenarios, even though technically both are outliers conditions. So, we can use scenario analysis to help us discern which days are truly outliers within the outlier and which days are just highly constrained. Though even the true optimization of all available capacity may not yield the results we desire, we may find relief from some of the pressures of being over capacity.

For this particular ED, the OR may get a priority on certain bed types, causing long LOSs in the department. So while some capacity is made available, it currently seems sporadic for the ED, as they get the "leftovers" of the OR, which changes its demand by HODDOW WOMSOY. To the extent possible, we need to ascertain the capacity that can be expected (the entitlement) by the various components during specific hours (the acceptance pattern). So, this ED needs to understand the patterns by which it can expect beds to be available now and in the future, based on any revised or optimized capacity. The ED needs to understand its entitlement for planning purposes, as well as the entitlement of other feeder components so that in-range variability can be understood and managed by all.

Furthermore, we need to ascertain what other feeder components might need so as to alter the capacity patterns and free up the downstream flow. Failure to understand the bigger picture of capacity entitlement and how capacity is allocated will lead to confusion and conflict. If the ED is at the bottom of the proverbial "totem pole" and entitlement is limited to what is left over from OR demand, then the ED should at least understand the acceptance patterns granted to the OR, and how much in-range capacity remains to which they might be entitled, if any. This will allow the ED to pattern their staffing, processes, operations, and even diversion status to a more regimented allocation of capacity. Importantly, it will help the ED to recognize the impact of the outlier-within-an-outlier status and how to effectively react.

This puts the onus on all components and the inpatient units to better understand the patterns in their variable systems, seek out root causes and ways to eliminate variability, and begin "systems thinking" by viewing the system as a system. The entitlement concept focuses the attention on any available capacity and quantifies it, even though it will not be sufficient to meet the needs of the components. This, in turn, forces the components to understand how best to deal with the now-quantified excess, in addition to truly outlier situations. Simply put, if patterns can be derived, from which capacity can be expected on in-range days, both the components and the receiving units should be able to structure their workload more effectively.

All the components, not just the ED, will then need to analyze their own processes and evaluate them within the context of the capacity constraints. From this exercise, they will at least know what capacity they are entitled to receive, and to what extent there is excess within in-range days, and to what extent they are dealing with outliers within outliers. Evaluation should include the timing and patterns of demand, alterations to these patterns, and temporary management of waiting patients through DCAMM simulation models. The alteration of created demand might include novel concepts such as:

■ Delaying or speeding admissions to better meet the (optimized) unit capacity patterns—Testing such scenarios is simple, with good DCAMM simulation.
■ Scheduling entitled admissions—If (a) we understand the patterns of capacity, (b) that capacity has been optimized, and (c) we have analyzed and quantified the capacity entitlement for each feeder component, then we should be able to regularly schedule admissions from those components. Not only should there be no mystery about the demand, there should be no changes to the acceptance patterns if all our parameters and processes are in-range. Naturally, there will be days when we won't need those beds (though, in highly constrained hospitals, this rarely seems to be the case), and in those situations the scheduled admission is canceled or used by another feeder component. If, on the other hand, outlier conditions require additional admission slots, those might be allocated from other components or allocated as capacity comes available.

However, again, during in-range situations (80 percent-plus of the time) we should expect to schedule an admission at a given time.

Stunning and strange as these concepts may sound, they are entirely achievable as we begin to work on the upstream processes and plan to create capacity as demand requires. Staff will immediately see the benefits to scheduled work, as opposed to the chaotic, seemingly randomized workload with which they now deal. Indeed, the next chapters will elaborate on this concept to demonstrate the concepts of workload analysis. Furthermore, such regularity will aid in developing less costly staffing patterns, focusing nursing staff on nursing tasks and reallocating other tasks to specialized resources, be they techs, med nurses, or licensed practical nurses (LPNs). This is simply a means by which to "scientifically" run a complex, variable, and interdependent system.

Bed Huddles, Acceptance, and Entitlement

The ever-common bed huddle is often an exercise in the last-minute bartering and exchanging of to-be capacity between component feeders and receiving units. These bed huddles often seem chaotic, since the staff has yet to use predictive analytics to detect and understand any patterns and outliers with which they might improve their operations. Rather than managing to the variation in the system, we are managed by it. The bed huddle takes on a firefighting feel, with staff scrambling to do what should have been predictable and proactively managed. Yet, even with DCAMM, these huddles might not go away completely.

Bed huddles should become less common and not continue to be the hassle they often become. This is due to the predictive nature of the DCAMM methodology and the ability to foresee a great deal of the demand in the system. If we can predict 80 percent of the system's demand and capacity patterns, by HODDOW WOMSOY, logically those patterns will allow us to better manage the daily bed availability. Of course, communication is critical, and predictive analytics requires proactive management and vice versa. However, the way bed huddles are conducted, and the information that is exchanged, should change dramatically. The nature and feel of these meetings should become more proactive and strategic rather than reactive and panicked.

When effectively using DCAMM, the reasons for bed huddles in a facility with available capacity change:

1. Reporting an outlier day in a feeder component, such as "bus-crash day" in the ED.
2. Reporting on the failure of dynamic capacity matching, such as can occur when staff call-ins or an unpredicted LOS causes a delay in capacity availability.

3. Reporting an outlier capacity situation, such as a unique group of med-surg patients with unusually long LOSs.
4. Trade-offs of predicted capacity between feeder components, based on the standard HODDOW WOMSOY variability of total demand. Since each component has some degree of variability in its demand, which yields a total demand pattern with variability, there may be some horse trading between components as needed. So, if the ED admits to the high end of its 80 percent range for the day, inpatient units may need to accommodate by managing flow from other components, or using predetermined hold times to prevent or alleviate any component pressure buildups. This all can and should be determined well in advance, using DCAMM simulations to ease the feeling of "every day as an outlier." So, even though there may be some horse trading among the feeder components, we should lose the feeling of chaos running our lives.

NOTE: This will occur even if we have bed-board/patient trackers available. Bed-boards do not eliminate the need for predictive analytics of the continuum. Rather, they can support it with real-time data such that decisions can be made faster and with more precision.

Similarly, the reasons for bed huddles in a capacity-constrained facility include:

1. Reporting an outlier day in a feeder component, such as add-on or emergent cases in the OR.
2. Reporting on the failure of dynamic capacity matching, such as can occur when staff call-ins or unpredicted LOS causes a delay in capacity availability.
3. Reporting an outlier capacity situation (as opposed to an outlier demand day, as described in the next section).
4. Trade-offs in available capacity, such that a component's entitlement might change slightly based on variances within in-range demand or outlier status. Capacity-constrained facilities will, of course, plan slightly differently for the inevitable pressures. For these facilities, it is even more critical to predict demand and capacity patterns throughout HODDOW WOMSOY, since these facilities will need to tightly manage all available capacity. Nonetheless, outlier days must still be monitored separately from in-range days, since the in-range days will be far more common and therefore require the most attention. (We'll discuss this more in Chapter 12 on outlier management).

As you can see, the focus on the huddles changes from reactive to more proactive, strategic, and cooperative. Moreover, the capacity-constrained facility's bed huddle is focused on the analysis of predicted and pre-allocated entitlements, which might be swapped as required.

Bed Huddles and the Occasional Outlier (Demand) Day

Of course there will be "those days." Demand outliers will continue to occur, their impacts rolling throughout the system for days. The fact that an outlier day can be felt for days on end, particularly in an available-capacity facility, is why every day can seem like an outlier. In reality, outliers have specific sources and should have expected outcomes. It is only through the management and focus on outliers that we begin to understand them in the context of their relatively limited occurrence. Naturally, the bed huddle changes on these days and during the aftermath as the outlier flows downstream. For this situation, bed huddles for outlier days include:

1. Finding and reporting the outlier day in its feeder component, such as "bus-crash day" in the ED, or flu-season Monday in direct admits.
2. Understanding the precise impact on capacity via a quick analysis of the quantification of the outlier (via a DCAMM Model).
3. Using a series of predetermined strategies from the predictive analytics playbook to mitigate the situation.
   a. Holding patients in a given feeder and making predetermined, necessary changes to operations to accommodate.
   b. Following the patient outlier downstream to gauge changes in future resource demands, perhaps using the DCAMM models for quantification of results, timelines, and resources allocations.
4. Ensuring that subsequent days and hours do not exacerbate future patient flow as future demand is within range. In other words, make sure that the outlier is limited in its impact on the system.

Strategies for addressing the outlier day and the concept of using predictive analytics to manage those days will be covered in Chapter 12.

Summary

Capacity is variable, as is demand. Thus matching capacity to demand can be a bit like repeatedly hitting a constantly moving target. Fortunately, like demand, capacity has patterns. These patterns tend to be, or at least can be, more stable, less variable than demand patterns. Additionally, capacity can be more or less controlled through the use of DCAMM's predictive, proactive management approach, and should be matched with the HODDOW WOMSOY dynamic demand. To the extent possible (and yes, there are outliers here, too), capacity should be effectively predicted and controlled through HODDOW WOMSOY matching to variable demand patterns throughout the same periods. Using the percentage of time capacity meets demand, we can better ascertain the

- Degree to which variability on both sides of the equation impacts our ability to manage our systems
- Degree to which in-range demand is influenced by outlier capacity scenarios
- Extent to which variation impacts the rest of the up- and downstream systems

Changing the way we think about capacity from a static and uncontrollable variable to thinking in terms of its variance, its range, HODDOW WOMSOY, and the potential for outliers will have a tremendous impact on the way we manage our systems. As we begin to *manage to* the variable demand from the community and focus on the variable capacity we can make available, we change our thinking to a systems view of the demand–capacity continuum. This will aid us in leaping forward toward the predictive management of the continuum and the enhancement of our financial, capacity, and quality metrics.

Note

1. Ownership versus accountability is an important distinction. Best described by consultant and author Joe Tye in his book *The Florence Prescription: From Accountability to Ownership* (2009, Values Coach, Inc. Publications) ownership means far more, and is far more effective at eliciting change, than accountability. Not only are the concept and the implementations different, the results can be dramatically different.

Chapter 10

Dynamic Resource Allocations, Dynamic Standardization, and Workload Analytics

It is often said that the greatest cost of healthcare provision is in the staff—the nurses, techs, administrators, support personnel, and so forth—that make up the real work of care delivery. Some 60 percent of the cost of care is in the staff. The world of healthcare is as dynamic as perhaps any, save a battlefield. Theirs is a world that can seem chaotic and full of randomness, uncontrollable circumstances, mysterious external forces of unknown origin, and conflict-creating personalities, egos, and attitudes. Yet, they are expected to perform flawlessly, regardless of the working environment in which they are placed. Fortunately, while the perception is workplace in chaos, these dynamic environments have been shown to be relatively patterned, predictable, and manageable. What we now must do is apply what we know about dynamic demand and capacity patterning to workload analysis and staffing. To do this, we must expand the horizons of the current analysis to include length of stay (LOS) as well as the multiple tasks required of staff. Some of this can be done using current dynamic capacity analysis, matching, and management (DCAMM) concepts. Some will require some good, ol' fashioned engineering.

To start our analysis, let's go back to the same demand patterns from which all our discussions have thus far derived. The concept is simple: if we can predict the demand patterns coming to a unit, by HODDOW WOMSOY, and thereby predict the capacity required to match that demand, we can predict the workload directly associated with the demand–capacity continuum. If demand and the creation of capacity involves specific tasks, we should be able to accurately predict the resource requirements and timing of workload associated with those tasks 80 percent-90 percent of the time. Since the initial upstream patient demand for inpatient units instigates all other downstream demand, and offers requirements for capacity, this is where we start. This demand for inpatient capacity, driven by demand from the feeder components, correlates with the two large boluses of unit activity, admissions and discharges. So, in this initial step we will evaluate the demand for resources based on the arrival and departure of patients from the unit, using our DCAMM diagram yet again (see Figure 10.1). The bottom left-hand corner of the diagram shows a graph that depicts the aggregate demand pattern on a given unit, for a given HODDOW WOMSOY (hour of day, day of week, week of month, season of year) period. We have already seen a similar graph in Figure 9.1. To recap, Figure 9.1 shows the aggregate demand pattern and variability as well as the capacity and its variability for a given unit and time period. Though the demand graph refers specifically to the total aggregate demand from the various feeder components, we can work backward in our analysis, back into the feeder components, to determine the patient types, volumes, and so forth expected to come from each.

When we begin to think of staffing and workload, we want to think specifically in terms of the demand for service created via the various tasks involved in patient care. The premise is that if we can pattern at least some of that service demand, we can go a long way toward predicting actual workload, by HODDOW, rather than simply reacting to incoming demand and making adjustments on the fly. And if we can predict workload, we can thereby better predict resource requirements and task assignments by HODDOW. Simply, if we know the demand patterns generated as patients arrive from various feeder components by HODDOW WOMSOY, we can begin to ascertain the demand for services and hence the resources required to provide the necessary care. We already know that admissions and discharges represent two large and mission-critical boluses of activity for inpatient staff. Failure to keep up with these important tasks means reducing the throughput of the system. And since we know we can pattern 80 percent to 90 percent of the arrivals onto the units, we should logically be able to predict 80 percent to 90 percent of the resource demand.

There are a number of vendors who offer acuity-based staffing systems as well as some that combine acuity, workload, and census into calculations of nursing and staff ratios. Some deal with all staff types, others just with nurses. These systems have, in some cases, incorporated some limited simulation capability, so as to predict future staff needs based on current staffing or patterns in key metrics, such as acuity. Some are more real-time, offering data on the immediate and near-term staffing needs. However, the predictive capability of these tools seems to be limited to a few hours in advance. Few, if any, have taken the leap into looking for patterns weeks or even months in advance, such that DCAMM-style analysis might be

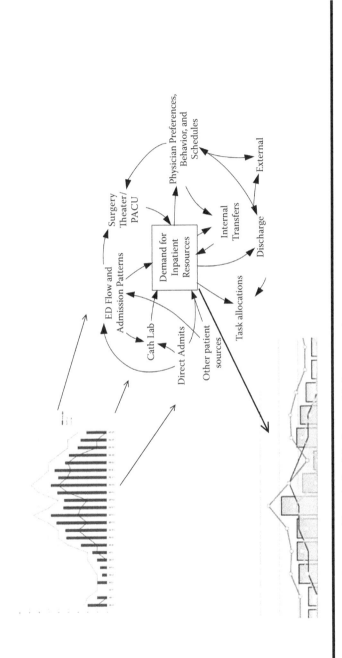

Figure 10.1 Capellini diagram of hospital-wide flow, with inputs and outputs.

initiated. This might be due to the limited scope and scale of the software, and the tendency to pull from existing ADT or finance data for inputs.

The Old Way of Creating Unit Capacity

As mentioned in previous chapters, consultants and gurus recommended capacity be regulated by the clock rather than demand patterns or workload, such as "discharge by noon" and "discharge by 2 p.m." Statistically legitimate concepts, these hard-stop capacity rules were meant to create enough capacity early in the day so that demand in the afternoon could be handled. The thought was that a hard stop on capacity would prevent later bottlenecks.

However, these concepts rarely see full success, due to myriad issues. Even if successful, these hard stops put a great deal of strain on nursing staffs by creating capacity when it wasn't necessarily required. Interestingly, these solutions might be considered wasteful in purist Lean circles, since overproduction when the output isn't immediately needed requires extra effort and resources.

Additionally, this methodology typically tells nothing about the sources of patients. Patients coming from different components may require different amounts of work and time. So a patient coming from the OR might require less work than a patient admitted from the ED, for whom more paperwork, clinical workup and testing, and care might be required. This differentiation can mean significant workload differences and can thus impact total resource demand.

Last, this methodology doesn't assist us as much as it could in determining the various staff requirements and algorithms throughout the day, which could include transporters and housekeeping in addition to nurses.

The New Way

Rather than using a single timestamp as the hard stop for discharge, we should instead look to the demand patterns, by HODDOW, to determine the capacity required. Although it may turn out that 80 percent of the patients need to be discharged by 2 p.m., the latter timestamp says nothing about capacity requirements during the other hours of the morning and afternoon. The amount of capacity required during the hour of, say, 11 a.m. may be different than that required at noon or 1 p.m. Furthermore, the amount of capacity required at 4 p.m. would be left unknown, since the focus is on the capacity before 2 p.m. Aggregating the capacity requirement onto a single hour could even lead to imbalances throughout the morning and unknowns later in the day despite success around midday.

The preference is to use a more granular demand pattern to determine capacity requirements, so as to avoid boluses of work, to differentiate days of week and patient sources, and allow for predictive analysis to order and help manage the actual workload and staff requirements. Rather than fabricating workload measurement based on a generalization of expected capacity requirements, a more precise and realistic assessment of the actual demand patterns and feeder components will be more beneficial to unit managers and staff. Such an analysis will help managers pace the work, staff more closely to the actual demand, differentiate skill-mix requirements by HODDOW, more specifically determine task allocations, and better manage the capacity side of the continuum.

Workload Analysis: Two Activity Boluses

When we begin to think about staffing and workload, we want to look for the indicators of work. Many software vendors use acuity as an indicator of workload, since manually or electronically calculated acuity totals yield various comparative rankings and ratings to differentiate patients in the population. These in turn indicate the total (average) amount of work or worked hours for a given patient type. The acuity tools are helpful, particularly when it comes to scheduling the appropriate number and mix of resources. We simply want to make these kinds of analyses part of the DCAMM hospital-wide optimization effort by relating the demand patterns to workload, by whatever metrics chosen.

Since we know can predict when a patient will likely arrive onto the unit and when capacity should/could/is made available, we can at least begin by predicting these two elements of the workday. Fortunately, these two events represent large boluses of resource activity. An admission can take between thirty minutes and an hour of nurse and other resource time. A discharge can take almost as long, depending of the efficiency of med reconciliation, patient education, and other nurse and non-nursing tasks. Thus, graphically, we get Figure 10.2.

You will note that Figure 10.2 is the bottom left-hand portion of Figure 10.1. It represents the demand arriving into inpatient units, as measured by tasks and

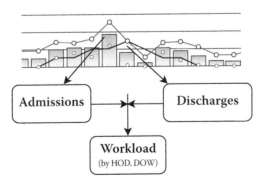

Figure 10.2   Determining demand-generated workload, by HODDOW.

resource demand. From this we can determine, by HODDOW WOMSOY, the demand patterns for staff to complete the tasks generated.

Simply, we can total the aggregate amount of work associated with admission and discharge by HOD and DOW. More important, we can predict when these events are likely to occur. These predictable workloads for admissions and discharges represent a significant percentage of the total work to be achieved on the unit and some of the most significant work for the ongoing functionality of the larger system. Failure to effectively manage these two tasks in a timely fashion can have a ripple effect throughout the hospital. We see this as admitted ED patients who are suddenly delayed during shift change, or the late family-provided ride home which delays discharge until after family work hours. Therefore it is critical to be able to manage these processes throughout the day and week. Since we know we can predict a high percentage of admissions, we can logically begin to predict the admission and discharge activities throughout the staff's day.

As noted in Chapter 9, being able to effectively predict the demand is critical to the ability to satisfy the demand. If the demand were truly random (as can be the case with some patients in small facilities, such as trauma patients into a small, rural hospital), it would be nearly impossible to pattern the capacity requirements. Furthermore, if we had no control over the processes and operations around capacity creation, it would be impossible to strike a continuum. Since neither is entirely true, we should be able to get a strategic handle on predicting at least some of the workload, and proactively structuring the continuum such that both demand is regulated and capacity is managed. By regulating demand, we simply refer to the control exerted over demand as the continuum is known and understand by both sides. Capacity is in turn managed through capacity entitlement and the recognition of the patterns of demand, for which capacity should be made available.

From Admit and Discharge to Census

Let's start the next step in our workload analysis with an examination of census. Hourly census data are usually obtained through patient tracking systems, bed boards, and other tools. However, hourly census, as it relates to workload and workflow, is directly correlated to the demand patterns created upstream in the feeder components. Changes to those upstream, component demand patterns can alter the demand patterns at the inpatient unit level, and thus might have an impact on hourly census. Thus this needs to be derived, rather than imported, for the purposes of what-if scenario analysis in a DCAMM model. This will also allow for incorporating interdependencies and variability (Figure 10.3).

Thus some of the census quantities can be gauged, based on admissions and discharges. One additional element in the analysis of census is length of stay. Without a specific understanding of the LOS of the patients on the unit, the admission and discharge data become less meaningful, since the total number of patients already

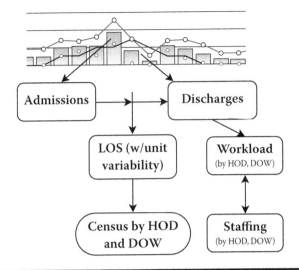

Figure 10.3   From demand to workload to staffing demand patterns.

on the unit would not be known. We could analyze the workload of admissions and discharges, which would be quite valuable, but would lose sight of the other work to be done on the patients already there and remaining.

Let's examine what we want to get from this analysis. What we are striving for in this analysis is:

- The total queue of patients awaiting discharge on a given day and on the appropriate day of a given patient's stay
- An understanding of the LOS for each patient granular enough to inform the model of the day of discharge, but not necessarily the exact time
- Discharge patterns by HODDOW (and WOMSOY, if differences are significant)

What we want to learn is the day upon which the patient is likely to be discharged, from which we can generate a queue of discharges. A specific patient's discharge time from 4-West needn't be tracked. Instead, we need to know the pattern of hourly discharges from 4-West. Next, we need the additional LOS data that will tell us how many patients will be staying on the unit. The admission patterns will give us the hourly arrivals (unit demand) of new patients. This is all coupled with the discharge queue, developed via the model, to build an anticipated pattern of admissions and discharges. So, from this we can derive Figure 10.4. What we can tell from this quick and relatively simple analysis is:

- How many patients are on the unit during any hour (assuming the accurate predictive analysis of demand and capacity [or, in this case, admissions and discharges] is accurate)

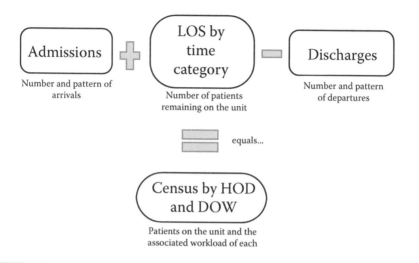

Figure 10.4   Simple census determination for DCAMM analysis.

- The relative admission and discharge rates
- The workload associated with the admissions and discharges, by HODDOW (at least)

From this analysis, we can keep going to determine the workload associated with patients who remain on the units. For instance, look at Figure 10.5. We already know that we might have a bolus of activity as patients are admitted and discharged from this unit throughout the morning. From Figure 10.5, it appears that on Mondays there is a spike of admissions at 1 p.m., followed by a gradual decline in the rate of admissions throughout the afternoon and evening. Since, again, these activities are critical to the overall flow of the entire hospital, we need to fill in the other tasks around the hospital's own "critical operational path" of admits and discharges in order to create an efficiently flowing system. This can be done by analyzing and prioritizing the many tasks that nurses and other resources need to accomplish during a given period.

Workload and Workflow

Let's first differentiate between workload and workflow. *Workload*, as used here, refers to the totality of tasks for a given process or set of processes. *Workflow* is the order in which we do those tasks. Before determining the flow, we need to understand the load. Now that we understand at least some of the latter, we can construct the former around the significant tasks.

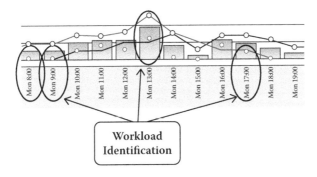

Figure 10.5 **Workload identification by HODDOW demand patterns.**

We can construct the workflow around the workload (known tasks and task times), whether that is an admission, expected discharge, med distribution, or shift change. Work with patients already on the unit, including those just admitted, is obviously part of the day's activities (Figure 10.6). The care for these patients must be considered in the overall scheme of the workload analysis and placed into the day's workflow. To manage this properly, prioritization should be made for the processes that are most important to patient care and those that are mission-critical to the hospital. So, processes such as med reqs, rounding, and shift change can be filled in around other tasks, so that we can actually begin to organize the day around our mission-critical processes. This will allow nursing staffs to split up responsibilities among themselves and other staff members, and prioritize their work according to the predicted workload and necessary tasks to be done. The key point here is as we move away from feeling that our environments are randomized and out of control, we can move towards a more scheduled and prioritized flow of tasks and work.

For instance, if a nurse comes out of a patient room after having just spent some time changing dressings and so forth, the next task she chooses should not be randomly selected. There should be some science to the choices, because her workload has already been anticipated by HOD. The nurse may need to pull from a list of (scheduled) choices, perhaps on a cheat sheet she keeps in her pocket, with prioritization given to specific tasks and times such that care is optimized and patient flow is steadied.

Furthermore, we can use analysis and task modeling to determine the appropriate staff for certain tasks. Just because the nurse does a task doesn't make it a nursing task. In an inevitable future of more expensive resources, the growth of unions, and the reduction in the numbers of qualified resources, task allocation will be critical to the effective function and financial viability of our facilities. This methodology will aid us in maximizing the patient care with the resources available through the predictive analysis of the important and time-consuming tasks.

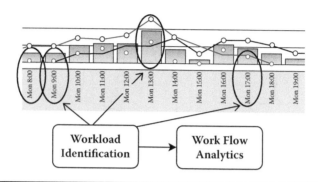

Figure 10.6 Workload and determining proper workflow.

Naturally, we do not expect to be able to schedule every minute of each day. Few, other than perhaps a factory line worker, can manage such. The way to achieve this is to analyze the important tasks expected within a given period of time, determine what can be scheduled (including patient admissions and discharges), then align the tasks with the resources.

Acuity-based staffing models can be aided by this analysis. As each day unfolds, patients of varying types are admitted. Each requires a slightly different amount of work. Patients requiring significantly more work can be assigned so as to balance the workload throughout the staff or assigned additional support personnel to aid in caregiving.

Thus, several inputs to decision making are coming together for this new management style:

■ Predictable boluses of care activity in the form of HODDOW admissions and discharges
■ Known tasks that must be achieved throughout the staff's day
■ Patient types, acuity patterns, and other workload-related data on the specific patients in the system

With this, we can begin to both proactively manage the expected workload and the flow of tasks throughout the day, based on the predictive analysis of demand and the knowledge of resource capacity. We can also begin to allocate tasks more effectively, examining resource allocations and staffing patterns along the way.

A Word on Variability

What happened to all that variability we've been screaming about since the first page of this text? Well, it's still there. Indeed, the variability of demand and capacity still have a tremendous impact on the systems we are trying to manage. Here, the variability can and likely will show up in the variability of the workload in the system. For instance, if our unit 4-West will receive between four and six patients on a given Tuesday between noon and 4 p.m., there could be a tremendous difference in the workload. The higher workload may cause upstream delays as staff members struggle to manage the tasks associated with the larger number of arrivals. Variable capacity may mean a simultaneous reduction in the available spaces for patients, which can have the effect of either reducing that workload (because fewer patients can be admitted during those hours) or increasing the workload (more work must be done earlier to clear capacity normally made available later in the day). Confusing? You bet. (And we haven't even mentioned outliers yet.)

The impact of dynamism will depend on the robustness of the process design and the capabilities of staff to accommodate the flow variances. This is why scenario analysis and the "what-ifs" are so important to the predictive analysis and management of the system. Both scenarios described earlier, as well as literally hundreds of other parameter combinations, can and should be analyzed to gauge impact on workload and resource requirements. As we begin to understand the impact of resource demand variation on the system, we can better determine how we might react to it to achieve higher performance and continued optimization of the system's key metrics. We can examine the workload impacts of a variety of upstream scenarios to study the impact on our units and how we might properly react to the variability that will inevitably reach there. The aforementioned six-patient scenario on 4-West, which is at the high end of the normal range, should be thought of in terms of the time required to perform the necessary work, the staffing options available, and potential negative impacts on the system's performance. This, again, is why discrete event simulation is so valuable, since with it we can study our systems within the realities of the variability and interdependencies of the system's flow.

Because the systems are variable, the workload will be variable as well. This realization begs us to consider the strict management of upstream demand variability to the extent possible, create capacity entitlements and acceptance where applicable (even within in-range demand scenarios), and generally proactively manage the in-range variability of our systems more effectively. To capsulate: If demand varies, quantify it and then predict it. If it varies more than you can tolerate, look for ways to control it. If you cannot control it, learn how to manage to it. If you can neither predict nor control it, predict how to deal with it if and when it occurs. This will eventually bring us to two other DCAMM concepts—dynamic standardization and break-point analysis—which will be covered in Chapters 11 and 12.

Task Allocation

The optimal configuration of care patterns while minimizing the cost of care is in part dependent on the task assignments of our resources. If all our care resources were nurses, we'd have much more expensive operations. There are a number of other resources we can tap, which might be more readily available in the marketplace, and who can support operations effectively.

In an assembly line environment, a given worker does a specific tasks or set of tasks, and repeats. The worker, with a standardized set of specific tasks, produces products faster and more efficiently and allows for better workflow and reduced stress. The best example is Kenji's automobile assembly line (from the Prologue of this text), wherein a pile of parts moves slowly from one end of the plant to another, becoming a shiny new vehicle along the way. This concept can teach us a little about *work breakdown structure*, or the breaking up of a large collection of tasks into individually assigned subtasks that yield the completed project. Work breakdown structure can apply, to a limited degree, to the work of patient care. The overall care of a patient during his or her stay on a unit, as the aggregate work to be done, is split into tasks and assigned, as needed, to the various resources on the unit. The appropriate allocation of these tasks among care providers is the key to optimizing care while reducing the total cost of care provision.

Even nursing tasks can be split up so as to offer greater efficiency, reduce travel time and stress, and improve care provision. A good example of this is the revitalization of the med nurse (MRN). The MRN was popular many years ago, but went away as nurses became more ubiquitous in the overall work of patient care. The MRN is assigned the task of ensuring that all patients receive the right meds at the right time throughout the day. Proper distribution of medications can be an issue for nurses who get caught up in the work of the day, resulting in delayed medications, displeasing both physicians and patients.

Furthermore, the MRN can individualize the med distribution to accommodate more options, such as two, four, five, or more meds per patient day. By being the sole resource in charge of med distribution, the MRN reduces errors, improves timeliness, and reduces workload and stress on other nursing staff. Other tasks can be allocated to support staff, who can work in teams with the nursing staff to achieve more efficient care with reduced stress and cost. Yet many team environments fail due to lack of proper planning, failure to communicate effectively, and distrust among team members, which leads to confusion about roles and responsibilities. Thus, teams become no more efficient than a group of "lone rangers" all doing the tasks that pop up. Instead, proper process mapping of care requirements, study of scheduled events and tasks, proper allocation of tasks based on skill, and effective communications and documentation are critical.

One recommendation for this kind of analysis is the common "swimlane" process map. This map allows for users to see the task assignments and even the timing of the tasks within a given process flow, so as to determine the best sequence of events to alleviate delays and optimize efficiencies or other key metrics. In Figure 10.7 and Figure 10.8 note how each resource has its own pieces of the overall flow. Notice too how the separation of tasks within the flow yields an excellent visualization of the overall operations and timeliness of tasks.

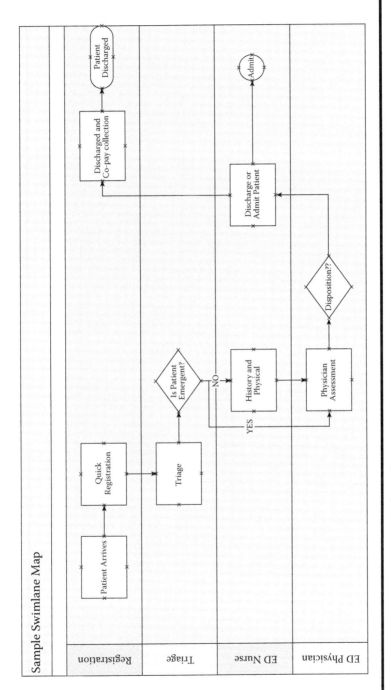

Figure 10.7   Simple ED triage swimlane diagram.

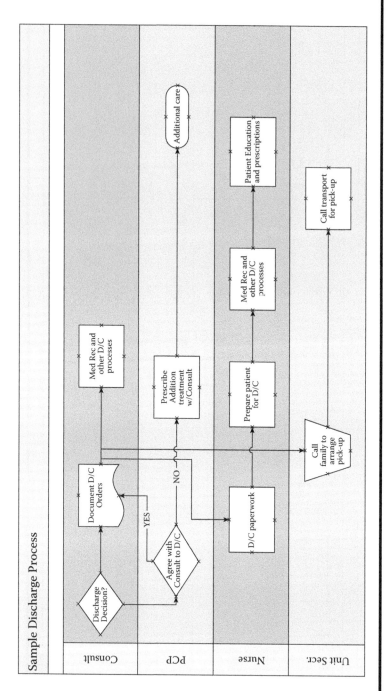

Figure 10.8 Simple discharge swimlane diagram.

Simulation is an excellent follow up to a static swimlane diagram. By incorporating the appropriate dynamism, simulations offer a much more realistic vision of how a task allocation will actually work for a given team. Simulation can locate and quantify the bottlenecks in such an allocation and allow for "what-if?" testing of scenarios for possible improvement opportunities. Simulation also allows for the dynamic analysis of the processes and resource allocations, so as to develop any necessary dynamic reactions to the changes in the environment. Importantly, we can test resource and task allocations for quality, appropriateness, and cost-benefit. By altering the allocation of tasks within a resource pool and using a variety of resource types, we can allocate tasks and understand the outcomes for a variety of performance metrics, whether they be productivity- or cost-related. Then, we select those that offer the best outcomes for our particular goals and situation, while accounting for constraints such as 1) takt times and skill-set trade-offs, and 2) quality and task requirement legalities.

Dynamic Standardization

The concept of *standard work* comes from decades of process improvement expertise, though it was codified as a concept in the Lean methodology. Intuitively, it makes sense. Essentially, standard work refers to the elimination of process variation and intraprocess waste, and the creation of repeatable, standard processes that all workers follow.[1] The goal is the achievement of standard and expected output and results. Structured and followed properly, standard work reduces or eliminates output variation, and thus rework and waste. This concept applies well to many processes where workers might take liberties in performing a task in their own way or in which there might be multiple ways in which to accomplish a task. When this happens, variances in productivity can erupt as one worker's methods are more or less efficient than another's. Furthermore, any errors that occur are more difficult to trace back to a root cause, since it may be difficult to tell which process produced an error and which did not. Lack of standardization can also yield too much flexibility in the way tasks are performed, which can yield takt or process time variation, resulting in up- and downstream bottlenecks. The outputs can therefore see more defects, waste, and errors. Standard work says that there should be a single way to complete a process, such that the expected result is ensured.

In healthcare, standard work can be important to process flow and the reduction in process time variation, reduction in errors, management of quality in caregiving, and training of new staff. However, we must remember that we are working in very dynamic environments. This dynamism has been shown to lead to changing parameters and circumstances, both internal and external to our systems. If processes remain rigid in the new environments, the processes themselves may contribute to a breakdown in system performance. In other words, a process flow that performs admirably under a given set of conditions may not perform as well under another. Therefore, while standardization of the actual performance of a process is still needed to ensure quality and proper outcomes, certain process flows may need to dynamically flex to meet the variations in demand, capacity, and other inputs. Therefore, in certain circumstances, what may be needed is *dynamic standardization*. That is, the use of multiple versions of standard work, the use of which depends on the circumstances under which the work is performed. Dynamic standardization could and should be employed when some system variation might cause a single version of standard work to fail to offer its expected outcome.

Take, for instance, ED triage. Let's assume that under normal circumstances, standard work dictates that a triage nurse manages all incoming patients, with a specific set of tasks. However, in outlier volume scenarios, this triage nurse may become overwhelmed, reducing her ability to effectively manage the incoming stream, possibly putting the emergent patient at risk. Under this outlier scenario, several options might be offered. First, the number of triage nurses performing the standard work of triage could be increased. Or, alternatively, an entirely new process might be developed in which an ED physician comes to the triage area to manage the patient streams. While both processes might be standardized, their dynamic use can be based on specific criteria, such as number of patients awaiting triage, door-to-triage time, or door-to-physician time.

Standard work, used dynamically, allows for quality to remain high under varying circumstances of parameters and variables. To set up a dynamically standardized workflow, one can use simulation models, value stream maps, or flowcharts. Knowing the breaking points in the system, the outcomes of various processes, and the required quality and performance metrics are all critical to the implementation of this concept. It is important to remember that if dynamic standardization leads to lower quality, lesser care, or inefficiencies, it is not achieving its goals. The goal is the same as that of standard work: to reduce variation and increase the likelihood of an expected or desired outcome. One of the important reasons for dynamic standardization is to establish clear and structured processes and operations that will apply in a number of different circumstances. This eliminates the "this happened, so I had to do it this way" excuse, which is the same as violating the standard work principle. The reason isn't variation in the process itself, rather in variables related to the process. In fact, the use of dynamic standardization might serve to improve quality, as it gives staff a way to deal with the dynamic environments in which they work in ways that still allow for the maintenance of quality.

As an example of the need for this concept, according to Dr. Jeffrey Liker, Lean advocate, author, and guru, "many manufacturers lose their ... gains after a few years because managers fail to monitor their viability as sales volumes or other conditions change."[2] In other words, gains are lost because manufacturing systems vary and fail to evolve. Because of the volatility of healthcare environments, and the dynamism within healthcare systems, the loss of gains Liker describes could happen in hours rather than years. External variables, such as arrival patterns or downstream flow constraints, can cause our current standard work to break down leading to confusion and frustration. Since the healthcare environment is more susceptible to the vagaries of dynamism, it makes sense to allow for a dynamic reaction. So, we need to meet the dynamism with dynamic standardization, producing the quality and outcomes we expect through a variety of standard work configurations.

Dynamic Resource Allocation

If dynamic capacity is required to meet dynamic demand, and our resources make up much of our service capacity, then resource allocations should be dynamic as well. This is particularly true of staff, since some resources (e.g., space) cannot readily change and staff make up a great deal of the requirements for care.

(Before moving on, it should be noted that the following concepts could also apply to equipment, especially commonly used, and commonly over-supplied, equipment such as infusion pumps. Thus, anytime you see "resources" and "nurses" in this chapter, you can also think of the other resources used such as beds, equipment, supplies, etc. Indeed, a more optimal allocation of pumps and equipment can save a large hospital millions of dollars per year in cap-ex and rental costs. It is not at all uncommon to see many more pumps than beds, to the point of extreme excess. Predictive analytics may therefore allow for better supply chain management, in that the variability in demand may allow for the reduction of inventory during slower periods, the lessening of cushion stock, and a better understanding of the nature of outliers. Although certainly not within the scope of this text, the proactive management of the dynamism of the system, and the relative predictability of the patterns of demand may yield opportunities to eliminate waste in inventory, meds, and biologicals.)

For the moment, let us focus on staff, defined as the nurses, techs, licensed practical nurses (LPNs), transporters, and so forth, that make up the larger patient care team. For many hospitals, a set pattern of staffing is used, regardless of the circumstances, DOW, or SOY. The excuses for this include:

- The "you never know" scenario, aka an outlier day
- A percentage of staff invariably calling in, meaning a required cushion to manage constant staff outages
- Old habits
- The sense that the always-full hospital dictates that units staff to full regardless of the scenario
- Union demand and legislated requirements. Far too often, flexible staffing means sending staff home when work gets slow and we have "outliers on the short side."

Otherwise, the aforementioned fixed staffing applies. Or, even worse, flexible staffing applies to nurses but not to support staff, such as transporters, techs, housekeeping, and clerical.

However, dynamic staffing of all staff types applies the same principles as the other dynamic analysis herein. Analyzing and predicting the demand in the system, all the way back into the community, yields the demand patterns we now know exist. If the demand is variable and patternable, so too are the boluses of activities associated with the demand, from its initiation through to its exit. Any and all predictive analysis we can do to help us proactively manage to the demand and capacity variation should be conducted, so as to glean as much workload and workflow information as possible. This can be achieved for not only nurses, but transporters, registrars, financial assistance and billing, ancillary services, and, on the back end, community resources such as EMTs and nursing homes. All we need do is:

■ Discern the demand patterns, by HODDOW WOMSOY, patient type, bed types, and other relevant characteristics
■ Calculate the (dynamic) capacity required to match the demand
■ Determine the appropriate resource allocation based on the task requirements and assignments
■ Dynamically allocate capacity in the form of resources to match the demand

By now you probably understand the continuum of demand and capacity. Look at Figure 10.9, which is now a familiar illustration, enhanced to show this principle.

Break Points and Task Allocations

Figure 10.5 shows what we already know; that demand and capacity are variable. But this variability complicates our efforts to allocate tasks and manage to demand, since high and low demand may require different resource and task allocations. Since we have determined that we can pattern both, we need to examine the impact of the variance of in-range and outlier demand so as to determine if, how, and when resource and task allocation changes are required.

In Chapter 12, we describe in detail the concept of "break points": the points at which system performance begins to degrade (see definitions at the beginning of this text). For our task and resource allocations, we modify the definition slightly to a "resource break point." This refers to the point at which demand creates the need for a change in a given task and/or resource allocation in order to maintain performance levels. This is combined with Dynamic Standardization to create a dynamic yet inherently more stable and efficient means by which to accommodate variance.

Resource break points can occur both within and beyond our ranges, and might even occur under multiple circumstances. Therefore, a deep knowledge of the impacts of system dynamism and the demand–capacity continuum is critical for the proper and ongoing allocations.

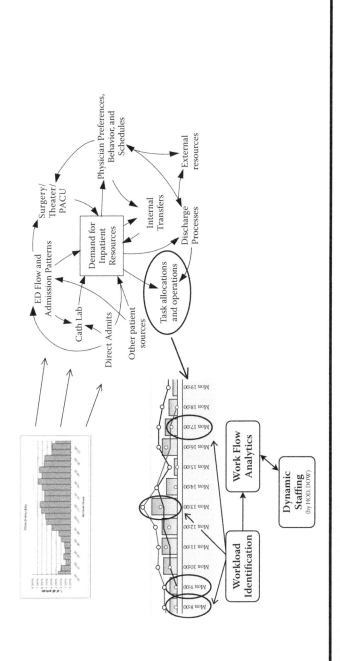

Figure 10.9 Demand-based dynamic resource allocations.

Using DCAMM and simulations of the continuum, we can determine the resource break points, and manage to these as they begin to occur. Say for instance the pattern of demand on 4-West is commonly between 10 and 14 beds on Tuesday afternoons between noon and five o'clock. Let's assume that this range is adequately met with a sufficient amount of capacity. However, the demand of the 13th and 14th patient tends to overwhelm our staff and cause a more chaotic work environment. Worse, if the latter patients come within a short amount of time, as they might from the ED, then we can see a bottleneck created on our unit.

The solution is, of course, to determine a better means by which to manage the additional patients. This might mean a re-allocation of tasks and/or resources, or perhaps upstream process changes such as scheduled admissions. Keep in mind that we have quantified the demand, and know the respective probability that patient 13 and 14 will follow patient 12. This will tell us the degree to which we should create consistent solutions, and the percentage of times a wait will be created if we choose not to react. So, when patient 12 arrives, we may consider an immediate change in process for either or both upstream and unit staff in order to accommodate the next two patients. In other words, as patient 12 arrives, we can predict the impact of the next patients and therefore create an operational environment that manages to the situation rather than reacting suddenly and sporadically.

Naturally, our DCAMM simulations help with this. "What-if?" scenarios should have been run to determine the outcomes of various demand and capacity circumstances, along with the impact on resource and task demand. Proper analysis of the workload and workflow should have proactively been achieved, so as to offer us tangible actions and necessary changes. As our environment is altered by variability, we should be able to react rationally and "scientifically" rather than randomly, so as to allow for better and more consistent performance and greater work predictability for our staff. Task and resource allocations are created as "dynamic standardization" requires, so as to accommodate the variable nature of the demand–capacity continuum.

Summary

One of the key underlying principles of this text is the ability to pattern, and therefore predict by HODDOW WOMSOY, some if not much of the demand coming into the system and the capacity we make available. The proper utilization of this predictive capability should entail an effort to effectively and dynamically match the demand with the available supply. The dynamic management of capacity, as it relates to matching dynamic demand, is therefore critical to the optimization of everything from patient flow to throughput and total system capacity.

This should, in turn, lead to logical changes to the management of resources. If demand can be predicted, even if only to a limited degree, we should strive to match that demand with available, appropriate capacity, such that wait times, LOS, and costs are reduced. This means the patterning of the relationship between demand and workload, especially for those large boluses of activity that can consume so much staff time. Workload patterns can then be discerned, from which we can derive workflow and the prioritization of tasks and allocation of appropriate resources. These workflows can be standardized, but only within the context of the dynamic environments in which they function. Dynamic standardization will allow for the regimentation of process design, with all its beneficial quality and consistency, while providing for precise and choreographed reactions to changes in external variables.

Thus, from dynamic demand and its corresponding dynamic capacity we come to the dynamic allocation of resources and the dynamic standardization of work. This will allow us to more effectively manage the system, with a constant eye toward the variability within the patterns of service demand. As we work with the in-range variability, we begin to understand that there are break points and outliers in the system. It is these two issues with which we will deal next.

Notes

1. Productivity Press offers a number of titles on standard work and Lean concepts in general through its Web site at www.productivitypress.com. A division of Taylor & Francis, Productivity Press is the largest publisher of such materials in the United States.
2. Paul Davidson, Lean manufacturing helps companies survive recession, *USA Today*, November 3, 2009, http://www.usatoday.com/money/industries/manufacturing/2009-11-01-lean-manufacturing-recession_N.htm

Chapter 11

A Word on Mandated Nurse–Patient Ratios

Perhaps one of the worst ideas to come from state and federal legislators is mandated nurse–patient ratios. The concept is simple: legislate the ratios of nurses to patients that hospitals must use at all times. The justification is also simple: mandated ratios will drive up quality and ensure better patient safety by ensuring the right number of qualified staff for a given population of patients at any given point in time. The unfortunate reality is the premise is false, and there are better alternatives.

Driven by powerful unions, legislators in states such as California, Illinois, and Massachusetts have already decreed how hospitals must run their businesses and staff their facilities. The current and pending legislation disregards cost, efficiency, and the dynamism of the work environments described in this text, and demands a fixed staffing pattern regardless of the conditions and circumstances.

In truth, the goals of mandated ratios have little if anything to do with patient care and quality. Rather, mandated ratio supporters seek to bolster the need for more nurses by legislating an increase in demand. This legislated demand artificially forces wages up, as would be the case in any situation where a given supply meets a growing demand. This also benefits nurse unions by driving up their membership, making them more affluent and powerful, and giving them a carrot by which to entice more unionization.

In states where unions are prevalent, such as California and Illinois, unions have successfully pushed through statewide mandated ratios. However, the results of the changes are very clear: no impact on quality, patient safety, or even patient satisfaction. Multiple studies in those states have shown no direct positive causal impact on any of these metrics. In fact, some are concerned that care quality may actually decrease due to the resulting cost reductions required in nonnurse staff (more nurses means less of something else). This is a classic "downstream impact" that is so often missed by well-meaning legislators.

The problems with mandated ratios are simple yet critical:

- Mandates fail to account for differences in
  - Patient populations
  - Process efficiency and workflow
  - Availability of work-reducing technologies
  - General differences in workloads between hospitals
- Mandates also fail to account for:
  - Differences in workload by hour of day and day of week
  - Additional staff support from licensed practical nurses (LPNs) and other resources
- Variability and interdependencies of a given system

Ironically, mandated ratios can actually skew the amount of work each nurse will have, due to the variations in acuity patterns, technologies, support staff, and so forth. Though one stated goal is to smooth the workload by standardizing the exact number of nurses available, thus making all nurses carry the same workload, the actual results are far different. Table 11.1 is provided by Frank Overfelt (president of Delta Healthcare LLC) and the HIMSS Nurse–Patient Ratio Workgroup, which was assigned the task of analyzing the mandates and their possible repercussions.

The chart reveals the different workloads, as measured by hours assigned and patient class levels, between three nurses. Each nurse has a 1:3 patient ratio, but clearly some will work much harder than others, given the variations in patent acuity. There is as much as two-hours difference in the actual work time required. Furthermore, this doesn't account for any *other* variations within the work systems.

Another way of thinking about this is the differences between night and day shifts, and weekdays versus weekends. Without accounting for the differences in workload, we might have the same staff on Saturday night at midnight as we do Monday at lunch. This, on the surface, appears preposterous, since the workloads and patient demands are dramatically different. Similarly, depending on the units in question, and the relative activities, admissions, and discharges, workloads can be quite different even during the same hours of day. Thus, to mandate a specific and fixed ratio belies the realities of the dynamism of this workplace and reduces the ability to effectively match capacity with variable demand.

The reason this is important to this text is that the concept flies in the face of everything purported herein. The same staff ratio, every hour of every day of every season, regardless of the multiple variables that impact the actual workload,

Table 11.1   Variance in Workload within Identical Staffing Patterns

Nurse	Skill Level	Bed Assigned	Class Level	Hours Assigned
A2N	RN	0973	2	2.8
	Ratio	**1:1**	**Total**	**2.8**
BJS	RN	0963	1	2.5
BJS	RN	0970	2	2.8
BJS	RN	0982	1	2.5
	Ratio	**1:3**	**Total**	**7.8**
BOM	RN	0968	4	3.4
BOM	RN	0969	5	4.2
BOM	RN	0972	1	2.5
	Ratio	**1:3**	**Total**	**10.1**
CAN	RN	0977	1	2.5
CAN	RN	0981	4	3.4
CAN	RN	0983	4	3.4
	Ratio	**1:3**	**Total**	**9.3**

is anathema to the efficient management of our systems. Indeed, mandated ratios would most likely be worse for patient care than the alternatives.

Dynamic Staffing

A better alternative is the *dynamic staffing patterns* described herein. These are also known as *engineered safe staffing ratios* by the aforementioned HIMSS Workgroup. Engineered and dynamic, these ratios use important data on the acuity patterns, arrival patterns, workload and workflow, and spatial design to better align the actual demands and workloads of patient care with an appropriate allocation of tasks and resources. This creates a much more effective and efficient allocation and allows for dynamic adjustments to changing workload and the evolution of demand and capacity.

Importantly, Dynamic Staffing allows for the creation of the resource allocations we've suggested. By using proper task assignments and team work environments to match dynamic workload, we can improve quality and efficiency while reducing cost, waste, and risk.

Current Legislative Efforts

Currently, Sen. Barbara Boxer (Democrat, California) is pushing Senate Bill 1031, which is worse than even the California mandates. It specifically precludes hospitals from accommodating the mandates through the use of alternative resources, even though those resources may be more efficient and appropriate. Additionally, Rep. Jan Schakowski (Democrat, Illinois) is sponsoring an equally heinous House Bill 2273. Both these bills will get a boost if healthcare reform passes and unions continue to have a significant seat at the policy table.

Summary

Hospitals can and should be able to make their own decisions about staffing. These decisions can now be based on better and more information about the dynamism of the systems, and the realities of their physical plant, technologies, and patient populations. Greater efficiency and efficacy await us if we employ the concepts herein, as well as the performance and process improvement (PPI) methodologies from our friends in manufacturing. Certainly, we don't need legislators dictating how we run our facilities.

We should strive to engineer a dynamic staff allocation based on the dynamism of healthcare systems and the many variables that impact workload and workflow. Only then will we optimize care and the effective utilization of resources.

Chapter 12

Outlier Management and System Balance

There are three more concepts to cover before you can go forth to profoundly change the way your hospital is managed: outlier management, break points, and system balance.

Outlier Management

To grasp the essential concept of outlier management, let's ensure that we understand everything that leads up to it. As we near the end of this text, let's review what we know.

Healthcare systems are dynamic. Variability and interdependencies combine to create systems that are inherently more difficult to understand, manage, and predict. Dynamic demand comes to us from our communities and is met with our dynamic capacity. The dynamism (the combination of the inherent variability and interdependencies in complex healthcare systems) in the demand–capacity continuum means that commonly used averages don't help much in the analysis and optimization of healthcare systems. Averages rarely happen in real life—everything else does. Because dynamism impacts the system so much, averages simply cannot be trusted. Even slight variability can throw off expected performance of an interdependent system if not adequately accounted for. The result is a system that is not the sum of the averages of its parts. Capacity, throughput, efficiency, and productivity are all negatively impacted by dynamism.

Since we cannot rely on averages to foretell the future, we need a more powerful form of predictive analytics that will aid us in managing these systems. But precisely predicting a dynamic system is inherently difficult. The greater the dynamism, the lower the predictability. Fortunately, healthcare systems are not as randomized and chaotic as we might think, else there would be little hope of optimizing them at all. At least some if not all of the dynamism has patterns by which we can discern future behavior. These patterns offer the understanding that the systems in which we work are not totally random and unpredictable, and therefore can be effectively managed. Indeed, in many instances, some 80 percent to 90 percent of the dynamism occurs in relatively tight ranges such that it can be patterned and more thoroughly understood. When and where patterns exist, they yield the means by which to study the system in the context of its dynamism and thus manage to the changing environment, rather than being managed by it. The patterns in the dynamism are also key to the ability to predict future performance, by HODDOW WOMSOY (hour of day, day of week, week of month, season of year). Furthermore, to the degree that the patternable dynamism is relatively stable and tight, inclusive of HODDOW WOMSOY variation, it can and should be viewed as commonplace, standard, and in range. This alters the analysis we would do and the way we think about improving the system. Thus we come to realize that healthcare systems are dynamic yet still manageable. We can begin to discern how one component's dynamism impacts others upstream and downstream, and how the initial demand patterns drive all other system demand and the requirements for capacity. As we understand this dynamic demand–capacity continuum and its impact on performance, we begin to see how we can influence the up- and downstream demand patterns in the system so as to have a truly systemic impact. And furthermore we can more effectively and proactively allocate resources (remember, to include staff, equipment, supplies, etc.) to dynamically match dynamic demand.

As outliers occur more frequently, we may witness the evolution of some part of the system and the system writ large. *Evolution* occurs when system variables change both internally and externally, such that outliers become the norm and new outliers appear. This can result from efforts to improve the system as well as from changes to external variables such as competitive offerings and demographics. Since evolution of the system is inevitable, it requires us to constantly monitor outliers and look for developing trends becoming new patterns.

As we learn the dynamics of our systems, we begin to view them and manage them differently. Using the tools of discrete-event simulation as well as common process improvement methodologies, we discern that at least some of the operations and processes can become dynamically standard, flexing as needed to the dynamism of the system performance. This dynamic standardization helps us to better control performance that we heretofore considered unmanageable. Dynamic standardization thus helps us deal with both in-range and outlier conditions, such that the performance and quality metrics of our systems do not falter.

And as we come to understand how to better manage the standard dynamism that is inherently in range, we naturally begin to focus on those outliers that cause us such pain. Hence, the next step in dynamic capacity analysis, matching, and management (DCAMM): outlier management.

Since the standard range does and will occur in a high number of instances, it must be managed well in order to manage the system optimally. The remaining, relatively small percentage is the truly random and unpredictable events that drive the systems over the edge and cause breakdowns. These are the outliers, and they are caused by the dynamism of the system that occasionally goes beyond the norm. Outliers can have a tremendous impact on system performance, and are often the root cause of process bottlenecks and breakdowns. Furthermore, because they are relatively unpredictable, they are inherently more impactful. However, they should be recognized for what they are: relatively unique events. The points at which the system leaves its standard range and moves into these more unusual circumstances are the *"break points."* Break points must be recognized and quantified, so as to help discern when the in-range performance can no longer be expected and when perhaps some change to the standardized processes needs to occur.

Beyond a break point, the system may tip into an outlier status—circumstances and conditions that are among the more rare and unusual, but that are relatively unpredictable and cause great impacts on the system's overall performance. The system's flow and balance begin to fall apart, and bottlenecks seem to appear everywhere as the demand-capacity continuum ceases to mesh. The interdependencies cause the outliers to ripple throughout the system wherever causal impacts lead. Planning for the normal range of circumstances fails us, as the unexpected circumstances cause unanticipated results, leading to a feeling of chaos.

Look at Figure 12.1. A demand outlier appears outside the normal expected range, occurring less than 20 percent of the time. As mentioned, outliers can appear on the "low" and "high" side of the range, but are most commonly associated with the end of the range that causes us the most angst. An outlier in demand can overwhelm the capacity before it has time to react, while an outlier on the capacity side can constrain incoming demand like a pinched hose. While outliers are relatively uncommon, they are often the situations we remember most. We can all rattle off stories of a few favorites.

Outliers are so impactful in part because of the interdependencies of the system. If a bolus of arrivals of patients to the ED only impacted triage, we might not complain. If slower-than-normal discharges only impacts families awaiting the release of their loved ones, it wouldn't be so bad. However, because surgical services demand impacts demand for hospital discharge (a portion of our capacity), we must be concerned about the systemic nature of outliers as they erupt.

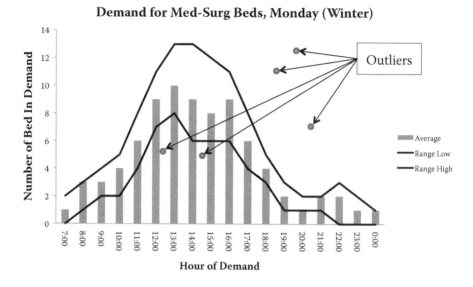

Figure 12.1   Outliers and their appearance.

Outliers can erupt wherever there is variability. The degree to which outliers impact us depends on several factors, including:

■ The relative variability of the process or system. For processes with "tight" distributions (meaning, little variability around the average), outliers may not be very impactful except in high-volume, high-speed processes. For instance, if the registration time distribution is between three and four minutes 90 percent of the time, a five minute outlier will likely have little impact.
A process or system with a wider range of variability is likely to see most distant outliers. Recall some of the Figures we've used in this text, and recall the long "tails" on the distributions, such as Figure 2.3 from Chapter 2 on Variability. From that Figure, we can see that an eighteen (18) minute triage time is likely an outlier, and would certainly cause delays for the next patient(s) and perhaps downstream resources.
Of course this concept can apply to arrival patterns, process times, system performance metrics, etc.
■ Their relative degree and probability of occurrence. A 1-in-20 occurrence is closer to the "typical" than a 1-in-1000 occurrence. The further an outlier is from its norm, the more likely its impact will be more widely felt.
■ The degree of up- and downstream dependencies. If an outlier occurs at, say, registration throughput time due to a staff member calling in sick, it is unlikely that hospital discharge processes will be effected three days later.

However, other upstream outliers could have impacts from end to end. Thus is it critical to fully grasp the nature and quantifiable impact of the system's interdependencies.

■ The complexity of the interdependencies. The ED touches so many areas of the hospital that its outliers are widely noticed. A high volume outlier in the ED can impact demand on ancillary services, transport, inpatient and observation units, Physician rounding, Hospitalist and/or admitting Physician demand, case management, and discharge. The same degree of an outlier in direct admits or cath lab might not have similar systemic impacts.

Examples of outlier scenarios include:

■ "Bus crash day" in the ED, in which a higher than normal volume and/or acuity of patients arrive.
■ A high number of add-on or emergent cases in the OR. Though we might accommodate them, they can still throw off the normal patterns of work-flow as demand overwhelms capacity throughout surgical services as well as downstream components and resources.
■ Longer than expected LOS for a high number of patients on a unit causes upstream bottlenecks and shuts down the normal flow from the feeder components.

As we have discovered, the interdependencies of the system cause the impact of outliers to be felt throughout. Bottlenecks from the above scenarios can last for hours or even days. For instance, the above "bus crash day" in the ED may result in a higher-than-normal number of admissions, which clog inpatient or observation units for several days. Same with a high number of add-on's from the OR. The inpatient unit LOS example may result in worse-case impacts such as cancelled cases in the OR, or ED diversion and high wait-times.

Ironically, extreme outliers, such as disaster scenarios, are often studied. While their occurrence is perhaps the most rare, we tend to spend a relatively large amount of time and energy planning for them, while we ignore planning for the more common "really really bad day". Indeed, it is not uncommon to see cities and towns run a "live scenario" meant to mimic a terrorist attack, earthquake, or other natural disaster. I recall vividly the city of Chicago spending some $16 million of Federal and State dollars to run a half-day disaster scenario, complete with fire trucks, ambulances, and hundreds of "volunteer dead and wounded". For the minimal lessons and information gathered, I would suggest it was not money well-spent. What a simulation could have built with those same dollars! Remember, however they are studied and understood, disasters are just outliers in the extreme.

Outlier Management

Outliers must be dealt with as the unique events that they are—as outliers—such that we do not manage each and every day as if it's an outlier. Since the in-range metrics can be predicted relatively well, and since it is the outliers that cause us the most pain and suffering, we should focus on the latter and not the former. This becomes *outlier management*.

Of course, everyone remembers "bus-crash day" in the ED, or flu season on the med units. Too many bad days are remembered as normal when they are not. We need to discern specifically what makes up an outlier, as indicated by the performance and outcomes of the circumstances, and the statistical analysis of the data. What is important about this concept is that we can quantify what constitutes an outlier, rather than assuming that a tough day is always an outlier day.

Outlier management is simply the focus on impacting outliers in order to significantly improve performance. Since much of a process' or system's performance can be managed through the predictive analytics derived from the analysis of the patterns of dynamism, in-range performance is inherently more manageable than the random outlier. Furthermore, altering the in-range parameters presumably has a finite and inherently limited impact on the results, since there is only a limited amount of change available—the parameters are already within a given range. However, any outlier is a risk to not only performance metrics, but also breakdowns in quality, patient satisfaction, costs, and revenues. Since a small number and degree of outliers can have such a significant impact on system performance and metrics, outliers should become the locus of analytical, tactical, and strategic analysis and efforts. Eliminating an outlier can have a tremendous impact on the system's overall performance as well as quality and cost.

Outlier management does not mean that we ignore the in-range performance or the parameters that lead to dynamism. In-range performance will still be of concern, so long as there is room for improvement. Outlier management should be the first goal of the management team so as to minimize outliers and their impacts to the extent possible. There are a number of ways of proceeding into outlier management. The first step is to understand what outliers are and what their impact(s) might be. This requires the kind of analysis already recommended in this text. Assuming you have already begun your DCAMM analysis, then you'll have already likely found some of the instances of outliers and their outcomes. Since any variable component or process can have an outlier, we also need to ascertain which outliers do or might cause significant impact(s) on performance standards and metrics. Once this step is achieved, you should begin to ascertain the root cause(s) of their occurrence. There may be several interdependent causes, so each should be isolated for analysis (this, as we have seen, is readily achieved in a simulation model). Assess what can be changed, and by how much, and to what degree any associated variability can be reduced or eliminated. Running the "new outliers" through a DCAMM model will tell us the [predicted] systemic impact of the changes made by the outlier.

Furthermore, it will aid us in determining the source(s) and extent of the root cause(s) of outlier appearance. Knowing the root cause(s) will then aid in the development of meaningful and effective remediation steps. Of course, some will cause greater impact than others, and should be prioritized for removal or prevention.

And as we determine those outliers that impact us most, we then can proceed to develop the necessary PI improvement solutions. We can also use our simulation scenarios to test possible dynamic solutions, including dynamic standardization, dynamic staffing, and other measures. These scenarios aid us in determining several key elements of proactive management:

1. What are the break points? In other words, what triggers the tip over into outlier status?
2. How can these break points be detected? How quickly can they be detected? And what mechanism gives the indicators of performance change?
3. How granular do we need to be in the definition of the outlier? Is a single number enough or do we need to go deeper into the characteristics of the numbers?
4. What dynamic changes need to take place to accommodate them?

For instance, in an ED, a break point for admission volume to med-surg on a given Tuesday winter afternoon between 1 p.m. and 5 p.m. is seventeen. After this break point, (as we should have already determined through root cause and simulation analysis using "what-if?" simulation scenarios), the current OR schedule and the resulting total demand for inpatient beds begins to create conflicts and constraints on certain inpatient units. The key questions become: (1) How early can we detect this condition in the ED? (2) What can we do to proactively alleviate it, so as to mitigate the impact of the outlier? Perhaps the answer might be to look all the way back to triage arrival patterns (by volume, acuity, etc.) to discern what a seventeen-admission afternoon looks like at the front end of the system. Is there any discernable difference between a seventeen admission afternoon or, say, an in-range fourteen-admission afternoon in triage? What makes the front end of the system different? Perhaps the difference lies in morning flow bottlenecks, which lead to a bolus of afternoon admissions not seen on in-range days. Before we charge forward with solutions, we need a solid understanding of the impacts of perhaps a variety of causes.

Using a DCAMM simulation model, we could test various combinations of the actual timing of demand so as to discern how the capacity is made available for patients being admitted. As another example, capacity analysis might reveal incongruities in discharge patterns between days, which can be traced back to physician rounding caused by a busy Tuesday surgical schedule. Importantly, *testing scenarios can reveal how much capacity needs to be made available during specific hours, so we can use the entitlement concept to appropriate a specific additional amount of capacity such that the outlier is eliminated and becomes "in range."* There are myriad ways to go about this analysis. However, as described earlier, you will be inherently limited in your analysis without simulation and a systems approach. The sort of root cause analysis described herein is very simple, for demonstration purposes.

But management engineers are schooled in the art and science of many methodologies of complex and sophisticated root cause analytics, and can guide your facility to these sorts of revelations. Once the revelations are made, then the task of discovering how to better proactively manage them, as or preferably before they occur, will be a tremendous help in improving the overall performance of the system.

Focusing on the outliers, and bringing out-of-range performance into range will enhance the overall performance of the system. But remember as you achieve change, you must go back to the DCAMM analysis to ensure that the next bottleneck is always accounted for. You'll be dealing with that one next.

Dynamic Systems Balancing

Thus we come to the culmination of everything we've worked through in this text. *Systems balancing* is the predictive, proactive, holistic management of the demand–capacity continuum by dynamically, continually, predicatively, and efficiently matching dynamic demand with dynamic capacity. Through the progression of the methodology:

- Understanding of variation and interdependencies (aka dynamism)
- Recognition of patterns, outliers, and break points
- Control of both up- and downstream demand and capacity patterns such that the continuum is more harmonious
- Use of predictive analytics to foresee the impacts of dynamism, change, and outliers
- Implementation of proactive, dynamic standardization of operations to manage both in-range performance and outliers
- Focus on outlier management and bringing outliers into a more predictable range

Systems balancing allows for attainment of the optimal available capacity. System balance, then, is little more than understanding and managing a system as a dynamic system, such that the dynamic component parts harmoniously and precisely intertwine as the system changes over time. The more smoothly and often the system can mesh in this way, the closer to true optimization the system will come. With the right tools, mindset, and vision, even the balancing of the complexities of patient care can be attained.

Our now well-worn capellini diagram (Figure 12.2) again shows the interdependencies and variation that plagues healthcare systems. We experience its dynamism every day and are constantly challenged to keep up with its evolution and outliers.

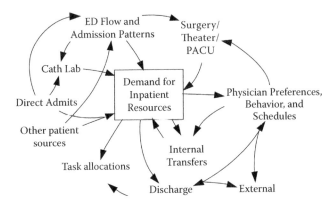

Figure 12.2   Hospital-wide capellini diagram.

Through the use of capellini diagrams, several well-made simulation models, and the tried and true process improvement methodologies such as Lean and Lean Six Sigma, we can now better understand how the pieces and parts dynamically fit together, and what causes those connections to become corrupted and congested. Using the various tools in our tool belt and applying our models to achieve strategic what-if scenarios, we can test the robustness of the system, the outliers by which the demand–capacity continuum is broken, the possible solutions, and the outcomes of change before we actually implement. System balance, therefore, is the natural outcome of the implementation of all the tools, methodologies, and concepts we have discussed thus far. It should require little, if any, explanation, since if we use these tools as have been described, and surmount any challenges such as the ones described later, we should be able to move toward outlier management and beyond to system balance.

System balance is an ongoing, evolving process. What we seek to manage dynamic systems. We have already seen how healthcare systems change and evolve as components, communal demand, and internal efforts morph these systems over the short and long term. Therefore, the degree of system balance is somewhat dynamic and the degree to which balance is achieved will change over time. Recall the quote by Dr. Jeffrey Liker, from previous chapters. He stated that advances brought on by Lean improvements can ultimately fail as external variables of a system change. These external changes lead Lean improvement to regress. Similarly, even DCAMM-based solutions require tweaking and changing as evolution takes place, seasons change, and variability increases or decreases. As the system evolves, it may fall out of balance as the various component capacities are adjusted. We will inevitably struggle to maintain a consistent balance over time. Fortunately, we now know that the analytics and capabilities we need to achieve balance are available to us; it is just a matter of strategically deploying them as needed.

Yet, system balance is still only a part of DCAMM. And DCAMM, in turn, is a mindset, a strategic objective, a toolset, and a philosophy. It will require an entirely new way of thinking, and an abandonment of the Lean-is-the-only-answer mentality. It requires a new set of technologies, deployed in a very strategic way, and combined with strategic thinking and vision. This is neither easy nor quick, as we have discussed. Nor is it a perfect science, in which A plus B always and invariably equals C. Our systems are still dynamic, still have outliers, and still can seem as random as the shape of a snowflake. Nonetheless, the use of the these tools, concepts, and methodologies will take us to new heights of systems management if implemented with rigor, vision, and passion.

To get there, you'll have to go on quite a journey. The journey starts with the initial chapters of this text, capturing, analyzing, and understanding the demand of the system and the variability within it. Next, you'll have to precisely map the interdependencies of your system. You'll need to fully grasp the HODDOW WOMSOY changes that take place within your systems and how the dynamism of the system is altered over time. Using some relatively elegant (meaning, simple yet sophisticated) simulation models, you'll need to begin to understand how your system's dynamic demand is matching with dynamic capacity and quantify any gaps. You'll begin to see patterns and outliers, as well as the means by which to predict your system's performance over time. The root causes of bottlenecks of performance will become clearer as you peel away the factors that influence your key metrics. As you begin to see how your system needs to react to this dynamism, you'll begin to develop dynamic yet standardized operations to deal with the inevitable variances. You'll then begin to discern the differences between true outlier days and those days that are within a standard range of expected conditions. You can then develop contingency planning for the inevitable outlier and even disaster scenario days, knowing better what constitutes an outlier day. And as you realize that many days can be dealt with as standard, you come to outlier management and the understanding of what is required to keep your system in balance.

This journey is neither easy nor quick. It will require staff and manager training, so as to spread the understanding of dynamism throughout your facilities, just as the concepts of waste have begun to pervade hospitals. As the understanding of variability, interdependencies, and systems take hold, hospitals will be able to perform better as the dynamic systems they are based on a better knowledge of the systems in which we work.

Possibilities

Would we then be able to account for the entirety of the demand of a patient's flow once in the system at the component level? At this stage, might we be able to effectively predict all the possible downstream demand generated, through to the discharge back into the community? Might we be able to develop models of care that efficiently incorporated *all* resources in the community's care system, not just our hospitals, so as to optimize the communal capacity on a much larger scale and enable a more effective total allocation of resources? Clearly, this is well ahead of the thinking in ACOs (Accountable Care Organizations) and the new business and payment models currently being purported as solutions to our healthcare cost "crisis."

Might we proactively manage the demand of our systems such that variation is reduced or even eliminated in all but the most dire conditions? Might we predict arrivals and capacity such that we can instinctively and proactively match the two without the need for complex modeling or analytics?

Perhaps this is not yet possible given the current state of the thinking and analytics of our systems. Nonetheless, all this is ultimately possible if we lose the notion of the randomness and chaos of our systems and embrace the patterns and predictability within. As we do so, we can begin to see how the demand in the system can at least be, to a large extent, understood and perhaps controlled. To the extent that capacity is constrained beyond our ability to impact it, we can still understand the entitlements we are due, the precise capacity necessary to alleviate the problem, and the percentage of time and to what extent a given amount of capacity will assist us. Armed with this, we can begin to gain more control over our systems and the dynamism inherent to them.

Challenges

Of course, challenges await. Despite the best efforts to see the patterns in systems, sometimes the patterns do not exist in a meaningful way. For instance, the arrival patterns of trauma patients into rural EDs will invariably seem quite random, as will the arrival of specific, low-volume patient types into our EDs, such as mental health and drug overdose patients. Thus perhaps the biggest challenge is detecting and using the patterns that allow the predictability of the system. Without those patterns, this effort admittedly becomes much more difficult and results in less impact. The lower the volumes of demand, the more difficult it is to discern meaningful patterns. The low-volume, rural hospital will admittedly have a tough time predicting its arrival patterns unless the volume is substantial enough to create more granularity than a daily volume pattern. Breaking the volume out into larger time segments, such as four- or six-hour blocks, or segments that match staffing patterns, may be an option to help you grasp these low-volume situations. Regardless of how they are created, any and all efforts to detect and use the patterns will inevitably teach us much about the functionality of our systems and the predictability of the demand–capacity continuum.

So, even if we cannot pattern all demand, there is much that can be patterned, whether on the unit level or the source or component level. Although all demand may not have a defined pattern, some will. Thus whatever we can glean should be used as effectively as possible.

Another big challenge is getting staff and managers to think process and systems. These are critical to the success of efforts to change the system. Process and Systems Thinking require education using new concepts and tools as have been described in this text. You won't be alone in these efforts very soon. Beginning in 2011, the Society for Health Systems (SHS), through its parent organization, the Institute of Industrial Engineers (IIE), will begin teaching a course on process thinking. Additionally, SHS will soon begin teaching process thinking in medical schools to residents, so as to train them for a future in the complex world of healthcare operations.

Another seemingly daunting challenge is that those who will play the biggest roles in making DCAMM happen are the ones who currently cause the most resistance to change. Certain physicians, some unions, and specific nursing leadership all have a vested interest in the status quo. Yet we all know that the status quo is not sustainable or preferable. Change must happen if we are to keep the system afloat without sinking the country's finances. DCAMM requires not just a change to management, processes, and operations, but also a change to the way we think. This will come easier to some than to others. The very concept of scheduling admissions from the ED will seem ridiculous to some. The idea of dynamic staffing will upset others. And the idea that Lean is not the end-all-be-all might be anathema to certain consultants. Yet, based on the simple yet powerful concepts purported herein, it is clear what the new thinking will bring forth. Therefore, change must necessarily take place, and it will be up to hospital leadership to make sure that the right staff and physicians are on board.

Other challenges include data sources and the validity of available information. Indeed, I have heard Lean consultants insist that data isn't necessary to fix process and that hospitals don't have the necessary data anyway. This, to me, is a false premise and a bad concept to teach. Going to Gemba is always helpful, but only if the snapshot of time you see reflects the constant state of the operations. In healthcare, this is rarely the case. Gemba on Tuesday looks different than it will on the weekends or on an outlier day. Thus data is needed. A few words on the challenges and efficacy of data collection:

■ When someone says, "That data is wrong," the response should be "How wrong is it?" Is it 20 percent wrong, 50 percent wrong? Data is rarely completely wrong, unless the process that generates it is severely broken. (If the latter is the case, then the data could be corrected by fixing the processes that generate it). Even if its accuracy is indeed questionable, is it "directionally correct"? Meaning, does it indicate the general condition of the process, even if not exact? Putting data into this perspective will help users to get past the precision of the data and on to the practical implications of what the data indicates. Furthermore, even if the data is as much as 50 percent wrong, there is still 50 percent of it that is correct! Discern what is right and wrong, and use what you can within the aforementioned context.

■ Electronic data doesn't necessarily make good process data. Many of the critical timestamps of patient flow and operations are simply not collected in modern electronic systems. Many electronic systems collect data more for financial analysis than process improvement. The new electronic medical records (EMRs) are often devoid of good timestamp data of operations if not programmed in upon customized installation. Thus key process timestamps continue to be missing, making the role of data collection more tedious and troublesome. Nonetheless, it is critical to the overall effectiveness of our efforts. Without good data, we cannot measure our systems, use HODDOW WOMSOY differentiation, or understand the degree to which improvements are necessary.

Summary

The effective management of dynamic healthcare systems requires an entirely new way of thinking. Gone are the days when simple process and departmental improvements are enough to drive the results we need and desire. Gone are the days when we can casually build our way out of capacity constraints while discounting the need for the optimization of current systems. And gone, too, are the days when cost shifting can prop up inefficient, ineffective, low-quality, and low-productivity systems. Since the static methodologies we've borrowed from manufacturing can only take our systems so far, we need a healthcare-focused, healthcare-invented improvement methodology to go where we want to be. Such a methodology must take into account the unique conditions and parameters in healthcare, including and especially its unique dynamism.

In the concept of dynamic system balance, we have come to the culmination of the use of the concepts, tools, and methodologies outlined herein. It is the final element in what is a new approach for the improvement of these highly complex environments. Through this ongoing and proactive dynamic management approach, we will use our knowledge of the dynamism of our systems to better attain the optimization we seek within the context of the complexities that plague us. Without this approach, our static tools will forever frustrate us and keep us from proactively managing what should be more manageable.

Conclusion

As this text was being written, "healthcare reform" was passed and was making its way to implementation. Yet this reform package is seemingly neither about health nor care nor reform. Sadly, it has become the ultimate example of the stereotypical fate of an idea in committee. Though it has provided at least an impetus to change, it will leave healthcare providers to fend for themselves in solving critical operational issues of capacity, patient flow, quality and safety, and patient satisfaction while dealing with the aftermath of a largely partisan and ideologically entrenched political process. The future policies made, as well as those too politically difficult to make, will likely leave hospitals with lower reimbursements and reduced revenues, lower pay for physicians, tighter capital, and smaller budgets. None of this bodes well for the status quo.

Meanwhile, the management of healthcare systems has long had the reputation, particularly among its frontline employees, of being slow to adapt and adopt. The miracles of the bleeding edge of modern medical are juxtaposed against seemingly outdated management styles, stifling bureaucracies, and belated information technologies in far too many facilities. The genius of new medical discovery itself seems mired in a restrictive administrative structure, which impedes rather than strengthens it. Nonetheless, many healthcare managers have already determined to set a new course and develop systems that will be robust and inventive enough to survive the coming era.

As we look for ideas, methodologies, and concepts to aid us in the journey to improved performance, we have traditionally looked to those industries more advanced than ours. Toyota, GE, Motorola, and other famed manufacturers appeal, due to the achievements garnered from the regimen of their successful approaches. Indeed, they can offer valuable insights and lessons from their years of learning.

Yet, healthcare systems are uniquely dynamic, more so than nearly any other work environment. Thus we require something else: more appropriate methodologies and concepts to achieve our goals. These must come from within, not from outside, the industry. Since healthcare systems are dynamic, changing every hour of each day, we need dynamic analytical tools and methodologies to improve and optimize them. Manufacturing applications simply do not hold the ultimate solutions.

Dynamic capacity analysis, matching, and management (DCAMM) is little more than a different way of thinking, a new methodology and approach, and an addition to the currently available library of tools. It is meant to allow you to take the inevitable dynamism and turn it into predictive analytics, and go from reactive management using uninformative averages to dynamic management of in-range variability and a focus on outliers. It should change your perspectives, analytical focus, and management approach. In short, it is hoped that it will profoundly change the way hospitals are managed.

I wish you all the best in the implementation of these ideas and tools. Godspeed to your success.

Epilogue: Kenji's Story (Continued)

Kenji's son was eventually seen in the small community hospital emergency department (ED) where his father had taken him. Kenji chatted with his wife via cell phone during the night and she'd agreed to stay at home, since she was "very" pregnant with their second child. No sense in her suffering through that agony! By Kenji's standards, the process was painful to witness. Though he knew little about the art and science of caring for patients, he knew much about process control, wasted time, and misdirected effort. How could this world be so different than his? Were the environments that much different?

By the time Kenji and his son arrived back to their home over twelve hours later, light was beginning to shine through to another overcast day. Kenji wasn't so much angered as he was intrigued by the long wait, uncomfortable conditions, frustrated ED staff and physicians, and clearly visible waste. Perhaps frightened was a better term. There was so much wrong it was almost difficult to put his finger on a starting point. "How could they operate in those conditions and not kill people by accident?" he thought.

After he put his thoroughly medicated son to bed, Kenji lay down beside his sleeping wife and tried to decide if he would go to work in two hours. Things were a little slower than normal at the plant, so he thought he might get away with a family leave day, but he'd need to check with his boss first. He'd call at 6:30 a.m. when Stephen arrived.

As he lay there, Kenji couldn't get his mind off the chaos he'd seen in the ED, once they'd been admitted to the "back" (as they called it—odd name, he thought). Had he not been so tired, he might have watched the staff long enough to offer suggestions on how they might work more effectively. He smiled to himself; he knew nothing about healthcare. Still, he couldn't escape the thought of perhaps being able to help them. Did they really know how inefficient they seemed to be?

The short nap went by like a flash. Kenji woke to the sound of the local FM radio station on his alarm clock. His wife had already gotten up to check on their son. As he rolled over to get the phone, Kenji's mind flashed back to the dream of the night before. "I wonder if the plant is still even there," he thought aloud. The gray ooze, the chaos, the factory at a standstill, caving in on itself. Perhaps it had imploded and his job was gone. He reached for the phone and dialed a number he knew by heart, to the desk of his boss, Stephen Frasier. Stephen understood completely. Though his two girls were in college, he recalled the same phone calls made to his boss when he was in Kenji's job.

As Kenji hung up the phone, easily getting a pass for the day, he considered lying back down to get some sleep. But he knew he wouldn't sleep. Something was eating at him ... hard. He thought again of the dream he'd had in the ED: the frozen plant, the stacks of arriving containers with nowhere to go. A twinge in his back instantly reminded him of the ED where he'd had the dream. Talk about bottlenecked. He sat silently on the bed for a few moments, gathering his thoughts. He looked around at the comfortable setting he'd built for his growing family, based on years in manufacturing. It would be hard to leave to take a chance, especially with another little one on the way. He stiffened his sore back, rose, and went to the closet and began to dress in one of his only two suits.

He'd be going for an interview today. His local hometown hospital needed his help.

Index

Author

Pierce Story, MPHM, DSHS, is the senior consulting manager for GE Healthcare's Hospital of the Future Division. He is also founder of Jumbee.com, a Web site dedicated to the advancement of profound change in healthcare and health policy. During his twenty-plus-years healthcare career, Story has dealt with complex systems redesign, operations improvement, and performance analysis throughout hospitals and health systems. He brings years of experience, unique perspectives, and new concepts to patient flow, patient care, and health system redesign. Having developed several new applications and toolsets for the analysis and redesign of key clinical operations and patient care capacity strategies, Story knows the needs of the industry and the failings of traditional industrial methodologies. His vision is a new way of managing the provision of healthcare in the United States.

Story earned a master's degree in health policy and management from the Muskie School of Public Policy in Portland, Maine, and is trained in both Six Sigma and Lean methodologies. He is also a Diplomate, past president, and active member of the Society for Health Systems (SHS), a volunteer organization of more than 900 healthcare performance improvement specialists and engineers. Through SHS, Story has become committed to bringing engineering principles and concepts to the clinicians and administrators who so desperately need them. He is also a member of the Leadership Council of the American Society for Quality's Healthcare Division. Story currently resides in Maine and North Carolina, where he enjoys his work in healthcare, riding his vintage Harley Davidson, and growing championship roses.

T - #0013 - 230425 - C0 - 234/156/12 [14] - CB - 9781439819753 - Gloss Lamination